Stanislavski's
Encounter with Shakespeare
The Evolution of a Method

Theater and Dramatic Studies, No. 14

Bernard Beckerman, Series Editor

Brander Matthews Professor of Dramatic Literature
Columbia University in the City of New York

Other Titles in This Series

No. 13 *Living Pictures on the New York Stage*   Jack W. McCullough

No. 15 *The Art of the Actor-Manager: Wilson*
Barrett and the Victorian Theatre   James Thomas

No. 16 *Male-Female Comedy Teams in American*
Vaudeville, 1865–1932   Shirley Staples

No. 17 *Distance in the Theater: The Aesthetics of*
Audience Response   Daphna Ben Chaim

No. 18 *French Theatre Experiment Since 1968*   Lenora Champagne

No. 19 *Evreinov: The Theatre of Paradox*
and Transformation   Spencer Golub

No. 20 *William Poel's Hamlets:*
The Director as Critic   Rinda F. Lundstrom

No. 21 *Gertrude Stein's Theater of the Absolute*   Betsy Alayne Ryan

No. 22 *Revolution on the Boulevard: Parisian Popular Theater*
in the Late Eighteenth Century   Michèle Root-Bernstein

Stanislavski's
Encounter with Shakespeare
The Evolution of a Method

by
Joyce Vining Morgan

UMI RESEARCH PRESS
Ann Arbor, Michigan

Produced and distributed by
UMI Research Press
an imprint of
University Microfilms International
Ann Arbor, Michigan 48106

Library of Congress Cataloging in Publication Data

Morgan, Joyce Vining.
Stanislavski's encounter with Shakespeare.

(Theater and dramatic studies ; no. 14)
Revision of thesis (Ph.D.)—Yale University, 1980.
Bibliography: p.
Includes index.
1. Stanislavsky, Konstantin, 1863-1938. 2. Shakespeare,
William, 1564-1616—Stage history—Russian S.F.S.R.
3. Shakespeare, William, 1564-1616. Julius Caesar.
4. Shakespeare, William, 1564-1616. Hamlet. 5. Theater—
Russian S.F.S.R.—History—19th century. I. Title. II. Series.

PN2728.S78M64 1984   792.9'5'0947   83-17979
ISBN 0-8357-1485-3

To my mother and father

Contents

List of Illustrations   *ix*

Preface   *xii*

Introduction   *xix*

1 The Nineteenth Century Background   *1*
    The State of Russian Theater
    The State of Russian Acting
    Shakespeare on the Russian Stage: Translation,
        Interpretation, Scholarship

2 Naturalism: The 1903 *Julius Caesar*   *17*
    The Meininger Innovation and Stanislavski's Early
        Shakespeare Productions
    The New Theater of Stanislavski and Nemirovich-Danchenko
    Julius Caesar: The Shaping of the Production
    Julius Caesar in Chekhovian Tones
    The Fate of the 1903 *Julius Caesar*

3 Symbolism: The 1912 *Hamlet*   *81*
    Search and Experimentation
    The Invitation to Gordon Craig
    Preparations for *Hamlet*
    The Production
    The Aftermath

4 Two Later Productions   *127*

5 Conclusion   *135*

viii   *Contents*

Notes   *139*

Bibliography of Works Cited or Consulted   *151*

List of Illustrations

Othello at the Society of Art and Literature, 1896. (Photographs courtesy of the Moscow Art Theater Museum.)

1. Othello (Stanislavski) in Venetian dress.

2. Exterior set: Venice, I, i.

3. Exterior set: Cyprus, II.

4. Interior set: Venice, the Senate, I, iii.

5. Othello's study, IV. Othello (Stanislavski) is shown in Arab dress, with Rodrigo, Emilia, and Desdemona.

Julius Caesar at the Moscow Art Theater, 1903. (Photographs and ground plans from V.I. Nemirovich-Danchenko, *Rezhisserskii plan postanovki tragedii Shekspira "Iulii Tsezar"* [Moscow, 1964], except No. 10, from *Moskovskii khudozhestvennyi teatr v illiustratsiiakh i documentakh* [Moscow, 1938].)

6. Roman street, I. Caesar's procession.

7. Roman street, I. Nemirovich-Danchenko's ground plan.

8. Brutus's garden, II, i. The conspiracy.

9. Brutus' garden, II, i. Nemirovich-Danchenko's ground plan.

10. Caesar's study, II, ii. Calpurnia pleads with Caesar.

11. Caesar's study, II, ii. Nemirovich-Danchenko's ground plan.

12.. The Curia of Pompey, III, i. The assassination of Caesar.

13.   The Curia of Pompey, III, i. Nemirovich-Danchenko's ground plan.

14.   The Forum, III, ii. Caesar's funeral.

15.   The Forum, III, ii. Nemirovich-Danchenko's ground plan.

16.   The camp near Sardis, IV. Brutus' tent.

17.   The camp near Sardis, IV. Detail: Brutus (Stanislavski) and Cassius (Leonidov).

18.   A field near Philippi, V, i.

Hamlet at the Moscow Art Theatre, 1912.

19.   Ophelia (O.V. Gzovskaia) and Polonius (V.V. Luzhski). Courtesy of the Moscow Art Theater Museum.

20.   Hamlet (V.I. Kachalov). Courtesy of the Moscow Art Theater Museum.

21.   Model of a set for act IV. Courtesy of the Moscow Art Theater Museum.

22.   Model of a set for act V. Courtesy of the Moscow Art Theater Museum.

23.   Sulerzhitski's ground plan for I, i. Courtesy of the Moscow Art Theater Museum.

24.   Sulerzhitski's ground plan for I, iii. Courtesy of the Moscow Art Theater Museum.

25.   Sulerzhitski's ground plan for I, iv. Courtesy of the Moscow Art Theater Museum.

26.   Sulerzhitski's ground plan for I, v. Courtesy of the Moscow Art Theater Museum.

27.   Sketch of I, i, by A. Lyubimov. Courtesy of the All-Russian Theater Society.

28.   Preliminary sketch for I, ii, by Gordon Craig. N.N. Chushkin, *Gamlet-Kachalov* [Moscow, 1966].

29. Sketch of I, v, by A. Lyubimov. N.N. Chushkin, *Gamlet-Kachalov* [Moscow, 1966].

30. Sketch of II, by N. Istomina. N.N. Chushkin, *Gamlet-Kachalov* [Moscow, 1966].

31. Detail from Sulerzhitski's rough ground plan for II, drawn by J. Vining Morgan.

32. Sketch of III, iv, by A. Lyubimov. Courtesy of the All-Russian Theater Society.

33. Sketch of V, i, by A. Lyubimov. Courtesy of the All-Russian Theater Society.

34. V, ii, final tableau. Courtesy of the Moscow Art Theater Museum.

35. V, ii, detail.

Preface

When, in 1966, I first became fascinated with Stanislavski's early work, my colleagues expressed their dismay at my lack of adventure. Why not Meyerhold, they asked, or Evreinov? There is so much yet to be said about the avant-garde Russian theater of the early twentieth century. The implication was that there was nothing new to say about Stanislavski.

Indeed, considerable attention had been paid to Stanislavski's acting system and its contribution to modern theater. However, other than the overviews provided by the autobiographical *My Life in Art* and the biographies, relatively little had been written about the artistic development of Stanislavski himself. Since then, several Soviet scholars have concentrated on Stanislavski's artistic growth, notably M. N. Stroeva in her two-volume study of Stanislavski's work as a director and E. I. Poliakova in her analysis of his experience in acting. These books are part of a veritable explosion of Soviet Stanislavski scholarship over the past two decades: analyses, reminiscences, chronicles. There has been plenty to say after all.

Aside from the biographies, *My Life in Art,* and the studies mentioned above, most books on Stanislavski treat his work at a fixed point or as a static phenomenon. Some of the most straightforward presentations of Stanislavski's acting, directing and teaching techniques have been written by Soviet men of theater like Gorchakov and Toporkov who studied and worked under Stanislavski. However, these refer to Stanislavski's later work and assume that all his artistic growth is behind him. Theater historians write from a similar point of view, concentrating either on the productions of the mature Stanislavski or on the acting methods recorded in *An Actor Works on Himself* (published in English as *An Actor Prepares, Building a Character* and *Creating a Role*). They discuss Stanislavski's earlier work through the looking glass of these volumes, written toward the end of his life to summarize and bequeath all that he had learned about his art. There is a certain justification for studying the early work in the light of the later theory but, in so doing, one loses sight of the artist in his development, in his relentless search for better answers.

The biographies and the studies by Stroeva and Poliakova present a chronology of search and growth, covering the entire span of Stanislavski's career. But at no point do these narratives dwell long enough on any one production to describe it, or the work process behind it, fully enough to present the struggles and doubts as clearly as the methods and results. More parochially, many of the productions under discussion are of Russian plays which are either untranslated or poorly rendered, and therefore inaccessible to the English reader who is then unable to evaluate productions of them. In fact, non-Russians are too often reluctant to find fault with any Russian production of a Russian play, even of those plays which have become part of the international repertoire.

However, during every major period of Stanislavski's growth, he wrestled at least once with the problems of producing Shakespeare. A thorough presentation of these productions could show Stanislavski at work during several crucial stages in his development. For an English speaker, Stanislavski's efforts to stage Shakespeare illustrate most clearly his approach to theater. Shakespeare is our home ground whereas Ostrovski is not, and we can assess Stanislavski's achievements with Shakespeare with an assurance that does not apply to Ostrovskii, or even to Chekhov.

In this book I propose to examine specific Shakespeare productions which demonstrate the various stages of Stanislavski's artistic evolution. My research has concentrated on Stanislavski's first two decades as a director, from 1890 when he was named stage director of the Society of Art and Literature until 1911 when the Art Theater officially adopted his new "system" or "method" of acting. His efforts during these twenty years determined the focus of his mature work. My intent is two-fold: to describe Stanislavski's early development through his work on Shakespeare; and to present the work process of his theater by scrutinizing the preparation of two major Shakespeare productions. Stanislavski worked on both these productions in collaboration with other directors; working with a partner seemed to give him the distance required for a tough objective assessment of his own work.

In many ways, Stanislavski belonged more to the nineteenth century than to the twentieth. As a theater artist he consolidated, completed and continued the work of his predecessors. After an introductory overview, therefore, I will sketch the nineteenth-century Russian theatrical milieu in which Stanislavski began his career. Discussion of his struggle with Shakespeare's plays requires the perspective of earlier Russian treatments of Shakespeare, so the first chapter provides a summary of them. This preliminary section is based on the extensive literature available in Russian.

Stanislavski's early work was dominated by an externalism of presentation which adopted two production styles, naturalistic and symbolist. I will devote a section to each mode, and will concentrate on the production which best exemplified it: for naturalism, the 1903 *Julius Caesar,* and for symbolism, the 1912 *Hamlet.* Each section will contain chapters on the development of the style, and on the genesis, preparation, presentation and significance of its major example. In the section on naturalism, specific attention will also be given to Stanislavski's earliest Shakespeare productions. Stanislavski produced two Shakespeare plays after 1912: the 1918 *Twelfth Night* at the First Studio of the Art Theater and the abortive 1930 *Othello* on the Art Theater's main stage. The significance of these productions will be discussed in a brief section which precedes the conclusion.

In order to study a production and to explore the work process behind it, the ephemeral theatrical event must be recreated. For some of Stanislavski's Shakespeare productions there is ample material from which to piece together a reconstruction; for others, only general outlines can be sketched from the evidence which remains. Photographs, recordings, reviews, set and costume designs, lighting plans, correspondence, memoirs, sketches and models, are all useful. Even itemized bills are useful. Perhaps the single richest source, particularly if well annotated and if seconded by the other evidence, is the promptbook—a copy of the playscript with notes by the director concerning interpretation, blocking, technical effects, and anything else he wants to have happen on the stage. The notes may be extensive, sufficient to guide a stage manager in conducting rehearsals; thorough promptbooks were written for most of the productions under discussion. Unfortunately, those for *Julius Caesar* and the 1930 *Othello,* though extensive and readily available in published form, are incomplete. The promptbook for *Hamlet* contains very few notes, but the production is well documented in stenograms of important conversations and meetings, myriad reviews, and an admirable collection of ephemera preserved at the Moscow Art Theater Museum. Furthermore, western archival materials have been published, with translations of published Russian documents, in Laurence Senelick's recent reconstruction. On the other hand, there is very little material about the 1918 *Twelfth Night,* barely enough to describe it.

To reconstruct the productions concerned in this book, I have used published materials when available, the archives and ephemera of the Moscow Art Theater Museum, and the Gordon Craig Collection at the Bibliothèque de L'Arsenal, as well as the unpublished materials of other museums, libraries and archives. I am not the first to study these materials, and I acknowledge my indebtedness to the work of those scholars who have preceded me: N.N. Chushkin and B.I. Rostotski in their studies of the 1903 *Julius Caesar,* most particularly in the long introductory essay which precedes their edition of Nemirovich-Danchenko's promptbook; the same N.N. Chushkin in his studies of Kachalov's performance of Hamlet; Denis Bablet in his book *Edward Gordon Craig;* Lawrence Senelick in his painstaking accumulation of facts and documents in *Gordon Craig's Moscow "Hamlet";* M.N. Stroeva and E.I. Poliakova as mentioned above; B.I. Zingerman in his analysis of Stanislavski's promptbook for the 1930 *Othello.* While readers can refer to Senelick for a vivid chronicle of the *Hamlet* production, many materials for the other productions are not available in English; I have therefore incorporated more documentation into those discussions.

I should like to express my appreciation to the Moscow Art Theater Museum for granting me access to its archives and the privilege of working in its reading room. Thanks is also due to the following libraries, museums and archives for their kindness in granting me permission to study their photographs, recordings and unpublished materials: the Library of the All-Russian Theater Society, the Bibliothèque de l'Arsenal, the Houghton Rare Book Library at Harvard University, the Leningrad State Theater Museum and the Bakhrushin Central Theater Museum. None of this farflung research would have been possible without the financial assistance provided by grants from the Concilium on International Relations of Yale University and from the Inter-University Committee on Travel Grants, for which I am most grateful.

I should also like to thank the Soviet scholars and actors who graciously shared their knowledge and reminiscences. The late Vasilii Osipovich Toporkov generously made me welcome at the Art Theater and in his home, and Igor Konstantinovich Alekseev showed me the treasures of the museum that was his father's house. The late Sergei Vaganovich Melik-Zaharov guided me through the Art Theater archives. At the All-Russian Theater Society, Eleonora Matveevna Krasnovskaia helped me locate material, introduced me to Soviet scholars, and steered me to the libraries and theater archives of Moscow and Leningrad. Later, when I returned to continue my research as a student at Moscow State University, Aleksandr Abramovich Anikst consented to direct my work. When seeking answers to specific questions, I was granted interviews by the theater historian N.N. Chushkin, the actress A.G. Koonen, and by V.V. Shverubovich, Dean of the Technical Faculty of the Moscow Art Theater Studio School and son of the actor Kachalov. These kindnesses, and those of many others in both Moscow and Leningrad, made my research doubly fruitful.

Upon returning home, I wrote under the gentle prodding of Robert Jackson at Yale University and rewrote with the editorial advice of my colleague at the University of New Hampshire, Peg Vreeland Aaronian. Dennis Waters and A. Irving Forbes also lent me their expertise. But my greatest debt is to my husband Brian, for encouraging me and reading my drafts and taking over the household so I could keep writing, and to my children David, James and Kira for their patience in putting up with a preoccupied mother.

Unless otherwise specified in the footnotes, all translations of Russian materials presented in this study are mine. In transliterating names and titles from the Russian, I have used the Library of Congress system in the footnotes and bibliography, and less technical but more familiar and readable versions in the text. And lastly, there is a problem with dates because the Russian calendar differed from the Gregorian calender by thirteen days until February 1, 1918, when a Soviet reform introduced the western calendar (so that February 1 became February 14). In this study, all dates are given according to the Gregorian, or Western, calendar.

Introduction

The artist at work, fallible and uncertain of success, is more magnificent than the icon which history will make of him after he is called great. The process is almost as interesting as the perfected idea, and perhaps more instructive. Hence the fascination with writers' notebooks and painters' sketchpads. Hence this study of Stanislavski at work on his creative idea.

Stanislavski is recognized as one of the great men of modern theater, perhaps even the greatest of them all. Twentieth century theater artists owe at least part of their achievement to the base he provided. Because of the immensity of his contribution, however, theater history has too often made him an icon.

A remarkably human and fallible artist, Stanislavski makes unlikely icon material. His great gift was the determination to realize his vision of theater's potential—a determination tempered by the humility to learn from his own mistakes. Even at the end of his life, Stanislavski denied having the last word on the art of the stage. There is no Method, he declared, only a few answers to some of the questions. What history would record as achievements, he saw only as stepping stones to further exploration. Only once did he presume more, after his successes with Chekhov and Gorky, and even then he soon admitted dissatisfaction with the limitations of those discoveries. Stanislavski's legacy, then, is as much his constant creative growth as it is the artistic conclusions he formulated in the process.

When Stanislavski began to stage Shakespeare, early in his professional career, he contested the traditional Russian approach to Shakespeare production. The Russian tradition was relatively young. After more than a century of vague Russian awareness of Shakespeare, his plays exploded onto the Russian stage during the second quarter of the nineteenth century. In no time, Russia accepted Shakespeare as a cultural god. It is not surprising that nineteenth century Russian romantic theater venerated him. Stanislavski, who rejected romantic theater, did not contest the veneration. But he did contest the romantic interpretation.

Stanislavski described his art as realist; he also considered Shakespeare a realist. Realism, as Stanislavski understood it, was rooted in the complexity of ordinary life. He equated romanticism with over-simplification. When romantic theater concentrated on the spiritual turmoil of Shakespeare's main characters, Stanislavski accused it of reducing the play to its principal character, and the character to a single strong passion. *Othello* became Othello, who became Jealousy. Stanislavski's revolt against the romantics was to shape his approach to Shakespeare.

Stanislavski wanted to make Shakespeare come wholly alive on the stage, and saw his realism as an optimal production style. Carefully, he demystified Shakespeare's heroes and made them mundane. He recreated the verity of their assigned time and place with all the experiential intricacy he could muster. Then he staged the conflict between the characters and their respective worlds, trying not to neglect the conflicts within the characters themselves. He was not satisfied with the results. All the details were there, but overall the productions fell short of his intention.

In his rebellion against the distortions of the romantics, Stanislavski created a distortion of his own. The problem lay in his emphasis on the worlds inhabited by Shakespeare's characters, and in his insistence on keeping the characters ordinary. The romantic distortions were founded on a grain of truth: Shakespeare's heroes are drawn to a larger scale than ordinary men and women. Shakespeare can indeed pit a character against his society, because the exaggerated scale of the character makes him equal to the conflict. The characters do not become dehumanized, but rather ultra-humanized: their conflicts are those of ordinary folk, but magnified to reflect universal experience. It was not until his last, abortive, production of a Shakespeare play that Stanislavski came fully to grips with the importance of the individual hero.

Stanislavski's problem is characteristically Russian. In assessing the relative importance of individual and society, the traditional Russian worldview has always weighted the latter, seeing the individual as one component among the many who together constitute the whole. To see the individual as the whole, important in himself, is a Western perception. This Western concept was imported into Russia during the eighteenth century, when Russia imported as much Western culture and technology as possible. The romanticism which dominated the Golden Age of Russian literature attests to the viability of the cult of the individual on Russian soil. But even romantic historical drama gave full play to the preeminence of the will of the people, of society. Later, in the work of Tolstoy and Dostoevski as well as in the intellectual climate of their time, the pendulum swung back to the older native worldview. Stanislavski grew up with it.

Stanislavski was thirty-three when he first tried his hand at producing Shakespeare. He was an amateur actor and director, beginning in family theatricals and then becoming active in Moscow theater groups. In 1890 he was appointed director of the theater of the Society of Art and Literature in Moscow. By this time, he had worked with and learned his craft from the theater greats of late nineteenth century Moscow: Lenski, Ermolova, Fedotova. Part of his ambition was to analyze theatrical truth, and acting in particular, precisely enough that one could thereby train oneself and others in the principles of the art. Eagerly, he studied the techniques of European actors and directors who passed through Moscow on tour. The German troupe of the Duke of Meiningen impressed him with its discipline and the extraordinary verisimilitude of its sets. The Italian tragedians Rossi and Salvini inspired him by the power of their performances. For years, Stanislavski would be torn between the external reality created by the Meininger and the spiritual truth conveyed by the master actors.

It was Salvini's Othello which initially impelled Stanislavski to stage his first Shakespeare production in 1896. The Russian amateur scrutinized Salvini's approach to the role and his preparation for performance in an effort to understand how he achieved such power on the stage. The urge to play Othello became irresistible, Stanislavski wrote later, when he visited Venice with his wife, the actress Lilina. In Venice, the pair researched future sets, accumulating enough information to enable them to recreate Othello's Venice with an accuracy worthy of the Meininger. On the way home, in Paris, Stanislavski met a graceful young Arab in native dress and in him saw Othello. The outward shape of both the play and its main character was decided before Stanislavski reached home.

Stanislavski's interpretation of the play emphasized the clash between two cultures, the Middle Eastern and the Western European. He not only recreated Renaissance Venice on stage, but developed a Cyprus so vivid that there was room for a Turkish-Cypriot uprising against the Venetian overlords. But Othello's problems paled in the glare of the powerfully portrayed historical realities of his time.

Next Stanislavski and his fellow actors attempted Shakespeare's comedies and found them more comfortable to stage. To some extent, Stanislavski began to concentrate more on the actor's performance than on the visual effects, although the genesis of the first of these productions would not so indicate. The 1897 *Much Ado About Nothing* was undertaken for frivolous reasons: Stanislavski had become enamored of swashbuckling on stage, by his own admission, and also wanted to find a play that would permit him to reproduce on stage a medieval castle-museum he had seen in Turin. Inevitably, the external resolution was paramount. *Twelfth Night* was produced the same year, with sets noticeably less important than the quality of the acting. Stanislavski chose this play in order to perform as Malvolio, and he gave his attention to acting from the outset. He was satisfied enough with *Twelfth Night* to revive it during the second season of the infant Moscow Art Theater.

The new theater was established by Stanislavski and Vladimir Nemirovich-Danchenko, a well known playwright and critic. Unlike many of the independent theaters with artistic ambitions, the fledgling Moscow Art

Theater began its existence in good financial condition; Stanislavski was a wealthy man. Having gathered a troupe of talented young actors from the troupe of the Society of Art and Literature and from various theater schools, Stanislavski and Nemirovich-Danchenko prepared to open on October 14, 1898, with *Tsar Fyodor,* a Russian historical play by Aleksei Tolstoy. It was a vivid reproduction of Russian sixteenth century life, as impressive as anything the Meininger had presented, and was well acted. The cast felt that the historical accuracy of the stage environment helped them to perform better. But *The Merchant of Venice* was a disappointment when it appeared on October 21 in spite of its careful mise-en-scène.

The future of the theater was uncertain on the evening scheduled for the première of a play which had not met much success when it was first produced in St. Petersburg: Chekhov's *Seagull.* Nemirovich-Danchenko had pressed for its selection as one of the plays for the first season. The production was a triumph. Chekhov, the Art Theater, and many of the young actors who performed in *The Seagull* made their reputations that night. Ever since, the seagull has been the symbol of the Moscow Art Theater.

Chekhov's plays were ill-suited to traditional methods of production, but the approach developed by Stanislavski seemed ideal. The Art Theater presented the inner truth of Chekhov's plays by carefully combining a mass of everyday details, in an attempt to mirror theatrically the poetic structure of the plays themselves. Stanislavski's emphasis on creating ordinary believable people found a perfect vehicle in Chekhov's understated characters. Through work on Chekhov, Stanislavski and the Art Theater created the beginnings of an integrated new understanding of theater.

Having used the new acting and staging technique to produce Gorky, Ibsen, Hauptmann and other contemporary playwrights, the Art Theater put it to a severe test in 1903. Nemirovich-Danchenko suggested that the theater use its discoveries to stage *Julius Caesar,* a play he had wanted to direct ever since he saw the Meininger perform it. Both he and Stanislavski wanted to present Shakespeare's characters with the psychological subtlety they had learned with Chekhov, and they decided to place them in a vividly reconstructed Julian Rome at a crossroads in history. True to Russian literary tradition, they saw the people of Rome at the play's center. The production was a resounding success at the box office, controversial in intellectual circles, and a partial failure according to Stanislavski and Nemirovich-Danchenko.

Disappointed that the style which worked for Chekhov and other modern playwrights did not seem to apply universally, Stanislavski tried to isolate those aspects of it which would. In 1906 he went to Finland for a summer of self-assessment, and returned confident that he had managed to condense all his theater experience into a few basic truths. This core of ideas was the beginning of what others would eventually call Stanislavski's method.

In spite of some opposition from the members of the Art Theater, Stanislavski embarked on a period of experimentation. If naturalism would not unlock the secrets of the theater of experience, another artistic approach might do so. In that hope, Stanislavski turned to symbolism. In western Europe, the symbolist designers Adolphe Appia and Gordon Craig were fomenting theatrical revolution. New plays were being written in the symbolist mode. Symbolism promised a new artistic truth, and had become a strong creative movement which was already taking root in Russian poetry.

In the theater, as elsewhere, symbolism was the opposite of naturalism. Symbolist designers did not assemble environments for the actor, but created an atmosphere which derived from the essential idea of the given environment. Their sets, shadowy and amorphous, were often composed of static structures made variable with the new technology of lighting. Appia and Craig built airy visions within which the actor communicated his spiritual truths. It was a fragmentary and elusive presentation, far removed from the mundane realities emphasized by naturalistic theater. Furthermore, it served to accentuate the actor rather than overwhelm him. When Stanislavski wanted to liberate his actors from the tyranny of the naturalistic set, the symbolist approach looked very promising.

Stanislavski first heard about Gordon Craig in 1907, when he met Isadora Duncan during her second tour of Russia. Fascinated by what he heard, he invited Craig to come to the Art Theater to produce a play.

The Craig-Stanislavski *Hamlet* premiered in 1912. Craig had evolved an experimental set, using immense screens to create a variety of abstract settings, and he brought it to Moscow for *Hamlet*. Within this nonrepresentational environment, the actors portrayed a dynamic Hamlet and the depraved world he was called upon to cleanse. The Hamlet, played by V.I. Kachalov, became a Russian theatrical landmark, but the brilliance of Craig's visual concept dwarfed the rest of the cast.

As a cooperative venture, the 1912 *Hamlet* was a monumental meeting of two theatrical reformers whose theories were diametrically opposed. While Stanislavski tried to present ordinary human realities in terms of "theater of experience," Craig worked to purify acting of its unpredictable flashes of human emotion and bring the actor closer to the marionette. Both were wholly devoted to creating a new theater, and were able to appreciate the dedication of the other even while disagreeing with him. It was, at least at the start, a unity of opposites.

Misfortune and misunderstanding were eventually to take their toll on the production. A last-minute catastrophe made Craig's curtainless scene changes impossible, so that the screens had to be moved behind the curtain instead of gliding from position to position as if by magic, in full view of the audience. Craig and Stanislavski found it increasingly difficult to work together, and the press eagerly hunted scandal in their deteriorating relationship. All this served merely to make this *Hamlet* one of the notorious, as well as one of the notable, productions of the early twentieth century.

After the 1911 *Hamlet,* Stanislavski began to free himself from his preoccupation with external resolution and to concentrate on acting. At last, he returned wholeheartedly to the art which had so fascinated him when practiced by the great star performers of his youth. Twice more he would stage Shakespeare, once in a studio with his students and once from temporary exile in Nice. The studio production of *Twelfth Night* in 1918 was performed in a small room and very simply set, but splendidly acted. Those who remain of the 1918 audience still praise the performances. The 1930 *Othello,* directed from half a continent away, was devastated by the collapse of its lead actor and Stanislavski's alter ego for the production, Leonidov. Cancelled after the death of the actor playing Iago, it was shown only ten times. Its prompt book has been published, translated, and is generally taken to be an example of Stanislavski's system in action. In both the studio production and the *Othello* that almost was, Stanislavski proved that his discoveries, refined and expanded by years of experiment, worked with Shakespeare.

Stanislavski's long professional career, then, can be divided into three major periods: a naturalist period which has its early and mature stages, an experimental period characterized by forays into symbolist production styles; and the period of psychological realism and the coalescing of his theories about acting. Approximate dates can be given to these periods, though there is some overlap as one style waned and another was coming into being. *Julius Caesar* sounded the knell for the naturalist period, although that style continued to dominate new productions of Chekhov and Ibsen. Stanislavski's brief collaboration with Meyerhold in the Theater Studio in 1905 evidenced the beginnings of experimentation even before the contemplative months in Finland during the summer of 1906. After *Hamlet,* Stanislavski continued to use nonrepresentational sets when he thought them appropriate to a given play, but by the end of 1912 he concentrated on his "system" of acting, and the last period can be said to begin at this time.

Stanislavski believed that Shakespeare's plays were an ultimate test of a mature theater. It is possible, though it is nowhere stated, that Stanislavski saw best in a Shakespeare production that which remained for him to accomplish. Certainly, the 1903 *Julius Caesar* and the 1912 *Hamlet* represented turning points in his artistic development. To see, in this early work, the difficulty with which Stanislavski's original vision was achieved is to better appreciate the achievement.

1

The Nineteenth Century Background

... Form does not arrive spontaneously. Neither does it arrive automatically to express a new message. Form must be created.

Gorelik

It would be difficult to assess the impact of Stanislavski's achievement, the significance of the Moscow Art Theater as an artistic unit, or the nature of the Art Theater's work with Shakespeare, without having some knowledge of what went before. After all, no cultural phenomenon springs into being from a void. It seems appropriate, therefore, to cast a quick glance at Russian theater of the late nineteenth century and at the approach to Shakespeare then current. Moscow theater is of primary interest here, not only because Stanislavski worked in Moscow, but also because the history of late nineteenth century Moscow theater is that of Russian theater as a whole. Both Moscow and St. Petersburg had a strong theater tradition, but it was Moscow that saw most of the drive for theatrical reform and change in the 1880s and '90s.

The interpretation of Shakespeare by scholars and literati usually had little influence on stage interpretation, but some are of interest and will be sketched. More relevant to this study is the quality of the available Russian translation of Shakespeare, and the kind of Shakespeare productions to which Moscow audiences were accustomed.

The State of Russian Theater

Imperial control of Russian theater began under Catherine the Great, intensified under Alexander I and Nicholas I, and reached its apogee in 1854 with the establishment of a complete monopoly of the performing arts by the Imperial theaters. Only café entertainment and variety shows were exempt, and these were not permitted any "dramatic" content, nor could the Imperial artists perform in them. Censorship was stringent: if a play had survived the censor and was published, wholly or in part, there was no guarantee that the Third Department would permit its production. In fact, even criticism of either the actors or the productions of the Imperial theaters was declared, in 1815, "unsuitable for any publication."[1] This particular law was not repealed until 1826, when one journal was allowed to publish a theater column in each issue. While the position of the critics grew steadily better, that of the playwright grew steadily worse. Double censorship was to continue throughout the century, ever unpredictable, never unsuspicious.[2]

All theaters, whether in the provinces or in Moscow and Petersburg, were under the management of a single Director of Imperial Theaters. He was, in turn, responsible to the Court Ministry. The Director appointed the regional officers, all of whom had an established government rank corresponding to their positions in the theatrical Directorate. From 1882 to 1898 the head of the Moscow office was a former army officer, the retired commander of the guard at the Summer Palace, who had been given this post in gratitude for his military service. His righthand man, the director of dramatic personnel, had been promoted to his post from head bookkeeper for the railroads. Most of the other officials of the Moscow office at this time were career army men who had been put into semiretirement by the grant of theater service.[3] Needless to say, this kind of staff was minimally, if at all, concerned with the artistic integrity of the theaters under their charge. There is no indication that the staff of the Moscow office was in any way atypical.

On April 7, 1882, Alexander II ended the monopoly of the Imperial theaters. It must be admitted that a few private theaters had existed during the 1870s. Various individuals and clubs staged plays for their own amusement, without official permission. In 1872, A.F. Fedotov organized a troupe in a theater built for him as part of the Moscow Polytechnic Exhibit. His theater had the support of influential leaders of the Commission for the Improvement of the Living Conditions of Workers and Craftsmen. With their protection, and without official permission, the theater regularly staged classic drama until 1877, well after the Exhibit had closed. The winter of 1880 saw the opening of Anna Brenko's theater in Moscow. In St. Petersburg, she had managed to obtain permission to stage "scenes from plays,"[4] and from them contrived full-fledged productions. Her Pushkin Theater attracted many fine provincial actors and was known for its ensemble acting—a great rarity at the time. Unfortunately, Brenko lacked the business acumen necessary to compete with the new theaters which were formed in 1882.

The new theaters were of two sorts: artistic ventures, like the Pushkin Theater, ambitious but usually short-lived; and business ventures, unambitious, but usually durable. The best example of the latter was the Korsh, established by an entrepreneur of that name. He gathered a talented troupe of performers, some of whom were destined to become well known dramatic actors at either the Maly or the Moscow Art Theater. His repertory was kaleidoscopic, but hardly avant-garde. The theater provided upper and middle class Muscovites with good entertainment, and survived until the October Revolution.

While the new theaters provided the Imperial theaters with long overdue competition, they also attracted young talent which would otherwise have added depth to the troupes of the Imperial theaters. Those troupes became increasingly weaker, and relied more and more on a few outstanding actors at each theater. By the mid-1880s, only these great talents held the Imperial theater together. On the whole, with the rise of the independent theater, the Imperial stage went into a serious state of decline.

As already noted, the Imperial theaters were not run by competent men of theater, nor even by necessarily competent men. The repertory they chose, never noted for its strength, was now selected with an eye to competing with the light entertainment of the private commercial theaters. The directorate was assisted in its choice of repertory by a series of "Committees on theatrical literature," which included playwrights as well as government functionaries. The Committees had been organized to provide lists of plays suitable for production, and thus to recommend good drama to the local theaters. But, since both the censor's office and the local theater directorates showed a marked preference for melodrama, vaudeville and farce, it is understandable that, despite the strongest recommendations from the finest playwrights, melodrama, vaudeville and farce comprised most of the normal theatrical fare. Only when a serious man of theater achieved some measure of power in the local directorate, as did P.P. Gnedich at the Aleksandrinski in St. Petersburg, could the situation improve. There were some exceptions to the usual repertory, resulting from the reformed benefit system.[5] Under the direction of some of the greatest actors of the time, the benefits presented first rate drama, classic and modern. In this way, often *only* in this way, the repertory included Shakespeare, Lope de Vega, Racine, Molière, Hugo, Goethe, Schiller, Ibsen, Pushkin, Gogol', Turgenev, Ostrovski, and Tolstoy.

There were no directors in the modern sense; the function of the director was then little understood and less appreciated. Most of those appointed to direct productions were men of little talent, artistic or organizational. As it worked out in the Maly Theater, the principal director was an appointed official, responsible for the distribution of parts and the ordering of sets. He organized preliminary read-throughs, and tried out aspiring actors for minor roles and understudies. Everything else was assigned to the stage managers and their assistants. There was usually little attempt to create an artistic whole. Any efforts of that sort came from certain star actors, and a few playwrights (notably Ostrovski and Nemirovich-Danchenko), who would take some rehearsals.

The troupe of an Imperial theater was made up of a few very talented star actors, and many lesser performers for the secondary roles. Extras were recruited when necessary; the Maly often used soldiers from the Moscow garrison for this purpose. Bureaucracy strangled hiring practices, so that too many minor actors were second-rate provincial players, for whom a walk-on in

Moscow was preferable to twenty lines in Kursk. These players were given to extreme gestures and effects, to "picturesque" posing. Their speech was affected and unnaturally accented. They used the conventions and devices sanctified by generations of second-rate actors, and they played for immediate audience reaction. The audiences, by the way, were no better—they were accustomed to walking around during performances, and chatting with friends. It must not have been easy to get a reaction from them.

Rehearsals for an average new production occupied two or two and a half weeks. Usually, only mornings and Saturdays were available for rehearsal, since most of the cast would be performing in another play in the evening. After the distribution of roles, the play was read to the cast either by the author or by one of the actors. There would then be a varying number of read-throughs by the cast. At this time, the playwright or a star actor might try to interpret the play for the cast and to explain the nature and significance of each role. Several days were devoted to learning lines. After line rehearsals, the play was blocked. Once the head director was satisfied with the blocking, a full dress rehearsal was supposed to be called. In practice, however, the full dress was omitted in all but historical plays and foreign classics. At this point, the production was considered ready to present to an audience.

Mass scenes were rehearsed separately by an assistant director. At the Maly, rehearsals were usually only held for garrison soldiers, who were largely disinterested in the proceedings. Stagehands, prop men, and other theater workers acted as extras without rehearsal. This perfunctory treatment of extras resulted in offhand confusion during performances. There were exceptions: one production of *The Maid of Orleans* had five rehearsals for all soldiers and other extras. Productions with a minimal number of walk-ons and small parts used actors from the regular troupe—but even they paid little attention to their roles. All of this shoddy rehearsal technique was, however, no worse than the methods which prevailed elsewhere in mid-nineteenth century Europe.

Nor can the Maly's approach to setting and costume be considered unusually backward. As in Europe of the mid-1880s, painted drops and wing pieces were used to provide the setting. A description of the general phenomenon is as apt for the Maly as for any other theater of the time:

> At this time the stage was a huge box with a curtained peep hole opening in the front. When the curtain was raised, the audience looked into a stage flanked by canvas wings, appearing frankly in rows as such, or with hinged flaps for variety, or as "cut outs" supplementing "leg drops" and "set pieces" in an effort toward a painty sort of reality.[6]

In addition to the many defects of this "painty reality," Ostrovski complained, sets for a new production were often chosen from among those used for every other production, and with which audiences had gotten bored long since. As elsewhere in Europe, each theater had a stock of sets from which it drew for any and all productions. Some might be renovated for a new production; others were used "as is." Once in a while, a new set might be made for a classic or an historical play. Props were gathered at random.

There were five or six standard contemporary sets in every theater, all made to fill the whole stage so that a palace interior and that of a peasant hut had the same length and breadth. Most of the sets were interiors: a rich living room, a poor living room, an office, etc. Shakespeare, Schiller, and Pushkin were usually performed in "gothic" settings. When the standard sets were deemed unsuitable, one could sometimes avoid building new ones by borrowing from another theater: the Maly's set for *Antony and Cleopatra* in 1887 was a loan from the Bol'shoi's *Aïda*. More often than not, any resemblance to the period and place of action was strictly coincidental.

After the two Russian tours of the Meininger in 1885 and 1890,[7] certain directors tried to emulate the historical accuracy of its staging techniques. There had been some demand for historical realism as early as the 1860s, and certain directors and star actors made efforts to respond to it, but were hindered by lethargic local directorates. With the Meininger, archeological realism became respectable, and therefore possible in Russian theaters.

As to costumes: according to contracts written during the last decades of the nineteenth century, actors were to provide their own costumes for contemporary plays, and the theater's directorate was to assume responsibility for the costuming of historical plays and character roles. The theaters, therefore, paid no attention to costuming except in the case of historical and classic plays. Star actors received a special grant for costumes, and took care to be beautifully and fashionably dressed; the audiences would be impressed, and no one was concerned about suitability for the role.

As to historical costuming, Stanislavski writes in *My Life in Art* that almost no one was interested in the history of costume. Three costume styles were popular: "*Faust, Les Huguenots,* and Molière, if one does not reckon our national boyar fashions."[8] He tells of one incident in which the Meininger players let a Moscow theater copy scenery and costumes from one of their productions; after each actor altered the costume to suit personal taste, the costume bore no resemblance to the Meininger model but looked as though made for *Faust* or *Les Huguenots.* Theatrical tailors, too, had their traditions and often refused to follow a designer's sketches, chalking up any innovation in costuming to the designer's inexperience. Although it concerns the German stage, Simonson's assessment of mid-nineteenth century costuming is appropriate here: "at best the general effect achieved was that of the usual costume ball."[9]

But in England and France, the Romantics had insisted on historically accurate costuming long before. Gorelik cites the careful historical costuming of Talma and Mlle Mars. He reminds us that, "by the early years of the nineteenth century, the English Romantic directors John Philip Kemble, Edmund Kean and David Garrick had already established the principle of historic and geographic documentation for stage scenery," and that "authenticity of settings and costumes were an established principle in the ensuing presentations of Macready, Charles Kean, Beerbohm Tree and Henry Irving."[10] This English principle did not come to Germany until the Meininger, or to Russia until the mid-1880s. The first tentative Russian venture in this direction was the Maly's decision, in 1882, to stage Griboyedov's classic, *Woe from Wit,* in period dress. In 1889, the Maly hired F.L. Sollogub to design costumes, which he did with great attention to historical and geographical accuracy. Unfortunately, his costumes were used for very few productions— but the tailors seem to have been cooperative in these cases.

The use of music was another disturbing element in productions of this period. When used during a production, it was only vaguely, if at all, related to the period and mood of the play. Most productions were accompanied by musical overtures and entr'actes, whose significance was described by the critic Leonov as "preparing the audience for the mood demanded by the particular play, and maintaining that mood until the end of the performance."[11] However, there seemed to be little connection between this ideal and the reality: polkas were played during the entr'actes for one production of *Hamlet,* for example. Only in 1898, when Lenski banned overtures and entr'actes at the Novy Theater, was there any change in the policy of the Imperial theaters.

All in all, Russian theater needed a thorough change. The repertory needed enriching; the visual production needed serious attention; the star system was deteriorating and needed reform, or even replacement by the new ensemble system used in several European theaters and in Brenko's Pushkin Theater. Responsible artistic direction and extensive preparation for performance were still rare. Theater management was in the hands of bureaucrats, whether government officials or financiers, who had little or no concern for artistic values. There were a few talented reformers fighting within the system, but the deadweight of the Imperial directorate combined with public apathy to crush most of the insurgents. If Russian theater was to be pushed in new directions, it would have to be from outside the Imperial system, in the cutthroat arena of the private theaters. The financial problems of such a venture would have to be overcome at the box office level, by awakening the general public to artistic quality.

The State of Russian Acting

Nineteenth century Russian acting was in the romantic tradition then current in most European theaters. Her star actors were the glory of the Russian stage. All the deficiencies of late nineteenth century Russian theater—weak direction, lack of concern with scenic illusion or integration of production elements—all were countered by the strength of Russia's star actors.

Generally, the romantic actor (Russian or otherwise) used a set, a costume, as mere background for the exhibition of his skill. He played to the audience, hoping to elicit its admiration. The personality of the actor could always be felt distinctly behind the stage character, so that a role seemed necessary only insofar as it served to project the "star." To some extent, the finest of the romantic actors developed character in their roles, but theatricalized it nevertheless by giving primacy to temperament. Thus they too made sure of displaying their virtuosity. Even the acceptance of the new realism did not essentially change a romantic actor—"like Sir Henry Irving, who resisted dramatic realism long after he began to play in 'solid' realistic settings. Not surprisingly, Irving usually turned even these into *coups de théâtre . . .* by subordinating every element in the production to his personality."[12]

Russian acting of the eighteenth century was in conscious imitation of the European classical style, as was Russian literature of the period. In the early nineteenth century, young actors, like the young poets before them, "discovered" the emotional romantic approach and rebelled against the older rational stylizations and formalities. The two acting styles lived side by side for some time in the two great tragedians of the 1830s and 1840s, V.A. Karatygin and P.S. Mochalov. Karatygin was an actor of pure reason, whose studied performances used to great effect the full range of his fine voice and agile body. His acting was consistently good, while Mochalov's was either breathtaking or abysmal (and sometimes both in one evening). The almost illiterate Mochalov was a romantic actor of the first water, and based his acting technique solely on emotion. His furiously vengeful Hamlet remains one of the greatest performances in the history of Russian theater. But when inspiration failed, his performances had all the vitality of a broken balloon.

At the same time, a short fat comedian was consciously developing a system of acting that was to affect every great Russian actor after him. M.S. Shchepkin was the finest comic actor of the century. The critic Aksakov described him as "a rare combination of talent, a clear brain, and a fervent devotion to art."[13] Coming onto the stage in the wake of the neo-classical period, he was early impressed by the naturalness of the amateur actor Prince Meshcherski. Shchepkin rebelled against the affectations of the old style, but did not, like the romantics, leap headlong into a morass of new affectations. He began to develop a style based on personal experience and observation, these being his guides to a believable presentation of emotion on the stage. No believer in *emploi,* Shchepkin played dramatic as well as strictly comic parts, and was famous for blending comic and tragic elements into his characterizations. He was capable of giving startling dramatic depth to farce, so that an audience might find its laughter suspended and themselves oddly touched by the character he played.

Shchepkin's approach was largely intellectual. Although he railed against effect, and argued for naturalness and simplicity, he did not believe in "living" a role, but rather in so thoroughly understanding it that it could be presented fully, with all its complexities, in the theater. He tried singlehanded to bring something of the concept of ensemble acting onto the stage. In fact, when a "star" comic performance would dwarf the work of the other actors in a given production, Shchepkin would gear his own acting to the level of that of the rest of the cast. He taught the value of constant work on a role, and the need to study life at every moment in order to inform one's interpretation of a role. "The theater is a temple," he wrote, and demanded dedication from its artists: "treat it with reverence, or get out."[14]

He instructed his colleagues, attended their rehearsals, and helped them define and solve acting problems. He taught students recommended by the ballet school, and took the most promising of them into his home, where he gave them a most rigorous training. Some of his students became the greats of the next generation.

By posing cardinal questions about the relation of art to reality and about the limits of theatricality, Shchepkin's system derived a series of basic tasks for the education of an actor. To ascertain the nature of these tasks involves considerable rummaging in Shchepkin's unfinished "notes," his extensive correspondence, and the memoirs of his fellow actors and his students. Shchepkin seems to emphasize the study of the play as an artistic whole, careful analysis of the character to be played and its role within the play, the study of life and the analysis of one's own emotional experience, control of the will and the development of one's physical and vocal abilities, constant attention to stage action and one's fellow players during a performance, naturalness and simplicity of behavior on the stage. All this seems pathetically elementary to the modern reader, but little of it was to be found in nineteenth century European theaters.

Students like Fedotova, Shchubert and Shumski taught Shchepkin's system to their colleagues and students. During 1888–89, Fedotova trained Stanislavski and his fellow actors from the Society of Art and Literature.[15] Every actor on the Imperial stage, whether he came there from an acting course or from the provincial theaters, was touched by Shchepkin's work. Thus the great Russian actors of the latter half of the nineteenth century shared a realistic tradition which added depth and versatility to a romanticism in constant danger of sinking into superficiality and stereotype. Lesser actors, however, aped the gestures and devices of Shchepkin with no understanding of the approach that spawned them.

During the latter half of the nineteenth century there are two directions to be noted: the move toward establishing good drama schools, and the attempt somehow to codify the practical knowledge of acting technique so that the achievements of great actors could be preserved and used to train young actors.

There had been schools attached to the Imperial theaters for some time, but the curriculum tended to be weak. An aspiring actor usually began by studying ballet; if he were selected to study dramatic acting, the ballet school would send him to a prominent actor for lessons. In 1868, the director Voronov wrote his "Project for a drama class in the St. Petersburg theater school," suggesting a very basic program for training actors. It was ignored. Developing Voronov's ideas, Boborykin published his program for the systematic schooling of actors, and seven years later, in 1879, helped establish a drama school. Books and articles on the art of acting and the training of actors appeared frequently, but few had any value.

In 1882, an Imperial committee was formed to draft a "Proposal concerning the administration of the Imperial theaters." Included in the committee were three playwrights, Ostrovski among them, as well as myriad court ministers and functionaries of the Directorate. The basic administrative system remained unchanged, and Ostrovski felt that his recommendations were largely ignored. But despite his pessimism, several minor reforms resulted from the work of this committee. Among them was the initiation of a project to overhaul the curriculum of the Imperial theater schools, and the foundation, in 1883, of several private theater schools. One of these latter, which was established by the Moscow Philharmonic Society, was briefly headed by Shchepkin's student Fedotova, and would later include Nemirovich-Danchenko on its faculty. Stanislavski attended this school, but only for three weeks:

> In my time they required a rather complete course of general culture, and many subjects of a general nature were compulsory. Learned professors crammed our heads with all sorts of information about the play we were rehearsing. This aroused thought, but our emotions were quiescent. They described the play ... very eloquently and vividly, that is, they described the final results of creative work, but told us nothing of how we were to do it. We were taught to play a given role, but we were not taught our craft. We felt the absence of any basics and any system.[16]

In 1888, acting courses were introduced at the Moscow theater school, and famous actors were brought in to teach. Following the suggestions of Boborykin's book, however, the school promulgated the acting style of the Comédie Française. The curriculum was similar to that of the school of the Philharmonic Society. Required courses included: history of Russian and foreign literature, history of drama and theater, church history, civil history, a foreign language, diction, fencing, singing, painting, "practical drama," and the preparation of examination productions.

During the 1890s, a number of serious articles by Russian actors appeared in the press. Among the best of these were several by Iur'ev who was one of the first to discuss the actor as creator, and the director as organizer of the production and interpreter of the play. The 1890s saw a series of articles by

A.P. Lenski, a star at the Maly and an instructor of "the practice of dramatic art" at the Moscow theater school. Already known as an innovator, he continued the line of thought initiated by Shchepkin. He claimed unlimited artistic freedom for the theater, insisting that theater was not a mere audio-visual illustration of literary works, but that it combined with the playwright to create a joint artistic statement. These articles, and others like them, reflected the new surge of creative thought on the part of Russian theater artists. Their theories and analyses of their art fired the imaginations of the young. But the excitement of their ideas did not penetrate to the directorates. Nor were the theatrical entrepreneurs interested; only the private theaters which styled themselves as "artistic" were likely to provide fertile ground for new ideas. So far, nothing substantial had taken root.

In 1895, feeling that the Moscow theater school was not giving its students enough practical experience, Lenski organized matinée productions with the young actors. The repertory was taken primarily from Russian and foreign classics. They rehearsed whenever the acting students could muster up some free time, and borrowed whatever sets and costumes they could. In spite of this necessarily haphazard approach, many of the productions thus staged were selected by the Maly to become part of their regular repertory. In 1898, dogged by the conservatism of the directorate and hoping to escape it to some extent, Lenski established the Novy Theater. It was based on the work of the matinée troupe, from which it took many of its actors, and was affiliated with the Maly, on which both Lenski and the new theater were financially dependent. Both opera and drama were performed at the Novy; Lenski served only as dramatic director. In this position, he was able to continue his exploration into acting methods—but not for long. The conservatism of his fellow directors, the destruction of Lenski's acting ensemble by the Maly's insistence on the inclusion of its "stars" into the troupe, and pressure from the Maly to abandon the classical repertoire, convinced Lenski to leave the Novy. He spent the last years of his life in appointed positions within the Maly directorate. He was to describe his struggle with the bureaucrats there as a labor of Sisyphus: he could not, for example, get Shaw or Ibsen or Gorky staged at the Maly even while their plays were appearing regularly at the Moscow Art Theater. He finally left the theater altogether in 1908, and died a few months later. His whole life seemed to him to exemplify the futility of reforming the Russian theater from within the Imperial system.

Lenski was primarily an actor, and his first concern was the actor's art. He saw the actor as central in theater, and all other elements of production as subordinated to him. Eventually, almost a generation ahead of anyone else in Russian theater, Lenski came to see the stage set as an environment for acting. He also saw that the actors must become an ensemble. While the actor creates equally with the playwright to shape a theatrical idea, in order to develop that idea all elements of the production must be subordinated to the whole. A strong director is therefore necessary; he coordinates all the factors which go into a production, and assumes ultimate responsibility for everything. Still later, Lenski came to see the director as creator as well as organizer of the production: it is the director who determines the interpretation of the play taken as a whole, and it is he who decides the style of its presentation. Rather than limit the actor, however, the director assists him: he helps the actor find the "essence" of his role, and express it as fully as possible within the given interpretation and style of the production. In general, Lenski continued the tradition begun by Shchepkin, but unlike Shchepkin, Lenski went so far as to say that the actor must live his role on the stage. Always he came back to the problem of acting. If there was to be any renewal of Russian theater, it must be generated by an improved understanding of the actor's art.

As actor, director, and theoretician, Lenski had a great deal of influence on the young amateur actor and director, Stanislavski. The younger man adopted many of the ideas of the older, and was to develop them with the independence of the private theater artist. Lenski, along with several other of the Maly's "stars," enthusiastically supported the younger man's efforts, and helped him in his work at the Society of Art and Literature. When both the Novy and the Moscow Art Theaters embarked upon their first seasons in 1898, there was a sense of mutuality about their endeavors. New things were going to happen in Russian theater, and both troupes were trying to bring it all about. If Lenski sometimes expressed envy at the accomplishments of his prospering admirer, it was because he, Lenski, had so often been thwarted by the directorate in his efforts to work along the same lines.

In fall of 1905, Lenski and Nemirovich-Danchenko discussed the possibility of merging the Maly and the Moscow Art Theaters, and hoped for a government subsidy plus independence from an official directorate. When a merger seemed unrealistic, there was talk of getting the Maly to invite Nemirovich-Danchenko to direct. But the directorate was leery of any reform that Nemirovich-Danchenko might bring with him, and Nemirovich-Danchenko was equally leery of the directorate, so that by 1907 all these projects were dropped.

It would seem appropriate here to focus briefly on the founders of the Moscow Art Theater before they joined forces. Konstantin Sergeevich Alekseev, whose stage name was Stanislavski, was the scion of a wealthy merchant family, and only a young amateur actor and director, when he helped found the Society of Art and Literature in 1888. His partners were well-established artists: the playwright and director A.G. Fedotov, the opera singer F.P. Komissarzhevski, and the artist F.L. Sollogub. (At the time, Stanislavski was a student of both Komissarzhevski and Sollogub.) The Society sponsored many activities, including classes in acting and singing, but it was not long before its dramatic presentations became its mainstay. The Society concentrated on staging forgotten, "untheatrical," and generally little-known plays—producing, for example, Tolstoy's *Fruits of Enlightenment* even before the professional theaters were allowed to present it publicly. Lenski, and Maly star actresses Fedotova and Ermolova sometimes directed and sometimes served as critical observers. The audience was mainly drawn from the intelligentsia and Moscow artistic circles. When Stanislavski was appointed director of the Society's theater group in 1890, it was this audience which accused him of blindly imitating the Meininger. Stanislavski was under the influence of the Meininger, doubtless; it was touring Russia that year and Stanislavski attended as many performances and rehearsals as he could. He was enthusiastic about its innovations. But Stanislavski was developing an approach very much his own: he planned each production thoroughly and thoughtfully, not only in terms of physical detail and external realism, but also with an increasing concern for understanding and interpreting the play and each role within it. There was at least as much of Shchepkin and Lenski in Stanislavski's work, even then, as there was of Meininger.

In June of 1897, three months after the futile first "All-Russian Conference of Theater Workers," Stanislavski received a letter from Vladimir Ivanovich Nemirovich-Danchenko, inviting him to meet and talk. Nemirovich-Danchenko was then a well known playwright and critic who taught drama at the Philharmonic Society's school, had some informal directing experience at the Maly, and acted occasionally in amateur productions. His reputation as critic and man of theater was considerable, and at the time his stock as playwright was much higher than Chekhov's. The two men met at a Moscow restaurant, the Slavianski Bazaar, and decided to establish a new theater together. At this famous meeting, they talked for eighteen hours to define their goals in undertaking the project. Their theater would be accessible, with tickets at reasonable prices and with productions which would speak to issues of general public concern. Their repertory would be taken from the best plays of past and present, both Russian and foreign. These plays would be staged so as to replace popular cliché with psychological truth and spoken simplicity. In no way should a production portray life as alien to that lived by its audiences; this theater was not to deal in escapist entertainment. Finally, and perhaps most important for the development of world theater, they wanted to train a new kind of actor, free from the despotism of accumulated theatricality. The core of the new troupe would come from among the most promising actors of the Society of Art and Literature, and the best of Nemirovich-Danchenko's drama students. As to the working relationship of the two founders, it was immediately decided that each would have the last word in his own particular specialty. Nemirovich-Danchenko was the final authority in literary and administrative affairs, and Stanislavski in matters regarding acting, directing, and technical production. It was to be a fruitful and remarkably long-lived working relationship.

Shakespeare on the Russian Stage: Translation, Interpretation, Scholarship

Shakespeare's plays began to wend their way into Russia as early as the mid-seventeenth century. The earliest traces are the "English comedies" (*The Jew of Venice, Hamlet, Romeo and Juliet, King Lear, Othello, Julius Caesar*) played at the court theaters of tsars Aleksei Mikhailovich and Peter the Great. These were probably not even close enough to the originals to be called adaptations. Beginning with Sumarokov's 1850 *Hamlet*, the eighteenth century saw a series of adaptations and translations from the Ducis and LeTourneur versions of Shakespeare—all more closely related to French classical drama than to anything Elizabethan. Sumarokov's *Hamlet* is the best from among these, but is clearly the work of a classicist who considered the English playwright to be in need of considerable civilizing. As the century drew to a close, however, a new sensibility brought more respect for Shakespeare's "barbarisms." When Karamzin's translation of *Julius Caesar* appeared in 1787, it seemed to be a generally faithful rendition, probably done largely from the original.

The translations of the early nineteenth century, of which there were quite a few, still drew mostly from the French versions of Ducis and LeTourneur. It was not until the 1830s that a significant number of translators began to work from the original. Vrontchenko's *Hamlet* (1828), *King Lear* (1832), *Macbeth* (1834), and Polevoi's *Hamlet* (1837) began this new wave. Gradually, Russian Shakespeare translation was freed from the shackles of French classicism. More and more of the plays began to appear in Russian. By 1841, thirteen plays had been translated and published and by 1855 there were only six plays left untranslated. Yet the quality of those translations left much to be desired; the critic Belinski lamented that a great number of bad translations were being published, while better translations languished in manuscript in various archives.[17] It was during the 1840s that the great debate about optimal methods of translating Shakespeare began: it was literal prose versus form-retaining poetry. Today, the debate is still unresolved. There are the magnificent verse translations of Boris Pasternak on the one hand, and on the other the prose translations of Lozinski, whose extraordinary academic literalism manages to retain some of the originals' poetic style.

The complete works of Shakespeare were published in Russian in 1865–68, as collected and edited by Nekrasov and Gerbel. In 1899, the fifth edition of the complete works was published, under Mikhalski. As better translations appeared, they would usually be included in the next edition. On the stage, however, habit reigned supreme. Polevoi's *Hamlet,* for example, had been superceded time and again by better translations—but theaters kept using the Polevoi version. It worked well enough on the stage; both actors and audiences were accustomed to it, and known inaccuracies could always be eliminated by patching in lines from better translations.

By 1899, the level of Shakespeare translation was reasonably high, if not staggeringly so. Further, a number of simplified adaptations made Shakespeare more broadly known. There had been a few attempts at translations for the stage, some of which were painfully bad. One of them, however, won the Pushkin Prize from the Academy of Sciences in 1886; it was a *Macbeth,* translated by the actor Iur'ev. Henceforward, stageworthiness was increasingly sought in new translations of Shakespeare.

Although Shakespeare was just becoming known in Russia at the beginning of the nineteenth century, Shakespeare studies were already included in the literature programs of several Russian universities thirty years later. By the 1840s Shakespeare had become sacred; even the censors were apologetic about suppressing a line from one of his plays (or a whole play from a theater's repertory) [18]—an unusual attitude in a Russian censor at any time. Articles about Shakespeare were translated from French, German and English. Belinski's 1838 article on Mochalov as Hamlet marked the real beginning of original Russian Shakespeare criticism. At once influenced by and repudiating the German "Hamletism," Belinski found in Hamlet a synthesis of several contemporary types. He saw Hamlet as forceful, energetic, and yet "afraid for man." [19] From Belinski on, the bulk of Russian Shakespeare criticism would deal with the characters rather than the plays, and that usually in terms of their relevance as symbols of current Russian types.

In the 1840s, Botkin and Zotov established a reputation as specialists in Shakespeare. By the 1860s the study of Shakespeare was recognized as a field in itself, and a sizeable body of original literature on Shakespeare already existed. The foremost foreign studies were almost invariably translated into Russian, as were a number of lesser monographs. The radical critics debated the relevance of Shakespeare and the Shakespeare cult to modern Russia, but in the 1870s the cult grew stronger than ever. Numerous "Shakespeare circles" were formed, where the bard's works might be read, discussed, translated, and even performed.

Turgenev's article, "Hamlet and Don Quixote," appeared in 1860. Like Belinski, Turgenev was more interested in literary characters than literary works, and he dealt with these two as representative of universal human types. The reading of Hamlet was new, however. Turgenev saw him as epitomizing the cold egocentric tendency in man: unloving, cynical, genuinely suffering— but from wounds largely self-inflicted, Hamlet was seen as ultimately ineffectual and isolated from the flow of human life. In Turgenev's short stories, the 1830s Hamlets-of-great-emotional-power were watered down to the Hamlet-of-Shchigrov-District, whose most salient characteristics were inaction and self-pity. If Shakespeare was relevant to the 1860s, the modern Hamlet was not. Elsewhere Turgenev localized Lear into "King Lear of the Steppes," and a story by Leskov had Lady Macbeth taking up residence in Mtsensk. By the time Chekhov wrote *Ivanov* in 1887, hamletism had become a cheap pose: "I've been playing Hamlet, and you've been playing a noble-minded young girl. . . ."[20] A decade later, Mikhailovski condemned young Hamlets and *the* Hamlet himself: "Hamlet is an idler and a milquetoast, and from this angle idlers and milquetoasts can recognize themselves in him."[21]

Serious scholarship, however, was not attuned to this popularized Shakespearism. The leading Shakespeare scholar of turn of the century Russia was N.I. Storozhenko, whose articles and studies dealt wiith the evolution and structure of several of the plays, and with the comparison of Shakespeare's works to literature of the Renaissance. Rather than deal in philosophical interpretations of Shakespeare's dramatic literature, he treated the plays as inseparable from platform and actor.

Despite Storozhenko's integrated and theatrical approach to Shakespearean drama, his studies were entirely ignored by the theater artists of the time. Russian theater of the 1880s and '90s still preferred to perform Shakespeare in terms of character study. One went to see Hamlet, Othello, and Macbeth, not *Hamlet, Othello,* and *Macbeth.* The romantic tradition of acting all but demanded this approach. Of course, this is not to say that there were not some brilliant Hamlets, Othellos, and Macbeths. But the acting gave precedence to individual virtuosity rather than to new interpretations.

There were exceptions; one of these was Dalmatov's 1891 Hamlet, in the Gnedich translation. The actor saw Hamlet as a sort of early Christian philosopher living in pagan territory, rather than as a Renaissance humanist. In fact, he saw Hamlet himself has having a good bit of the pagan in him. Ophelia, on the other hand, was simply a healthy wench, totally incapable of coping with the alien thinking of her lover. Gnedich, who also directed the play, did not subscribe to this interpretation, but Dalmatov was adamant. He played it his way, and the rest of the cast played it Gnedich's way. Feeling must have run very high; when Gnedich gave Dalmatov a specially bound copy of his translation, he inscribed it "in memory of mutual torment."[22] The production was extremely successful at the box office and with the critics, although Dalmatov's unconventional approach got poor reviews.

As might be expected, it was Lenski who insisted on staging Shakespeare's plays as dramatic entities, rather than as an excuse to present an interesting character. He wrote, "I am completely convinced that, apart from the quality of his poetry, the success of Shakespeare in his time, and in our own, depends not so much on the degree of talent in a given actor as on the harmonious performance of the plays, and on simple unaffected acting and a like production style."[23] When he established the Novy, Lenski was able to test these ideas. *A Midsummer Night's Dream* was presented in 1899; it provided the perfect starting point for a theater in which production style was to take precedence over star roles. Lenski sought to convey the spirit of the play, its intricate interplay of lyric and comic, of fantasy and reality. Music was an important element of the production and was used as a unifying factor. The great success of this production led to a series of Shakespeare productions both at the Novy and at the Maly. In all of them, the play itself was foremost. In *Coriolanus* (1902), the portrayal of Rome and its people was presented as central to the portrayal of Coriolanus himself. Some critics objected to the eminence given to the Roman crowd, and to the conflict between people and leader. But many others were enthusiastic. Although there is no written evidence, one must assume that Stanislavski and Nemirovich-Danchenko were also favorably impressed; there are many echoes of Lenski's *Coriolanus* in their 1903 interpretation of *Julius Caesar.*

In 1905, Lenski produced his last Shakespearean masterwork, *The Tempest.* Music was central to the presentation, and the set underscored the fantastic and the dreamlike. Lenski saw the play as speaking for the supremacy of human spirit over raw instinct. This interpretation was so strong an element in the production that the critics note that it was the interpretation of the play rather than the actors' fine performances that remained with the audiences as they left the theater. It would seem that Lenski had finally succeeded in his long drive to present a dramatic work as a whole, in so impelling a style that the audience would remember its ideas and images as well as its main characters.

Meanwhile, the Moscow Art Theater had taken root and its directors were putting their ideas into practice. Moscow audiences were witnessing the beginning of a new era in theater, an era foretold by the work of Shchepkin— an era which came into full flowering after Lenski, through the efforts of Stanislavski and Nemirovich-Danchenko.

2

Naturalism: The 1903 *Julius Caesar*

We must play Shakespeare differently than other theaters do; we must stage Caesar *in Chekhovian tones.*

Stanislavski

The Meininger Innovation and Stanislavski's Early Shakespeare Productions

Accustomed to fine performances from its star actors, Moscow was enthusiastic but not breathless over the performances of star actors on tour from the capitals of Western Europe. However, the revolution in theater organization and scenic presentation which a German troupe brought to Moscow and Petersburg stages astounded Russian theater goers. Stanislavski was among them, and recorded that, in 1885 and again in 1890, "the famous company of the Duke of Meiningen, headed by the stage manager Cronegk, came to Moscow. Their performances introduced us Muscovites to productions that were historically true, with mass scenes, splendid outer form and amazing discipline."[1]

Both Antoine, in France, and Stanislavski, in Russia, were profoundly impressed by this court theater from an obscure German state. The Duke of Saxe-Meiningen was not only its director, but also its scene designer. His handling of scenic production demanded historical naturalism and, to achieve it, the devoted collective work of actors and technicians together. His demands and methods were a revelation to the theater of nineteenth century Europe. Every theatrical element was woven into an elaborate tapestry; every detail was given the attention due to a contribution to the total impression. Setting was carefully related to play, period, and to the actor. Crowd scenes were planned, and rehearsed, for credibility. A large range of sound effects were used to heighten emotional impact, as were lighting effects (light was used in varying intensities, and often covered a remarkable range of visual impressions). The effect of all this has been described as the creation of an intensified reality, giving to remote events so strong a semblance of actuality that they seemed to be lived the first time.[2] Stanislavski recalled that "I did not miss a single one of their performances, and I went not only to see them but also to study."[3]

Stanislavski was not unaware of the deficiencies of the Meininger: the directors' lack of respect for the actor's art, and the resultant overemphasis on production elements. Meininger acting differed little from the German romantic tradition, save in the unity of ensemble playing. The romantic style was also associated with star-dominated performances, and audiences were disappointed that the Meininger gave them no star. After their 1885 tour of Russia, Ostrovski wrote in his diary:

> Their acting does not bestow the full soul-satisfying impression that comes from a work of art. What we've seen in their theater is not art, but expertise, i.e. workmanship. These are not the plays of Shakespeare and Schiller, but a series of living pictures from their plays. Nonetheless, the production makes a strong and pleasant impression while it is being performed.... The director is visible everywhere. It is obvious that even the leads act by command and by design.[4]

The problem was more than the lack of the customary "star," and Stanislavski began to understand that when he commented that the "necessity to create for everyone turned the stage director into a despot."[5] It would be some time before he grasped where the deficiency lay, and his admiration for the methods of the Meininger would prove as great a stumbling block as it was an impetus. For better and for worse, Stanislavski's early steps as a director would be guided by this new German naturalism.

He attended some of their rehearsals, and became acquainted with the Duke's righthand man, Chronegk, a strict disciplinarian who was to become Stanislavski's model for a time. From Chronegk, Stanislavski learned the importance of organization and the necessity for a strong director to visualize the whole and to integrate all the theatrical elements, and thus to create a single interpretative statement. The Moscow Art Theater was to inherit much from the Meininger: the tradition of equality among actors, having even the strongest actors play occasionally in crowd scenes; the tremendous discipline and perfectionism, as evidenced in their numerous rehearsals; the spirit of innovation and experiment; and, not least, the welcome reception of ideas from any member of the company. It is proof of the magnitude of the inheritance that a description of a rehearsal in the early Art Theater sounds very like a Meininger rehearsal, and vice versa.

Aside from the innovations learned from the Germans, Stanislavski—as director of the more or less amateur theater of the Society of Art and Literature—was effecting in his little domain many of the reforms that Lenski was struggling for in the Maly. The repertory was solid, chosen from among the best foreign and domestic plays, whether classical or contemporary. Each production was thoroughly rehearsed, in line with the lessons taught by the

Meininger. The actors were disciplined, if not thoroughly trained, and accustomed to playing in ensemble rather than as a constellation. Stanislavski and his troupe were in good form, and ready for challenge.

It was, however, the performance of Tommaso Salvini as Othello that inspired Stanislavski to produce that play and to take the lead role. The decision found support from the French critic Lucien Besnard, who wrote to Stanislavski, "after seeing your Society perform so beautifully in that awful play by Pisemski [*Bitter Fate*]. I am eager to see your troupe play *Othello*."[6] When Stanislavski visited Venice in 1895 with his wife, the actress Lilina, "the craving to play the Moor became almost unbearable."[7] Together, they spent much of their time in Venice collecting material for the production, "visiting museums, searching for antique objects, sketching costumes from frescoes, buying brocades, embroidery, and even furniture."[8] In Paris, they went to various theater suppliers to buy authentic-looking props, and material for costumes.

In Paris Stanislavski met the handsome Arab who was the second inspiration for his Othello. When the Arab learned that Stanislavski was interested in his costume, he took off his outer garment so that Stanislavski could make a pattern of it.

> Then I studied the Arab's movements. Returning to my hotel, I stood half the night before a mirror, putting on sheets and towels in order to turn myself into an elegant Moor, learning to turn my head quickly, move my hands and body with the grace of a startled deer, practising a smooth royal walk, and gesturing with rigid hands whose palms always faced whomever was being addressed.[9]

Work on the production began when Stanislavski returned to Moscow. There were casting problems, which resulted in giving the role of Desdemona to a totally inexperienced actress, and inviting a weak professional actor to play Iago. Since production costs had already eaten up the Society's financial resources and there was no way to rent space, rehearsals took place in Stanislavski's apartment, "in the one small room I could spare."[10] (Eventually the Hunters' Club found a room to lend for the rehearsals.) These sessions were scheduled daily, and often lasted until three or four in the morning. Not all of his actors could take this grueling schedule, and Stanislavski had to find a new Rodrigo halfway through rehearsals.

The intensity of this work is reflected by the elaborate notes in the prompt-book. Most of the notes are essentially mechanical, noninterpretive—but no detail was considered too small, no extra too insignificant, to be discussed thoroughly. Everything is noted: costumes, props, lighting, even the quality of sound to be produced by a crowd at a given moment. (There are so many complicated crowd scenes that this element is color coded: little squares of color represent the different kinds of crowd noises desired at any given moment as described in expansive insertions to the notes.[11]) Stanislavski indicates specific lines for members of the crowd, as well as blended overall sounds. While he does not discuss characterization here, he does determine external gestures and movement for each character. In I, i, for instance, we know when Rodrigo coughs, grows hoarse, wipes his forehead. Stanislavski defines the behavior of each character with the same precision that he fixes the external appearance of the set, props and costumes. N.A. Popov, the Rodrigo who dropped out of the production, kept his notes and described them in his reminiscences: "Now, when I look at this scrap of director's notes, it strikes me as technically rather naïve, but in 1897 [sic] these notes were a complete revelation to me."[12]

After an open dress rehearsal held earlier in the week, *Othello* had its premiere on February 1, 1896, on the little stage of the Hunter's Club. (Several months later, the production was moved into the more spacious Solodovnikov Theater, secured for Stanislavski by the impressario Lentovski.) Lucien Besnard, the Italian tragedian Ernesto Rossi, several actors from the Maly, and numerous critics sat in the house. From more than a few of them, Stanislavski could count on receiving a fair evaluation of what he had achieved with *Othello.*

As Stanislavski was moved by the sounds and sights of Venice to create his own *Othello,* so his Othello was portrayed as living in Renaissance Venice and Cyprus, surrounded by the sights and sounds of that time and those places. It was Othello on a human scale, rather than a romantic display of heroic passion. In fact, the critics were to find fault with the simplicity of Stanislavski's interpretation. Rather than the usual African, boiling over with tropical jealousy, Stanislavski played an Arab who, as Pushkin described Othello sixty years earlier, was "not by nature jealous; to the contrary, he is credulous."[13] A cultured man and a leader of considerable authority, he is nonetheless despised by the Venetians, and in turn he disdains them as mere intriguers. His abduction of a white aristocrat brings about a conflict which underscores this relationship between alien general and his resentful Venetian employers.

On Cyprus, the strife between Europe and Near East is given a broader focus. The Cypriots, only recently conquered by Venice, are far from subdued. Cyprus is shown as Turkish, with the extras in Near Eastern dress sharp contrast to Venice. To sharpen the sense of barely suppressed hatreds, the fistfight in act II, scene 3, is magnified into a short-lived rebellion. Iago orders Roderigo: "Away, I say! Go out, and cry—a mutiny!" and his next two lines are: "who's that which rings the bell? Diablo, ho! The town will rise!" Stanislavski used these lines to occasion the rebellion: crowds of Cypriots stole down the two streets on stage, toward the coffee house (center stage), armed with bared scimitars, sabers and even sticks, intending to attack their conquerers. To meet the attack, the Venetians were drawn up stage front with their backs to the audience. When at last the two groups of Cypriots fell upon the Venetians, a realistic fight ensued. In the midst of it, Othello rushed onstage, brandishing a huge sword with which he seemed to cut the contending factions in two. Then another brief clash—and Montano has been wounded. The actors' attention is focused on him, but while he is being carried off, a patch of light picks up a figure in the crowd. It is an old Muslim, impassively observing the fight, the wounded man, Cassio's arrest; nothing surprises him anymore—he has seen it all before.

The interior sets were striking, historically accurate representations of the Venetian and the Moorish. More striking were the exteriors. When the first curtain rose to the sound of the distant striking of a tower clock, there was a far-off splashing of oars. A floating gondola stopped on the stage; with a clang of chains it was fastened to a painted Venetian pile, after which it rolled gently in the water. (To intensify the realism of the set, Iago was directed to dip his hand into the canal, into noticeably real water—available in a hidden washtub next to the gondola.) Roderigo and Iago began their scene sitting in the gondola, then disembarked under the colonnade of a house which resembled the Palace of the Doges. After the alarum was raised and Desdemona's abduction was known, the entire house came to life: casements opened; sleepy figures looked out; servants put on their armor as they emerged from the house, picked up their weapons, and ran off to seize the Moor. Some jumped into the gondola and rowed under the bridge; others crossed the bridge on foot. The careful build-up to this frenzied activity caught the audience at once, and the realism of the set gave it all an irresistible immediacy.

In Cyprus, the principal street scene, on which the rebellion took place, showed a Turkish coffee house on the forestage center at the corner of two narrow Oriental streets. A constant bleak drizzle created puddles which hindered passersby. Near Eastern music and conversation emanated from the coffee house. In the early scenes Cypriots strolled in groups, holding their knives at the ready under flowing costumes and sneering at the drunken Europeans. It was easy work for Iago to foment an uprising in this atmosphere—and thus Stanislavski could invite the audience to learn first-hand of Iago's nasty talent for provocation. The revolt would also brand Iago as not above treason, and justify Othello's severity toward Cassio.

While Stanislavski made sixteenth-century Venice and Cyprus come alive on his set, he was less concerned with fidelity to Shakespeare's text. In Act I, the first two scenes were combined. The last two acts, those which Stanislavski found particularly onerous in performance, were heavily cut (and only slightly annotated, and that with a decided lack of originality[14]). In Act II, as we have seen, a single line became a whole mimed scene.

As a production, *Othello* was overwhelmingly successful. But the acting left much to be desired. While technical acting achievements like the crowd scenes were praised, Iago and Desdemona were poorly received and Stanislavski's Othello got mixed reviews. The magnificent sets, crowd scenes,

Figure 1.   1896 *Othello*. Othello (Stanislavski) in Venetian dress.

Figure 2.   1896 *Othello*. Exterior set: Venice, in opening scene.

Figure 3.   1896 *Othello*. Exterior set: Cyprus, in act II.

Figure 4.   1896 *Othello*. Interior set: Venice, the Senate.

Figure 5.   1896 *Othello*. Othello's study, with Roderigo, Othello
(Stanislavski) in Arab dress, Emilia, and Desdemona.

special effects and interpretative surprises like the Cypriot revolt carried the first half of the play, but after the third act the glitter faded and the threadbare acting was too poor to sustain interest. Othello himself lost color and strength: Stanislavski's voice began to give out, as he admitted in *My Life in Art* and as all the reviews noted.

At the time, Stanislavski's *Othello* was popularly understood to be no more than a brilliant, and intentional, imitation of the Meininger—who were not noted for their acting. But Stanislavski had intended more, and succeeded to an extent. He wanted to use the same kind of historicity as the Germans, but to use it in order to lend immediacy and credibility to a character usually played as much larger than life. The Meininger did not seem to use their vaunted scenic authenticity in this way; the art of acting and the problems of establishing a believable character do not appear to have been primary concerns in that theater. On the other hand, contemporary critics did not perceive this focus in Stanislavski's Othello either, which upset Stanislavski more than his problems in fulfilling his intentions for the role. He felt his efforts maligned when critics insisted on treating his sets as a spectacular bid for box office success.

Lucien Besnard wrote briefly from St. Petersburg and at length from France. He praised the mise-en-scène as unsurpassed by anything he had ever seen in France or in Germany, although the actors—aside from Stanislavski— were poor. Stanislavski himself, he said, though very good, played and directed with no reference to the traditions of Shakespearean theater passed from generation to generation and not to be ignored.[15] Stanislavski's response was delayed but interesting. He cites Hamlet's advice to the actors (III,3) as contradicting the traditions of nineteenth century theater, and condemns those traditions as being more to the taste of Ben Jonson:

> Remember, Shakespeare's contemporary Ben Jonson...preached precisely what they want to do to Shakespeare today. But it has nothing to do with Shakespeare. It was Ben Jonson, and not Shakespeare, who loved bombast and pretension, the picturesque and the theatrical.... He mocked Shakespeare's partiality for everyday characters.... If Ostrovski is called a playwright of manners in our day, so Shakespeare was one in his. Of course, I'm not comparing the two, but only claim that they are somewhat similar in their understanding of their art. It is not accidental that Hamlet says of the actors, in the second act: "They are abstracts and brief chronicles of the time."[16]

Stanislavski continues by denouncing scholars, "the Gerviniuses," as Shakespeare's chief enemies, because they rob him of all life and interest. And "Shakespeare is life itself, simple and therefore intelligible to everyone."[17] As to current theatrical tradition,

> I wage a desperate war with petty theater routine in our humble Moscow. Believe me, the task of our generation is to banish outmoded tradition and routine from art, and to make more room for imagination and creativity. Only thus will art be saved.[18]

Ernesto Rossi also wrote; it was a polite note in which he invited Stanislavski to come for a talk.[19] During that conversation, he declared himself unimpressed by the scenery:

> All these playthings are necessary when there are no actors . . . but you do not need it. . . . God gave you everything for the stage, for Othello, for all of Shakespeare. . . . All you need is art. . . . I can recommend you only one teacher . . . you yourself.[20]

Some decades later, these words would seem a touchstone to Stanislavski's creative thought.

Stanislavski's *Meiningerei* was a strong factor in his next Shakespeare production as well, the 1897 *Much Ado About Nothing*. By all accounts, comedy was more his forte as an actor—but it was not this that motivated him in choosing *Much Ado*. While in Italy, he and Lilina had visited Turin, and chanced upon a reconstructed medieval castle which had been turned into a living museum for an exhibition. The life and customs of the Italian Middle Ages were preserved in a walled feudal town much as colonial America is preserved in Williamsburg. Captivated, he and Lilina "decided to live for a time in the feudal town and to gather first-hand impressions of the Middle Ages."[21] Unfortunately, visitors were not allowed to spend the night, but the pair stayed until asked to leave. He later described the town, castle, and the recreated medieval life in detail in *My Life in Art,* and concluded:

> I did not need scenery and costumes for a play; I needed a play for the scenery and costumes. So I thumbed through Shakespeare, and decided that my ideas for a production could best be crammed into *Much Ado about Nothing.*[22]

The promptbook is revealing: it is far less annotated than the *Othello* promptbook, and largely concerned with blocking and, to a lesser degree, stage business. There is minimal attention given to any general approach to the play, except as a vehicle for "medieval Italy."[23] Several albums were filled with sketches and watercolor studies of sets and costumes. To judge from the reviews, and from comparing Stanislavski's pictures of the Turin castle with production pictures of *Much Ado,* that town and that castle were accurately reproduced on the stage of the Hunters' Club.

The critics were in raptures over the sets. One of them credited the production elements with making the play clearer than ever before on the stage, adding that "the public saw not merely a 'performance,' but *life* itself—which clarified and amplified everything."[24] In *My Life in Art,* Stanislavski's description of the experience of acting on this set emphasized that the cast (and the play itself) felt at home in his castle, the setting of the play had become real for them. There is, then, a certain justification for this stage realism from the point of view of the actors, whether or not it meets with the approval of the Shakespeare scholar.

No other theater did this kind of production so successfully. The acting was stronger than it had been for *Othello,* but was still not strong enough to hold its own on the magnificent sets. The reviews had little good to say about the individual performers, although one generous critic compared Stanislavski (as Benedick) and his leading lady to Lenski and Fedotova.

"At the time," wrote Stanislavski, "I thought that the director had to study and feel the everyday color in a life, a character, and a play, in order to convey it to an audience and to make it natural...."[25] Later, he was to give more emphasis to the actor's work in this regard:

> The usefulness of this production... lay in the fact that I had once more realized the importance of external characterization in defending myself from harmful theatricality in acting. I thought that creativity began with outer image and led to inner emotion. As I learned later, this was one method, but not the only one.
>
> . . . .
>
> Meanwhile, it was enough that I understood the necessity of visiting museums, travelling, collecting essential books, engravings, paintings, and all that portrays the external life of people and, at the same time, reveals their inner life. Until that time, I loved to collect—in general; from that time on, I began to gather things that were relevant to the theater and to the business of directing.

While formulating his theories on the methods of acting, Stanislavski had to act as well as to direct, so that he could test and temper his ideas. Not surprisingly therefore, his choice of *Twelfth Night* for December of 1897 was dictated largely by a desire to play Malvolio. A character less subtle than Benedick, Malvolio would be more amenable to an external approach, and would be a character in whose skin Stanislavski could feel more comfortable. He portrayed Malvolio, not as the traditional bitter buffoon, but rather as a "negative, pathetic figure, but hardly funny."[27] It was sympathy rather than laughter that he wanted from the audience. Malvolio was to serve as the link between the comic and the romantic elements in the play,[28] not as the most comic element in it. The critics were severe with the interpretation, while praising the talent of the interpreter.

Stanislavski's greatest achievement as director of this production was the harmony and balance with which he staged the play. He gave the production a musical-rhythmic structure, which corresponded with the play's alternation of comic and lyrical, of individual treatment and focus on groups. The structure was emphasized by music written for the production by Koreshchenko "in the spirit of the seventeenth century."[29] This extraordinarily rhythmic production was described in musical terms by almost every critic. As important as the success of the production was the fact that the cast, like a fine orchestra, worked together as a unit, in ensemble.

The sense of real life being lived miraculously on the stage, however, suffered from sets far below Stanislavski's usual standards. Stanislavski had commissioned Navrozov, a designer from the Imperial theaters and a painstaking artist of the "chocolate box" school who had designed sets for Stanislavski before. This time his sets had neither depth nor perspective. V.A. Simov, Stanislavski's set designer from 1896 on, remembers the scenery for *Twelfth Night* as minimal and undersized, completely incompatible with the stature of the lead actor and not much more suitable for those of average height. This deficiency was underscored every time the tall Stanislavski/ Malvolio had to bend double to enter or exit through the low door to Malvolio's "dark room."[30]

Twelfth Night was revived in 1899, during the second season of the Moscow Art Theater. There were no changes save in the cast. The preceding season had introduced another Shakespeare production into the repertory, but it was not particularly successful. The 1898 production was *The Merchant of Venice.* There was obvious thought given to general interpretation and production, and box office returns were not at all bad. From what little ephemera and notes remain, one can deduce that Stanislavski built the production on the contrast between Shylock's bleak and dirty Jewish ghetto and the festive and poetic world of Portia. The sets were praised for their striking authenticity.

But one mistake destroyed the production: in order to steer the actor playing Shylock away from his usual hackneyed performing technique, Stanislavski had him speak with a Yiddish accent—and thus reduced him to caricature. The press was merciless. And the director learned another lesson about the pitfalls of naturalism.

The evidence of these productions leads to interesting early conclusions. The 1896 *Othello* proved that breathtaking historical authenticity did not necessarily lead to breathtaking performances. *Much Ado About Nothing,* on the other hand, indicated that the naturalistic set need not smother the acting and could in fact stimulate the actor. It would surprise no theatergoer of the time that the uninspired set of *Twelfth Night* did not detract from the quality of performance, but both the dominance of a coherent interpretation and the emphasis on ensemble were still relatively innovative. Neither interpretation nor ensemble playing nor naturalistic stage environment, however, could redeem the one jarring distortion in *The Merchant of Venice,* and it was removed from the repertory after only ten performances. So the naturalistic stage environment would seem irrelevant, or even destructive, to the quality of performance in Stanislavski's Shakespeare productions. Perhaps this would have seemed significant to Stanislavski were it not for the resounding success of his naturalistic approach in the staging of contemporary plays. As it was, he simply decided that he was unequal to the challenge of Shakespeare.

The New Theater of Stanislavski and Nemirovich-Danchenko

Stanislavski's work at the Society of Art and Literature was continued at the young Moscow Art Theater, where he and Nemirovich-Danchenko had declared war on standard theater: its repertory, acting, interpretations, scene and costume design, rehearsal technique and organization. The two rebels sought to embody the truth of real experience in theatrical forms of expression and, during the early years of the Art Theater, began by basing their work on external naturalism in the hopes that scenic verisimilitude would give birth to inner spiritual truth. During the Art Theater's first season, the troupe discovered the profound theatrical revolution of Chekhov and came to grips with the new mode well enough to stage it successfully. In continuing to work with Chekhov, and later with Gorky, they developed new techniques and a new understanding of theater. Meyerhold described the development as one from naturalism toward theater of mood,[31] a misnomer. Stanislavski used a more accurate term, "theater of experience."

The first production of the new theater was *Tsar Fyodor,* a historical drama by Aleksei Tolstoy. The entire troupe was involved in the preparation of naturalistic reproduction of sixteenth-century Russia, so that they might become familiar with the world of this play and therefore portray its character better. Trips to Russia's ancient cities were arranged, the trip to Rostov Yaroslavski including an overnight stay in a restored Kremlin palace where Ivan the Terrible had once lived. The candlelit spaces of the museum helped the cast recreate the physical realities of the period during which Tolstoy's characters had lived, and stimulated their imaginations to create people shaped by sixteenth century fact rather than caricatures stemming from nineteenth century assumptions. The naturalistic sets and accurate historical costuming helped the theater to perform the play so that the tale of Tsar Fyodor seemed to come genuinely alive on the stage. The production was a great success with the public, and also firmly established the Art Theater's reputation for scenic naturalism.

The externalism of *Tsar Fyodor* was as much a hindrance as a help, in that it brought success at the expense of the inner content of the play. But during this first season, it was no mean accomplishment to create an exciting new external resolution, to perform better than adequately within it, and to arouse the interest of the public. Unfortunately, the next few productions were unable to accomplish even that, so that by December of 1898, the future of the Art Theater was in jeopardy.

Chekhov's *The Seagull* was scheduled to open on December 30. When the repertory for the first season was being decided, Nemirovich-Danchenko insisted on the inclusion of *The Seagull,* a new kind of play by Chekhov. He had already pressured Chekhov into allowing the theater to produce his play; after *The Seagull* had been staged at the Aleksandrinski Theater in St.

Petersburg in 1896 and had met with disaster (it was a traditional performance by a traditional theater of an innovative, nontraditional play), Chekhov swore to write no more plays and to work with no more theaters. Nemirovich-Danchenko persuaded Chekhov that the new Art Theater could stage his play with care and sensitivity, and promised that he could review the production plans before rehearsals began. Nemirovich-Danchenko then pushed Stanislavski into working on a play that the latter claimed not to understand, and calmed a young cast terrified at the thought that they must master a play that had failed when performed by one of Russia's oldest established theaters. Working on the play, however, turned Stanislavski and the actors into enthusiastic converts.

Stanislavski was not at the first rehearsal Chekhov attended, but was later told that, in general, Chekhov approved of their efforts. Whatever changes Chekhov suggested were carried out, including casting Stanislavski as Trigorin rather than as Dorn. Although Nemirovich-Danchenko assured Stanislavski that Chekhov was impressed with the detailed mise-en-scène Stanislavski had labored over, Meyerhold (who played Treplev) recalled that Chekhov was dissatisfied with Stanislavski's attempt at realism through a plethora of minutiae, through effects calculated down to the humming of dragonflies.[32] It was the first instance (and there would be many) illustrating a difference between Chekhov's and Stanislavski's approach to theater. Stanislavski was still in the throes of mastering naturalistic stage environment; he could not dispense with naturalism until it no longer presented a challenge.

As December 30 drew nearer, the members of the Art Theater became increasingly concerned about the success of *The Seagull.* Chekhov was seriously ill with tuberculosis in Yalta, and the cast was afraid that any failure would be physically dangerous to this man whom they loved and who had become part of their theater. Stanislavski and the actors were still not confident in their work on *The Seagull.* At the last minute, Chekhov's sister came to the theater and begged them to postpone the premiere until Chekhov had recovered enough to sustain the shock which could result from a second defeat for *The Seagull.* The directors wavered, but delaying the premiere would mean closing the theater. Determined to succeed, and terrified that their failure might kill Chekhov, the actors played to a depressingly small audience. After the curtain fell on the first act, the house was completely silent. Olga Knipper, performing in spite of a high fever, fainted. In despair, the rest of the cast began to leave the stage.

> Suddenly, after the long silence, the auditorium exploded into a roar of frenzied applause. The curtain opened, closed, opened again, and we all stood dumbstruck. Another roar, and the curtain opened again, and we stood stock still without enough sense even to bow. We finally understood and, incredibly moved, began to embrace one another....[33]

Each act was more successful than the last, and the theater joyously wired Chekhov that *The Seagull* was a colossal triumph. So began one of theater history's most fruitful relationships between actors and playwright.

At first, Stanislavski did not understand Chekhov's play at all. In order to make any sense of it, he wrote an extraordinarily detailed mise-en-scène. As the physical world of the play came to life under his fingertips, Stanislavski began to visualize the characters and to detect their inner life. From that point on, he was able to bring the play's inner world into focus so that it would be communicated to the audience. In producing other Chekhov plays, he relied on the same method: reproduction of the external environment in order to elicit the spiritual world of its inhabitants.

Both Stanislavski and Meyerhold claimed that Chekhov taught the Art Theater how to express the spiritual life of a play. But Stanislavski saw the lesson as one in selective naturalism, while Meyerhold understood it to be training in the rhythm of the stage. Stanislavski saw Chekhov's subtle psychological truths as breathing life into the verisimilitude he could already create on the stage. Meyerhold saw Chekhov himself transforming the artistic sensibilities of the actors as he taught them in conversations and at rehearsals. Finally, claimed Meyerhold, the heavy hand of the naturalistic director destroyed the harmony of Chekhov's plays and the Art Theater became unable to stage its own author. Meyerhold's criticism is partially justified, but it must be remembered that, in 1908, he was ahead of his time. Meyerhold's artistic career began under the influence of Chekhov, after many of the achievements of Stanislavski's revolt against romantic theatrical cliché. Scenic naturalism could be taken for granted by Meyerhold; it had been a revelation to the young Stanislavski. Understandably, Stanislavski saw the quiet world of Chekhov's plays as acquiring physical three-dimensionality through the new naturalism. Meyerhold would search for nonnaturalistic theatrical techniques to convey the psychological realism that the Art Theater was evolving.

Stanislavski depended on Chekhov, and later Gorky, to give him plays with which he could continue to experiment. After the premiere of *The Seagull,* Chekhovian drama was the Art Theater's bread and butter both at the box office and for the troupe's artistic growth. Working closely with Chekhov, Stanislavski and the actors continued to learn to make poetry out of the prosaic. It was a long and difficult process. No one was quite sure what the rules were. Stanislavski relied on his ability to create external truth, and hoped that it would always lead to the inner truth he and his theater achieved with Chekhov and Gorky. While the result of the Art Theater's efforts was called "theater of experience," no one at the Art Theater could yet define the term clearly.

The play was seen as the foundation of this theater—the whole play, not certain parts of it or even a sum of its parts. The theater's duty was to understand the play and to make it live with such immediacy that the audience would experience it rather than watch it happen. The director's charge was to determine the main idea underlying the play. This idea was perceived as that element which unified all the components of the play, and informed all the aspects of the production. All the artists of the theater worked on the play collectively, in ensemble. The director was the creator-in-chief: he interpreted the play, helped each actor and designer find his creative role within that interpretation, and maintained the balance and unity which are the basis of ensemble work. If the ensemble was successful, the play would live on the stage with full credibility.

In this theater of experience, the audience was also seen as cocreator. The audience was not a body of spectators to be entertained, but a group of human beings to be involved, touched, and brought into spiritual union with the life of the play. Years later, Stanislavski explained the concept:

> In the theater, the audience can either share the life of the actors and the author, or it can look at the stage with interest, curiosity, and enthusiasm about what goes on up there.
> In the first case, theater recreates life in a condensed and aesthetic form—this is theater of experience. In the second case, theater is a beautiful spectacle, a pleasant diversion, a pastime.[34]

Nor is the audience merely to be involved. Stanislavski and Nemirovich-Danchenko saw theater as the most powerful of the arts because of its ability to have a profound and immediate effect on hundreds of people at a time. They saw theater as ignoring its great force for good if, while entertaining and affecting its audience, it did not educate. "The public... unwittingly, leaves with an enriched understanding of life."[35] This function of theater was as important to Stanislavski and Nemirovich-Danchenko as the creation of a stage life which accurately reflected the reality of life outside the theater.

When Stanislavski and Nemirovich-Danchenko next staged Shakespeare, it is not surprising that they wanted to use their Chekhov-Gorky discoveries to achieve a new breakthrough in Shakespeare production. They believed that their new psychological realism would bring Shakespeare more sharply into focus. Unquestionably, it would be revolutionary to stage Shakespeare in Chekhovian tones—but whether or not that approach worked is still matter for debate. The production around which the arguments revolve is the 1903 *Julius Caesar,* directed by Nemirovich-Danchenko with the assistance of Stanislavski.

Julius Caesar: The Shaping of the Production

Julius Caesar had had a stormy history in Russia. In 1787, Nikolai Karamzin translated it into Russian. In 1792, Catherine the Great was so alarmed by any mention of regicide and revolution that she ordered the translation confiscated and burned. Although other translations were to follow, the play was never performed in Russian until A.S. Suvorin managed to obtain official permission in 1897. Due to his somewhat haphazard production, however, this first Russian staging of *Julius Caesar* had no particular impact. It was, in fact, completely overshadowed by memories of the celebrated 1885 Meininger production of the play.

After the stir created by the Meininger production, the question of continued suppression of the play is especially interesting. Just before Suvorin's successful attempt to get it released, P.P. Gnedich had a run-in with the censor: "When I said that the Meininger *Caesar* was allowed, they answered, 'it's possible in German, but regicide must not be shown in the Russian language.'"[36] Since *Macbeth* was possible even in Russian, perhaps the censor felt that the Roman conspirators, and Brutus in particular, made rather more attractive regicides than, for example, the Macbeths. At any rate, the censor's 1897 change of heart seems inscrutable. Politically, the air was charged. At a later performance of *Julius Caesar* in Kiev, the assassination scene was greeted with stormy and demonstrative applause.[37]

> "It's decided: we're producing Shakespeare's *Julius Caesar*," said Nemirovich-Danchenko, coming in and putting his hat on the table.
> "When?"
> "At the beginning of the next season."[38]

While still in his twenties, Nemirovich-Danchenko had seen the famed production of the troupe from Saxe-Meiningen. He was distressed by its reception: "Moscow bills this production as a complete and unusually accurate communication of Shakespeare's immortal work." He wrote an open letter to the Moscow paper *Teatr i Zhizn' (Theater and Life)* to state his position. He praised the troupe's external realization "in every regard," noting that "scenes, groups, thunders, and lightnings—all this is incomparable. . . . But not one character is sustained," and he criticized their distortion of Shakespeare's "inner meaning." He centered his reproach around the Meininger's idealization of Antony, Brutus, and Cassius. To their heavy cutting, which eliminated everything which would contradict this idealization, he reacted with ill-restrained disgust. By cutting the triumvirate scene, and all discord between Antony and Octavian in the last act, Antony—"this sly, talented pragmatist, able to play nimbly upon the crowd's stormy mood immediately following Caesar's murder, this obvious representative of a coddled age, himself almost totally immoral and later to prove a weak and filthy libertine,—appeared in the Meininger production as a noble youth." Shakespeare went to great trouble, he continued, to show the change that takes place in Brutus and Cassius after their murder of Caesar: not only does fate shower misfortunes upon them, but they are grown petty, discontent with themselves and one another. All the scenes reflecting this change were cut, so as to preserve the ideal Brutus and Cassius served up by the Meininger. This infidelity to the text rankled. Further, while delighted with the German's sets, props, and effects, the young Nemirovich-Danchenko felt cheated by the sacrifice of acting excellence to an imposing accuracy of external resolution.[39]

Nor was he alone. The playwright Ostrovski found some of the effects amazing, yet "saw neither Caesar nor Shakespeare," but only "an extraordinarily well-disciplined troupe." Caesar, he added, was in no way distinguishable from any of the other props.[40] Lenski commented that "the set overwhelms the actor, and the audience is busier looking at the props than at Shakespeare's ... play."[41] Despite the long work that the Duke of Saxe-Meiningen devoted to acting, his troupe met with much similar criticism during its sixteen years of touring. Many critics felt that the Duke's attempt at a synthesis of production elements tended to take the focus away from acting, to the detriment of its quality, at the same time that it accomplished wonders in terms of staging.

Later, Nemirovich-Danchenko decided that a good naturalistic production of *Julius Caesar* was possible. He believed that the Moscow Art Theater had both the technical expertise and the acting strength to present it as vividly as the Meininger, and with more artistic validity.

> "But how will we have time to draw up the production plan and prepare the scenery and costumes? ... "[42]

In a day or two, Stanislavski noted, the troupe would be going on vacation. There was still the theater's annual trip to Saint Petersburg to be considered, and the selection of a repertoire for the coming season. But, he added, when Nemirovich-Danchenko spoke with such confidence, he had already done a great deal of detailed planning. "Clearly, there was no time to argue; there was nothing to do but agree and begin doing the impossible."[43]

Stanislavski was exaggerating. The decision to produce *Julius Caesar* came as no surprise; it had been given much thought and no little discussion. In a letter to Chekhov written on May 8, 1898, when Nemirovich-Danchenko informed him of the new partnership with Stanislavski, he named several plays "under consideration for production, among them *Julius Caesar*.[44]

He continued to mention *Julius Caesar* in his letters to Chekhov: on January 17, 1903, and then on January 30: "I desperately want *Julius Caesar*. I think I already wrote to you about this. But there's no Brutus. And Alekseev wants neither to play Brutus nor to work on the play."[45] In fact, in a letter written about one month later, he briefly mentioned frequent arguments with Stanislavski. But, he said, the aguments drew them closer. There seems to have been a dynamic working relationship, if not perfect accord. And Nemirovich-Danchenko evidently liked it that way. Finally, on March 9, he announced to

Chekhov, "If the returns of *Pillars* [*of Society,* by Ibsen] are better than expected, I shall insist on *Julius Caesar.*"[46]

Meanwhile the theater was waiting for new plays from Chekhov and Gorky. The Association would make no repertory decisions until the plays arrived. And still they did not arrive. By April, the choice of repertoire could no longer be postponed.

> At the session of the board of directors in April of 1903... the repertoire for the coming season was discussed again and again. It was pitiful. The projected budget stood at 225 thousand rubles, but the anticipated returns did not warrant this sum. There was no "hit." Then I suggested raising the budget to 250 thousand, but with a production of *Julius Caesar....*

The suggestion of *Caesar* and, worse yet, that it begin the season, sparked the usual sober debate. Stanislavski was among those opposed to it.

> ... Konstantin Sergeevich expressed grave doubts as to the feasibility of so daring a project. Produce *Julius Caesar* after the brilliant Meininger production! And in so short a time! We won't be able to learn how to wear the cloaks! Or carry the shields! Before we can draw up the mise en scène, the period has to be studied!
>
> And Simov will never manage such complicated sets in two or three months![47]

Nemirovich-Danchenko countered with a preconsidered practical discussion of all possible difficulties: the time element, the acting personnel, and the whole complex of artistic, organizational, technical and administrative problems. "I... said that our mastery had become such that our *Julius Caesar* would be more powerful and interesting than the Meininger version had been."[48]

The mastery of the Art Theater was collaborative, as it is for any theater, and derived in particular from the readiness of each artist to learn from the others. The two founders of the theater set the tone. Nemirovich-Danchenko saw Stanislavski as his mentor in the practical world of theater production. In the July 4 letter, he wrote:

> My "merger" with you is particularly valuable, because I see in you the qualities of an artist *par excellence* which I do not possess. I can see content and its significance for the contemporary audience with foresight enough, but when it comes to form, I tend toward cliché even though I place a high value on originality. Here I lack your imagination and your mastery.[49]

Stanislavski, in turn, was to admit in 1911 that "literary analysis does not enter into my sphere of competence."[50] Theater historians N.N. Chushkin and B.I. Rostotski stress the fact that the two were mutually complementary: Nemirovich-Danchenko influenced Stanislavski's literary tastes toward the good contemporary literature represented by Chekhov, and Stanislavski led his partner toward a unique understanding of his approach to direction and production.[51] In 1898, by his own admission, Nemirovich-Danchenko was not ready to undertake a production of *Julius Caesar*, although at the same time he wrote to Chekhov that, as to artistic sensitivity, he considered himself anybody's equal.

As he grew more competent in theater production (having directed various plays at the Art Theater, both with Stanislavski and on his own), he grew more confident. In July of 1902 he wrote and delivered a report "To the members of the Association of the MAT" which reflects his concerns about the future of the Art Theater. In dealing with the problems of repertory, he agreed with Stanislavski that the theater should not rest on its past laurels, and must seek new directions. He defied those who wished to stage plays which the theater could handle without difficulty and which the public was sure to approve. Naming no names, he thereupon proceeded to carry on a polemic with those who felt that *Julius Caesar* is "of course one of Shakespeare's best plays," but that the Art Theater could not cope with it, because the actors "haven't the tone for this play yet, and the directors and designers haven't time to produce it as strikingly as this play demands." While allowing that it would be difficult to cast a play like *Caesar,* Nemirovich-Danchenko was convinced that the theater had to go all-out in its quest for new achievements. If they hadn't the necessary artistic strength, he concluded, it was doubtful that anyone had.[52]

> For this production, aside from its purely artistic qualities, the Art Theater clearly displayed both its organizational ability and its collective spirit. Neither Stanislavski nor I could have achieved such success if literally the whole *theater* had not taken part in the production.[53]

This collective spirit, which Nemirovich-Danchenko recalled in *Out of the Past,* was typical of the early Art Theater. In their memoirs, many of the actors also alluded to this intimate backstage esprit. It was the camaraderie of a young and often successful group, conscious of their daring and not yet so well established that they were not somewhat anxious for the future of their venture. The theater was as much theirs as it was Stanislavski's and Nemirovich-Danchenko's; the more senior members of the troupe belonged to the Association and were involved in its policy making. Without the Chekhov and Gorky plays the only possible hit for the coming season was *Julius Caesar.* They worked on it like madmen.

"In the life of the MAT, there was only one time when everyone involved in a production was given full initiative," Stanislavski recalled. "More material was amassed within the walls of the theater during a few weeks than could have been collected in years of individual work."[54] In *My Life in Art,* he described the organization behind the pandemonium that reigned in the theater that spring. To deal with the preparatory work, a separate office was set up in the theater, incorporating ten separately numbered departments each headed by an actor or stage director. Housed in the theater's foyer and adjoining rooms, the departments divided the work as follows: 1) literary matters including text, translation, changes and cuts, literary references and commentaries; 2) everything relating to life in Julian Rome, from architecture to customs and social conditions; 3) costumes; 4) weapons, armor, and props; 5) scenery; 6) music; 7) purchasing; 8) rehearsals; 9) crowd scenes; 10) administration, including the distribution of materials received to the other nine departments.

> The whole theater was placed under martial law and every actor and administrator and stage hand was mobilized. No one dared refuse to work on any pretext whatsoever.[55]

Anyone not kept busy in the theater was sent to solicit material from museums, libraries, antique dealers, private collectors and classicists. The response was generous and enthusiastic, and the theater was flooded with museum pieces and priceless books and antiques. Stanislavski claimed that the theater exhausted all the rich material in Moscow.[56]

In a letter written on May 21, 1903, Stanislavski said that all rehearsals had been abandoned in order to convert the theater into a combination library-museum-workshop. "Our work is in full swing. Interesting, but extremely exhausting."[57]

Of course, this work was done by the rankest of amateurs, not by specialists in the field. The rush to collect everything relevant resulted in a strange mélange of materials, and there were certain lacunae—but all this was merely raw material to be sorted, evaluated and used as seen fit. The amount of it was as staggering as Stanislavski indicated. The Moscow Art Theater Museum and archives hold the special albums (entitled "Costumes, Daily Life," "Furniture and Décor," "Armor," "Make-up, Hair Styles," and so on, in which theater workers collected excerpts relating to the history and customs of ancient Rome) and other untitled albums of tracings, drawings and photographs of ancient statues and buildings.

Meanwhile, many of the technical problems were being worked out. Stanislavski described the preparation of the costumes:

> Much of that which we cannot even dream about at present [1926] could be obtained before the war. For instance, the members of the properties commission were sent to the stores and brought back a tremendous amount of cloth in every possible quality and color.

The fabrics were hung on the stage, lit from every angle and examined from the house.[58] As in *Three Sisters,* for which the actors had to accustom themselves to military uniform,[59] the costumes for *Julius Caesar* took getting used to. For the natural effect desired on the stage, the actors had to learn to feel at home in togas. After only two weeks of work, Stanislavski already had himself and his actors decked out in the togas, and had begun to experiment with moving in them, and modeling their gestures on ancient statues.

V.A. Simov's whole workshop buzzed with the usual preliminary sketching and model building, so that a notion of probable sets was rapidly being evolved. At the desk of the "commander-in-chief," the initial work had begun on a general production plan.

> ... it had to be verified on location, in museums and on forums. We had to see places and things, even if only in ruins. We had to breathe deep of the ruins and give rein to our imaginations. We were staging "Rome in the time of Julius Caesar," not just Shakespeare's tragedy. The principal character was Rome.[60]

On June 13, Nemirovich-Danchenko and his wife left for Rome. They were accompanied by Simov. The assistant director, G.S. Burdzhalov, was also traveling abroad and joined the party.

Nemirovich-Danchenko had not ignored the possibility that *Julius Caesar* might be presented in a nonnaturalistic style. In fact, he wrote in his promptbook for *Caesar:*

> ... Shakespeare's plays must be staged either with completely new devices approaching those of Elizabethan theater, or with modern conventions—using everything the text allows to bring the text as close as possible to historical truth.[61]

He chose the latter, and throughout the promptbook wrestles with problems that the Elizabethan stage had solved easily, but which the realistic stage had not.

> Every stage director is familiar with the difficulty presented by small passing scenes in the construction of Shakespeare's plays. All the Elizabethan theater had to do was lower the curtain and hand out a sign naming the place where the next scene was to occur. Contemporary theater, realistic to the point of visual precision, demands that a set be provided for each passing dialogue.... But rapidity of scene change is indispensible to the effective staging of Shakespeare. (*Plan,* p. 372)

These problems intrigued him, but he left his notions about "impressionistic devices" aside and found workable if less exciting resolutions within the conventions of realistic theater.

Nemirovich-Danchenko sought a more intimate Rome than that of the Meininger. Though Duke George had also visited Rome to prepare for his production, he brought a grandiose and idealized antiquity to his stage. The MAT travellers felt that the Meininger had presented the Rome then approved by academia—more luxurious and magnificent than was warranted by the smaller, sterner harmonies of the first century before Christ. This older Rome spoke to the Russians of stoic severity, of the terse restraints of Caesar's prose, of early Roman discipline. Drawn to the simplicity and modest dimensions of pre-Imperial Rome, they decided to discard the usual clichés in favor of a new visual approach.

In his study of the "original topography" pertaining to the events of *Julius Caesar*, Nemirovich-Danchenko paid particular attention to the Roman streets and to the Forum. Upon close examination of the latter, Simov and he decided against the traditional view of the Forum with the Capitoline in the background. It was used by the Meininger and "is too exploited in all the landscapes of ancient Rome." Some of the results, and some of the spirit, of their research are revealed in Nemirovich-Danchenko's June letter to Stanislavski written after a visit to the Forum:

> There are quite definite indications of the rostrum from which Mark Antony spoke. The foundation and four steps are completely preserved. The rostrum was on this "platform," it was the same as the rostrum of Cicero, which is even better preserved. . . .
>
> . . . .
>
> It evolves into a first-rate scene—convenient, and full of variety and color.
>
> Since there is a street right in front of Antony's rostrum, we will block it up with a chariot (Hand-drawn . . .), the litters of rich Romans, little donkeys, etc.
>
> All this is historically accurate and infinitely more interesting than the trite Capitoline, which would now probably remain in the first balcony or in Chekato's store [across the street from the theater].
>
> We didn't hit on this immediately, but it's so smooth and accurate that I'm sure the great Chronegk was in Rome for no longer than between trains.
>
> (But someone should suggest to Vishnevski [playing Anthony] that he speak to the whole audience, not to the citizens standing closest to him. Let this daring device confuse the audience at first! That's nothing!)[62]

The Roman crowds and contemporary Italian life had a remarkable impact on the Russian observers. All this, most especially, could only have been experienced directly. Simov recalled that Nemirovich-Danchenko consciously derived his lighting plan from a "yellow-brown color, an Italian favorite and evident everywhere there."[63] The moods of the Italian streets were to be reflected in crowd scenes. In order to relate their impressions of this Italy to the world of *Julius Caesar,* Nemirovich-Danchenko, Simov, and Burdzhalov studied the realistic Roman art of the republican period.

A trip along the Via Appia resulted in another new approach. In Moscow, while working on his promptbook, Stanislavski had decided to represent armies and battles by a whole concert of sound effects: hoofbeats and the neighing of horses, the noises of a military camp, the tramp of a passing regiment, the clash of swords. Much of this was retained for the fifth act, but a visual representation was added. "In places, the Via Appia goes through hollows: the theatrical composition repeated this convenient tendency so as not to show an army as a whole, but only the heads, the tips of spears, tops of shields, and the proud and glittering helmets of Roman soldiers. . . ."[64] The general coloring of the shields and helmets was taken from the Veronese painting, "Triumph of Venezia," which Nemirovich-Danchenko saw some weeks later in Venice.

After two weeks in Rome, the four went to Naples to see a large collection of artifacts unearthed at Pompeii and housed at the Neapolitan Museum. Simov wrote again, "Here, the whole daily round of antiquity opened up before us." But the crowding of the material "and its isolation from the original surroundings deprived the material of its greatest value—i.e. the immediacy of its connection with life."[65] Describing the collection in more detail, Simov compared it to a display window, and dismissed it as *"nature morte."* He had to go to Pompeii.

Pompeii provided rich material for study. Smothered by volcanic ash little more than a century after the events recalled by Shakespeare, much of the city had been excavated by 1903. Many of the discoveries of Nemirovich-Danchenko and company in Pompeii were to find their way onto the Art Theater stage. One of the rooms in the restoration of the house of Cornelius Rufus served as prototype for the set for Caesar's house (II,ii). The shops for the set of act I were designed from Simov's photographs of those in Pompeii. Long rambles through the sun-scorched streets turned up a multitude of details which were repeated in the production: wall posters, a public well with a bubbling fountain, the very narrow sidewalks, the high flat stones which lay in the streets to allow easy passage after a heavy rain, and even the way Roman feet had worn down the ancient tiles.

From Pompeii, they went to Venice to rest and review the material they had collected. Necessary revisions in the maquettes already prepared in Moscow were discussed and agreed upon. Final drawings of all armor and weaponry required by the production were prepared and sent to Berlin where these articles were to be made. A statue of Pompey was ordered for the Senate scene. Then the four returned to Russia. Simov hurried to his summer place in Ivanovo to begin work on the sets. Nemirovich-Danchenko went to Moscow, visiting the theater on July 13. He assigned work to various assistants, and then continued on to the country, to "Neskuchnoe."

According to his letter to Olga Knipper-Chekhova, which he wrote from "Neskuchnoe" on July 30, Nemirovich-Danchenko had begun working on the promptbook some thirteen days earlier. Working seven and eight hours a day, he finished the first act on July 31. He took a short break, but felt the pressure of time: "I tire quickly. But I must return from the country with four acts."[66]

On August 5, he wrote a long letter to the actor Luzhski. Most of it concerned *Julius Caesar*. A cast list had been sent to the head of the makeup department; other sketches had to arrive before all the necessary designs for the makeup could be forwarded. He was worried that Simov might be behind schedule, and that the extras might not be working smoothly until September—relatively late in the rehearsal schedule. As to his work on the promptbook:

> ... The more I work, the more I see that the roles are far from being as thankless as the actors had thought at the first reading. ... I've done everything up to the Senate scene, and have

found many wonderful moments in Brutus, Portia, Ligarius, Decimus, Cassius, and especially in Caesar. What an astounding part! I haven't really gotten to Antony, but am up to his scenes,—if I were a Jack-of-all-trades in acting, I would choose Caesar.
... If Kachalov has the slightest faith in me, he will make his reputation with this role....
Brutus could be fascinating, but he depends totally on the personality of the actor. If the actor is spiritually gentle and pure, and has the delicate, refined feelings of a Brutus—a man head and shoulders above his times,—he will be marvellous. I seem to have been successful with Brutus' monologues and with the conspirators....
In general, I'm writing this mise-en-scène like a whole dissertation. It includes the most thoroughly evolved psychology, and incessant excerpts from history.[67]

The work on the promptbook marks a transition between the initial search for appropriate physical reality and the subsequent probing for interpretative values. Nemirovich-Danchenko began with the concept of Julian Rome as the central focus of Shakespeare's play, and he proceeded to shape a visual reconstruction of that Rome. That done, he analyzed each character and its role in the drama of political change. The detailed analysis began as he wrote the promptbook, and continued during rehearsals.

Two days later, he wrote to Stanislavski, but in this letter their disagreements are spotlighted. He repeats: "My mise-en-scène is a whole dissertation."

...I haven't begun the Senate scene yet, have finished everything before it. But I've already had a look at your scene, and I like a lot of it very much. I'm depending on it.
I've done everything up to the Senate scene quite carefully, and I mean to impose a great deal on the cast, by force,—I am writing with that much conviction. By the way, with Brutus—I know how difficult it is for you to take advice, and I have a premonition that there will be a heavy expenditure of time and nerves, but I hope to get my way. Just imagine: I've become so involved in this role that now it's incredibly dear to me. I find Brutus amazingly sympathetic; I know his tone, expressions, movements. I think I've even coped with the monologues! And I'm completely in love with Caesar! What a wonderful role!
In my version, the whole tone and tempo of the second act, especially the first scene, is *completely* different from yours. Nothing is the same—none of Brutus' scenes, not the conspiracy, not Brutus' scene with Portia nor his scene with Ligarius. And here I will ask you to acquiesce and follow me completely. I've worked too hard on this and given it too much thought. I wrote the scene in Caesar's house with great enthusiasm. In my version, Portia and Calpurnia—so similar in Shakespeare—are two opposites.

He was worried about the Senate and Forum scenes, which struck him as the most difficult in the play; "perhaps I think so because I haven't worked on them yet." Certain technical affairs had been delayed, and Simov still caused some concern. Nemirovich-Danchenko had only one week to write the mise-en-scène for the two scenes just mentioned; this left the last act (the fourth and fifth acts of the original) to be done later. He proposed to take four days off from rehearsals to deal with it. Many anxieties, "but, God willing, everything will work itself out in time."[68]

Even while he was struggling over the visualization of *Caesar,* Nemirovich-Danchenko had determined his interpretation of the play and its characters, and on the style in which he would treat them. The Meininger had presented a romantic, idealized "Schilleresque " Shakespeare, with an emphasis on grand heroes and supernatural phenomena. Nemirovich-Danchenko was closer to *War and Peace* or *Boris Godunov* than to Schiller. In place of idealized heroes, he saw ordinary men who are called to lead their fellow men. More significant than these leaders are the anonymous people of the crowd; all power comes from them and it is they who really change history. The central focus was to be Rome at the fall of the Republic—all of Rome, its people, its leaders, its mores, its faces, and its soul.

This interpretation, and the shaping of the play's production, were determined by Nemirovich-Danchenko's concept of Chekhov's dramatic technique. Inner meanings were conveyed by bits of real life trivia—a sense of Life was evoked by obscure individual lives. No heroes and villains here, but real people living in a real world, perhaps next door. If these new theatrical approaches were valid in the broader sense, they should also work with Shakespeare. Chekhov's plays had brought modern drama closer to the novel in terms of breadth and narrative detail; the Art Theater could present his work well. Shakespeare wrote plays of great scope without losing sight of the humanity of his characters. The Art theater hoped to present those characters and that scope by building on the selected naturalism it had begun to learn in staging Chekhov. The romantics dealt with great souls; the new naturalists dealt with life in the real world. And Nemirovich-Danchenko believed that life in the real Roman world of Caesar's day was Shakespeare's main concern in this play.

In *My Life in Art,* Stanislavski wrote that "Vladimir Ivanovich assumed the primary responsibility for directing the production, and we helped him."[69] In the program, Stanislavski is named only as the performer of Brutus. But he was far more than just one of the cast, or one of Nemirovich-Danchenko's technical assistants. As already noted, he wrote notes for the production which he submitted to Nemirovich-Danchenko as an aid, a guide for the final production plan. He spent a good deal of time directing, and attended to much of the technical detail. Nowhere does he speak of this himself, but it is evident from various letters and memoirs relating to *Caesar.* In 1905, Nemirovich-Danchenko was to write to him:

> Do you think I could have such delusions of grandeur as to forget that the best scene in *Caesar,* the Senate scene, was rehearsed by you, and not according to my mise-en-scène either, that you selected the costumes for *Caesar*—at least the tone for them,—and that even though I directed the crowd scenes for *Caesar* independently, it was three-quarters by *your* system . . . ?[70]

Stanislavski had taken it upon himself only to write a sort of running commentary to *Caesar,* and his notes made no claim to being either complete or particularly profound. They include the first three acts of the play (through the Forum scene), which are treated in varying degrees of detail. On the whole, Stanislavski was interested in externals, and did not approach the play from any firm artistic concept of it. He had not supported the inclusion of this play into the repertoire, and was not eager either to work on it or to act in it. On July 5, he wrote to Chekhov, "I feel like finishing with *Caesar* as soon as possible, and taking on some Chekhov."[71] In August, he wrote to Olga Knipper-Chekhova:

> ... but our theater is Chekhovian, and without him we'll have a hard time of it. If he gives us a play, the theater and the season are saved; if not—I don't know what we'll do. *Julius Caesar* won't take us far; we'll go so much farther with Chekhov....[72]

Stanislavski was reluctant to take on Shakespeare, whose plays he considered an ultimate test for any theater, until he felt more confident in staging Chekhov. Using a naturalistic stage environment to produce *The Seagull* or *Uncle Vanya* resulted in a vivid spiritual life that even the successful *Tsar Fyodor* did not have. Until the crucial difference was analyzed and understood, Stanislavski would not be eager to apply Chekhovian theater to Shakespeare's plays. But he had no choice; Nemirovich-Danchenko had taken the matter into his own hands. Nemirovich-Danchenko had watched the same creative process, and was determined to use it to produce a play he had long wanted to stage. The methods he would use were essentially those he had learned from Stanislavski. Stanislavski had helped Nemirovich-Danchenko before, and could hardly refuse this time. So, jotting down ideas and sketching ground plans, he did the creative spade work which is found in the notes dated "1903. June. Liubimovka." And despite Nemirovich-Danchenko's displeasure with some of his partner's ideas for the production, a good many others were used. Stanislavski also wrote addenda to his notes: bits of directorial advice, and "bundles of sundry details" in the historical-archeological vein.[73]

In his notes, Stanislavski did not see the crowd as white clusters of senators in togas; his comments are incisive and his crowd scenes include plebian, slave, and Roman low life. He wrote a whole series of sketches of the characters in the crowd. In so doing, he sought a reality usually lost by the idealized grandeur of theatrical Romes. He tried to blend both the poetic and the prosaic into his scenic detail, feeling as he did that this reflected Shakespeare's dramatic technique. Nemirovich-Danchenko used many of the ideas, both specific and general, which Stanislavski evolved in this discussion of the Roman crowd.

The technical details which Stanislavski worked out were generally adopted by his partner. Tossing off a brief schema for the storm scene in act I, Stanislavski suggested a "photosymphony and mime drama" using the widest variety of devices. He described lightning, the form and character of cloud movement, the uses of the magic lantern for zigzags of lightning and for "fiery rain," the various possibilities for making thunder backstage, and so on. "I'm writing down everything that seems feasible for our stage, so that you may choose." He went into the latest developments in stage technics: "They say that the cinematograph is used for thunderstorms in the main opera house in Paris."[74] Nemirovich-Danchenko later noted that all the technical work for the storm scene was directly supervised by Stanislavski. It was all carefully worked out in these June notes: where to place fans so that when the wind whipped across the stage at a certain moment, it would catch the actors in a certain way; how tarpaulins and the theater's "wind machine" should be used for given sound effects; how ventilators in the house could be used to create sound effects; how to adapt a device from *Uncle Vanya* for the sound of rain on the open street (rather than drop small shot onto metal, it should be dropped into water).

Other technical problems were posed by the short scenes. They demanded rapid set changes to maintain the flow of action, and yet this was impossible if the sets for these scenes were to be as elaborate as for the others. But the visual harmony of the production must not be destroyed. Stanislavski suggested various conventions, considering them realistic enough to agree with the general tenor of the other sets. The curtain could be drawn only partially, and the episodes played against a background of "bits" of realistic decor, or against a curtain painted in the style of the Pompeiian frescoes, or against a canvas drop and individual pieces—a fountain, a column or a bench. He did not so much propose concrete resolutions as outline a design principle new to the Art Theater. Nemirovich-Danchenko used this idea, and had Simov design several partial sets. Several of these short scenes were cut, however, after the final dress rehearsal, in order to reduce the running time of the play.

In his desire to do away with clichés and create new effects, Stanislavski could go to extremes. The detailed directions for the set of II,i (Brutus' garden), seem like a satire on Stanislavskian naturalism. Only a few of the suggestions were actually used. He would have had toys left behind by Brutus' children, which Brutus would notice during one of his pauses, and touch while he gazed over Rome. He had a parrot on a branch and a stork which would appear from behind a bush and screech when one of the conspirators tried to catch it. He developed a whole symphony of sight and sound to convey the pregnant hush of a southern night. So there would be falling stars and meteors (both visible and invisible), the cries of various night birds, the bubbling of either a brook or a fountain (with its stream of water reduced to a trickle), the barking and howling of dogs , the roars of wild beasts caged in the circuses, "the distant shouts of guards—various voices—now approaching, now withdrawing (to be panned in)... the cry of southern frogs like the tinkling of bells (I happened to get this sound recorded). Other night sounds."[75] This technique had often been used in producing Chekhov, and would have firmly established itself as an Art Theater cliché if it were repeated in *Julus Caesar*. Nor was Chekhov himself pleased with the symphonies Stanislavski composed for his plays: "Konstantin Sergeevich wants to set a train loose in act II [*Cherry Orchard*], but I think someone should restrain him. He also wants frogs and landrails." He tried to set limits: "... haying is usually done between the fifth and the tenth of July, and apparently the landrails, and the frogs too, have fallen silent by this time of year. Only the oriole utters any sound."[76]

Nemirovich-Danchenko was highly selective in using any of the so-called "Chekhovian" concert. "I definitely do not want to begin the act with pauses, noises, light effects, and a generally retarded tempo" (*Plan*, p. 309). The pause generated by the conspirators departure was not to be orchestrated: "*no other sound save that of the wicket gate;* just before morning, everyone is sleeping— people, animals, birds" (*Plan*, p. 335).

Nemirovich-Danchenko and Stanislavski continued to disagree until well after the premiere. In his promptbook, Nemirovich-Danchenko polemicized with his partner without actually naming him. He focused his attention on the heart of the play as he interpreted it, and did not feel that the success or failure of a given detail had any real significance. He wrote to Stanislavski in October that, "*first of all,* there must be a *harmonic whole,* the creation of a single spirit, and only then will the audience be moved.... The fact that you have far more talent than I to invent production detail does not in any way weaken my faith in *my own* views." He added that Stanislavski, in his enthusiasm, could sometimes "forget the point, the substance, the most *important* thing in any production—its inner meaning, the beauty and power of the whole picture."[77] Here, Nemirovich-Danchenko seems to have understood the strengths and weaknesses of Stanislavski's approach better than Stanislavski did. This did not alter his profound respect for Stanislavski's ability or his gratitude for Stanislavski's help and advice, as letters before and after *Caesar* attest. But at this time, the partners were involved in a theatrical effort, on the very worth of which they could not agree.

In terms of interpretation, there were several major disagreements. Essentially, Stanislavski was still under the influence of the Meininger production, whose technical brilliance still blinded him to its interpretational banality. Nemirovich-Danchenko labored under no such burden. Stanislavski saw Caesar as a sybarite, a poseur. Nemirovich-Danchenko saw him as a great man, little diminished even by his own weaknesses. It is the great Caesar which dominates the play, although it is the fallible Caesar whom we meet in the first three acts. Stanislavski emphasized the difference between Brutus' and Cassius' faith in the justice of their deed and its ultimate success, and presumed a lack of faith on the part of the other conspirators. Nemirovich-Danchenko saw no such split, and interpreted the conspiracy to murder as the unfortunate first step which the conspirators could not avoid in their mission to preserve the republic. He did not see Brutus as a tragic superhero, as Stanislavski tended to, and for which reason was uncomfortable in the role, but as an unusually just and courageous man who misread the political facts of his time. Nemirovich-Danchenko probed more deeply than Stanislavski into the inner conflict of Brutus, and hoped to show the audience how great was the spiritual price Brutus paid for his decision to murder Caesar. Brutus would often be lost in thought, torn by warring duties to country and to friend. This emphasis was alien to Stanislavski's view of Brutus as a man possessed of great determination, but eventually he managed to incorporate Nemirovich-Danchenko's interpretation into his performance of the role.

During these disputes, Stanislavski retreated into the technical details of directing and costuming the crowd—much to his partner's annoyance. Both lost themselves in their own fields of expertise, and grumbled at the other for lack of interest in the important things. But they ultimately gave way—Nemirovich-Danchenko usually yielded in technical matters, and Stanislavski bowed in questions of interpretation.

If technical detail occasionally seemed to preoccupy Stanislavski, his knowledge in that area was indispensible. Even before Nemirovich-Danchenko left for Rome, Stanislavski had molded the Russian actors into Romans ready to rehearse their roles in Shakespeare's history of ancient Rome. His eye determined a color scheme which divided the Romans into four general groups, thereby sharpening the contrast between various elements in Roman society. Caesar and his close associates were seen in purple and gold, presaging the luxury of Imperial Rome, and giving this group an implied stage center. The "last Romans"—Brutus and the conspirators—were in severe classic white. The pied and dappled crowd and the iron-buckled Roman armies comprised the other two groups. In the yellow-browns of the crowd, there was no screaming contrast, and when necessary, its general tone could even reduce Caesar's purple to the browned quality of clotted blood.[78]

Both Stanislavski and Nemirovich-Danchenko worked closely with Simov in designing the sets. Stanislavski was active in the planning, sketching, and construction of preliminary models. His advice to Nemirovich-Danchenko and Simov, which they seemed to follow during the course of their tour, was that they get the feel of Rome so that the sets planned by the theater and tested on its stage could be brushed with it. Here, his principal difference with Nemirovich-Danchenko centered on the set for the Forum scene. He had hoped to put the rostrum far upstage and thus make it possible to create the impression of a huge square, "free, with large spaces."[79] His blocking for the crowd in this scene was intended to convey its dynamic and tragic power; in order to accomplish this, he depended on having the use of these large spaces. Nemirovich-Danchenko approached this scene differently in terms of its visual resolution, and debated Stanislavski in his introductory notes to the Forum scene. Stanislavski could hardly be pleased with the new set; he had envisioned his version as providing the "hit set" of the production. But his version was too similar to the now hackneyed great Forum set established by the Meininger.

> It's not hard to present the Forum on the stage, even if the stage is smallish. But to have both the Forum and the undivided attention of the audience to those who speak on it—that's still a dilemma. Move the rostrum all the way upstage, and the actor is too far removed from the audience to be effective. Put the rostrum to one side—as they usually do—and the actor has lost a basic tool, mime, and has to carry the whole scene by his voice alone.
>
> (*Plan,* p. 435)

Nemirovich-Danchenko preferred to portray the Forum accurately, *but* with the actor's convenience in mind. The impression of a large square, so dear to Stanislavski, seemed irrelevant to Nemirovich-Danchenko. On this matter, he stood his ground.

Nemirovich-Danchenko returned to Moscow in August to take over the complex theatrical organization. By taking full charge of the administrative departments, as well as the artistic side of the production, he intentionally assumed full responsibility for the outcome. He hoped that this step would help create an air of calm in the theater; it seems certain that Stanislavski was relieved by it. An able administrator, Nemirovich-Danchenko realized that a solid effort had to be made by the whole theater if the play were to open on time, and was able to effect the united and spirited work necessary to that end. One of his most valuable assets was the ability to leave the actors, designers, and technicians very much on their own and yet make them produce what he wanted. He merely outlined the work to be done, and left the artists alone to do it.

Nemirovich-Danchenko's ambitious schedule for early August can be established from his July letters to Stanislavski and to Luzhski.[80] He seems to have kept to this schedule. Later he recalled, "I arrived in Moscow on the eighteenth of August, and the extremely complicated set for act I stood completely ready on the stage. And on the thirtieth of August we had a complete run through of act I."[91] On the latter date, he wrote

> Rehearsals every day, morning and night—now the crowd, now the principals. There is a new quality in the rehearsals themselves—more system and, perhaps, far fewer futile experiments, and less vacillating than there used to be.
>
> Another innovation—students for the crowd. It's much easier and pleasanter to work with them than with temporarily employed professional extras.... The rehearsals are coming along well, but the production side limps. The sets and the makeup are held up, and while the costumes are not late, they are simply bad—half-baked, neither artistic nor professional.
>
> Everyone is working earnestly, even amicably, if only in the crowd. There aren't more than one or two exceptions (to remain nameless). I haven't let anything spoil my mood yet...and am cheerful and confident. Konstantin Sergeevich and I are very friendly and have gotten our mutual effort well under way.

....

I still maintain that we will open during the second week in October (a full dress of *Caesar* on the 5th). Today is the 30th, and we began working on the 20th. We've done an unbelievable amount in ten days.[82]

As a director, "Konstantin Sergeevich participated mainly in the work on the crowd scenes," wrote V.P. Verigina, a student at the Art Theater in 1903. He stimulated the imaginations of the student extras by sketching out working examples of characters in the crowd. Verigina describes the first crowd rehearsal for the Forum scene: Stanislavski and Nemirovich-Danchenko sat the coworkers and theater students in the parterre, and spoke from the stage; they indicated the blocking and the reactions of the crowd to Brutus' and Antony's speeches.

Stanislavski spoke little, but stood there to demonstrate. He got carried away and, standing on the stage, portrayed the whole crowd all by himself. With bated breath, everyone watched how his mood changed, how Antony's imagined speech evoked a mounting sorrow and anger. The actor went into a furious rage, tangled his hair, and, tearing his clothes with the gesture, he ripped off his jacket. He showed us, alone and in a matter of minutes, the whole motley Roman crowd. If the crowd could act like that, it would be a staggering spectacle.[83]

From the "Chronicles of the Art Theater,"[84] it is known that the preparation of *Caesar* took over one hundred rehearsals. Specific information about them is minimal; the only records extant are the letters of Nemirovich-Danchenko, Stanislavski, and various actors in the company. But the letters reflect the mood of the theater well.

In August, Stanislavski wrote to his wife, who was tending their sick son at Liubimovka:

Vladimir Ivanovich works like a demon, and I help him. Rehearsals day and night, costume fittings, make-up, crowd scenes, in a word—hell. They rehearse with enthusiasm and, I think, success. Something may well come out of it all, but there's still a lot of work ahead, and very little time.[85]

The theater was in high gear. By the middle of September, there had been rough run-throughs of the first two acts, and work had begun on the third. Sets and costumes for act II were in the final stages, and were being tested on the stage. In Stanislavski's September letter to his wife, he listed at least one major rehearsal per day, and "on Tuesday the 8th—a run-through of acts I and II.... The work doesn't progress quickly, but seems promising."[86] Nothing interfered with work: when Stanislavski's wife wrote that she would come to Moscow for a few days, Stanislavski answered that he was anxious to see her, "but if you want to have dinner with me, don't forget that rehearsal is at seven."[87]

Nemirovich-Danchenko wrote a long letter to Olga Knipper-Chekhova in late September to tell her, and Chekhov, about progress to date. (Chekhov was intensely interested in this production, and later peppered his wife with questions about it in his letters from Yalta.)

> We began partial run-throughs a long time ago. Right now (I'm writing at night), we're running two acts: the first, "Brutus' orchard," and "Caesar's house".... The remaining scenes—except for the last (fifth) act—are well underway,... I count on getting to the fifth act on Tuesday. We've already tested the effects for it though; the sets are almost completely ready, and all the armor has arrived.
>
> One can already get some idea as to who is doing how well. The first item, obviously, is Kachalov. He could be magnificent, in every sense of the word. And he probably will be. The rest are coming along fairly evenly. Vishnevski's Antony will be far removed from the historical figure, close to the Shakespearean one, and—if yesterday's rehearsal wasn't deceptive (he and I see practically eye to eye)—he will be very good. He won't show you anything new, but will exploit his talents well.... Leonidov wavers and is pretty conventional, but will be pleasant and very satisfying to those who don't demand too much from Cassius.... Konstantin Sergeevich loses himself in his inability to conceal his lack of the tragic temperament.... When he approaches his role simply, beautifully, and *modestly,* he will be satisfactory.[88]

The set and lighting changes were so complicated that they required considerable experimentation and, therefore, many technical rehearsals. The intermissions were specially rehearsed in order to reduce the time needed to change scenery and lights. Knipper-Chekhova commented to her husband that all this fuss with the sets had thoroughly jangled the nerves of the director and his assistants. Later, Nemirovich-Danchenko gave a brief description of one such session:

> The whole cast was released for three days rest,... and Simov, Burdzhalov, Tikhomirov and I did not leave the theater until late at night. The scenery was set up, lit, examined, simplified if possible. And on the second day, we did it again. And again, and again, so that the intermissions would be no longer than the prescribed number of minutes.[89]

It was customary in the Art Theater actors to gather for a reading on the eve of a major dress rehearsal of a premiere. They would sit around a table, put sets and blocking and the rest out of mind, and concentrate on the inner life of the play and of their roles. So, too, for *Caesar.* In Stanislavski's papers, it is implied that this reading took place on the night before the premiere, but the correspondence between Chekhov and his wife puts the date several days earlier, on October 10, the eve of the first dress. There were three dress rehearsals before the premiere, and it is unlikely that the customary reading would take place more than once. On the eleventh, Knipper-Chekhova wrote to her husband about the reading:

> Yesterday I heard the reading.... It has simplicity and majesty. Kachalov read very well; each line is poured out in iron, beautiful, full of contrasts. Cassius-Leonidov hisses a little.

Vishnevski's usual deficiencies can be detected, but he makes up for it with undisguised temperament. Konstantin Sergeevich is good in places, and his beauty and plasticity are gripping.[90]

In a rough draft for *My Life in Art,* Stanislavski wrote that the reading "was dominated by an unusual excitement. It seemed to us that we had discovered...the inner terms on which we could live as naturally in a Shakespearean play as in one of Chekhov's."[91]

The play was to open a few days later than planned, so that the first dress rehearsal was not held until October 11. Knipper-Chekhova wrote Chekhov that it was run with great enthusiasm and that it boded success. But they got no further than the Forum scene that night.

An audience was invited to watch another dress, held on the thirteenth. "Everyone liked it; they said that not one European theater could match it. They're all crazy about Kachalov.... No one likes K.S., and that's a tragedy for the theater." But the performance was impossibly long; cuts were imperative. "*Caesar* ended at around 2:00 A.M., and that's without calls or applause. I think we'll end at one tomorrow."[92]

P.M. Pchelnikov had attended the first dress in his capacity as censor; as such he paid particular attention to the private Moscow theaters—with emphasis on the Art Theater. He made several "corrections" to the first act and to the assassination scene. After the October 13 dress, Nemirovich-Danchenko made a number of further changes, mostly cuts. Act II, scenes iii and iv, (Portia's and Artemidorus's brief scenes) were cut entirely. The other cuts were much less drastic. On the eve of the premiere, more technical rehearsals were held to speed up the tempo of the production and further reduce the length of the intermissions.

The critic N.E. Efros was present at the October 13 dress rehearsal, after which he wrote a short critical article entitled "Rome." It appeared in the Moscow paper *Novosti Dnia (News of the Day)* on the day of the premiere. As Efros himself admitted, it was an unusual journalistic move to review a dress rehearsal. *Russkoe Slovo (Russian Word)* had released only an eager announcement, and *Russkie Vedomosti (Russian News)* had published three pages of general historical and Shakespearean commentary, with a note to the effect that the characterizations were well done, but that the principal question was whether the theater could recreate Caesar's Rome.

Efros called the production "grandiose and, in many ways, exceptionally interesting." Emphasizing the lack of importance to Shakespeare of historical accuracy for his writing, and of archeological verities for his staging, he felt that the English playwright would only have been hampered by them. Caesar's Rome—and perhaps Caesar himself—was only a preface, a prop for the tragedy of Brutus, which Efros saw as the study of a soul no less complex than Hamlet's. Caesar was reduced to caricature for convenience's sake. (Efros confessed that he was consciously influenced in this by German romantic criticism. The foremost Russian critic of the 1840s, Belinski, also subscribed to this view, and it had remained a popular one in Russia.) But the Art Theater, he said, has taken Shakespeare's abstraction of Rome, and brought it solidly down to earth—at a cost, added the critic, of some sixty thousand rubles, "a whole fortune." In so doing, the "incidental" in Shakespeare was placed stage center. The Art Theater even corrected Shakespeare's historical errors. The resulting Roman panorama becomes the main interest of the production. But "I decidedly do not mean to say by this that, as Rome was 'incidental' to Shakespeare, so Brutus was 'incidental' to the Art Theater—further details on this to be published in a later review." Nevertheless the implication had been made. The review was not unfavorable—far from it. Efros noted that the theater had enemies in the press, and that many columns would no doubt be filled with arguments about *Caesar*. "But there will be no arguing about the fact that the theater took on a tremendously difficult task, and performed it brilliantly."[93]

Nevertheless, Nemirovich-Danchenko exploded. He considered Efros's views on Shakespeare "somewhat primitive" and "fatal to the genius of Shakespeare." He fired off a personal reply to Efros, defining his artistic intent and answering some of the critic's charges:

> If influential papers disapprove of our *Julius Caesar,* then it is not the fact of their disapproval which is offensive to me, but the erroneous interpretation of the theater's intent.
>
> I personally will be offended if you continue to err in your view of the play itself.
>
> So I'm writing for this reason. I feel that the author of today's "Rome" was barking up the wrong tree.
>
> 1) He stresses the interest of the theater in the set, property and staging elements, and this occupied a secondary place in the theater *from the start.* According to your comments, it would seem that the theater chose only those parts of the play which lent themselves to external resolutions. This is a crude and insulting mistake. Flagrant enemies of the theater blithely suggest that the strength of the production lies in a 60,000 ruble expenditure (it's half that) and a collection of European props. I consider such an opinion of our efforts directly insulting to the theater.
>
> 2) You view the tragedy erroneously (i.e. I can anticipate how you are going to view it). In no way is the "spirit of Brutus" the center of the tragedy. This is definitely an illusion. The play should not be classified with *Hamlet, Othello, Macbeth,* and so on, in this regard. (Otherwise it would be called *Brutus.*) In the given play, Brutus is merely the head of the conspiracy, of which he is the only assassin motivated solely by purely republican interests. In this play Shakespeare has already drifted from the concentration of interest in one human soul or in one passion (jealousy, ambition, and so on). In *Julius Caesar,* he painted a huge picture in which primary attention is focused not on individual figures, but on general phenomena: the fall of a republic and the growth of a nation—Caesar's *brilliant* awareness of the situation, and the *natural* ignorance of it on the part of an insignificant bunch of "last Romans." Hence the collision and the dramatic movement. With this in mind, isn't Brutus here no more than one—granted a principal one—of the figures? Granted too, Shakespeare makes a number of mistakes as to the historical details, but he seizes the *spirit of the given historical moment* and *attendant events* with amazing understanding of the psychology of *human history.* In this lies the center of the tragedy, not in the individual figures.

3) *And this was the main task of the theater.* To paint Rome, and her agony, at the fall of the republic.

. . . .

We staged the power of darkness [Tolstoy's *Power of Darkness*], and not Nikita and Matryona and *not the details of peasant life.* We are staging an historical picture, and not Brutus and Mark Antony and not the topography of Rome, plus Berlin-made armor.

In staging the power of darkness (always *via* the small things), we want Matryona and Nikita and peasant life to be there. In staging the fall of the republic and the dawn of monarchism over a nation at the end of its historical life, we want—in the same way—to have Brutus and Cassius and Caesar, and an accurate picture of everyday life. *Ideally* everything should be there. In practice—you can't have everything. But the over-all picture must come first—in the given situation: the spirit of an immense historical phenomenon, one through which every nation must pass. At first the commune, then the king, then the republic, and finally the hereditary monarchy covering its nakedness with external grandeur (Romulus and Remus, Tarquinius, the series of consuls, Augustus et al.).

These are the ideas which motivated our theater during the whole course of producing *Julius Caesar.* If we have accomplished it all, we have done a huge, a colossal, artistic deed. If not—we are impotent. . . . [94]

In his conflict with Efros over interpretation, Nemirovich-Danchenko states his overall view of the play more concisely than anywhere else. Efros pleads the case of nineteenth-century romantic criticism. Nemirovich-Danchenko is drawn to its opposite, the new naturalism whose focus is on social realities rather than on individual souls. Objectively, one must consider the fact that Shakespeare called his play *Julius Caesar,* not *Brutus* and not *Caesar's Rome.* Neither Efros nor Nemirovich-Danchenko were quite on target, but neither contradicted the play as much as he contradicted the other.

As far as modern scholarship has been able to determine, Shakespeare wrote *Julius Caesar* just after *Henry V* and just before *Hamlet.* It is, in many ways, a transitional play. Efros detects in it that which prefigures *Hamlet;* Nemirovich-Danchenko sees its spiritual kinship with the history plays.

The greater part of *Julius Caesar* deals with a political problem in the relationship of leader and mob, transplanting those same political interests expressed in *Henry V* to a Roman subject well known to Elizabethan audiences. Shakespeare's focus is on the practitioner of politics raised to the level of the mythic. Julius Caesar is a popular hero made superman, even though in the first three acts he is presented as the conspirators see him: a frail specimen, physically weak, spiritually arrogant, superstitious. The Caesar they see can be killed, but not the mythic Caesar—who is made stronger than ever by the destruction of the aging mortal shell whose existence (as Shakespeare describes it) must have been an embarrassment to the myth. The weakness which characterizes Caesar's physical presence in the early part of the play also serves to emphasize the might of his spiritual presence in the latter part. Brutus could not destroy the mythic ideal of power.

Nemirovich-Danchenko treats the political problem presented by Shakespeare, but from a different angle. He focuses on the mob rather than on the leader. While the approach is not Shakespeare's, who was interested in the complexities of the Elizabethan world, it is relevant to the early twentieth century. Shakespeare was revolutionary in stating that the power wielded by individuals depended to any extent on the consent of the people; Nemirovich-Danchenko was perceptive enough to notice that the people themselves were beginning to wield power. His interpretation, therefore, is more valid for his time than the Shakespearean approach.

Yet Efros has a point. In *Julius Caesar,* unlike *Henry V,* our sympathy is transferred from the power-wielding superman to the idealist who struggles against him and who is doomed by the very purity of his idealism. The center of emotional interest is Brutus, a figure who presages the Hamlet Shakespeare is soon to create. Brutus, who murders from philosophical motives, can be seen as representing the revulsion of humanity against the superman. Shakespeare deals at length with Brutus, as he does not with the other conspirators, making a complete study of a man predestined to failure but retaining his moral integrity to the end. But Brutus himself is not the subject of the tragedy, as Hamlet will be; Brutus is part of the tragedy. In *Julius Caesar,* the tragedy lies in the triumph of practical power over political idealism.

Efros's article also contains many inaccuracies, as well as his debatable romantic interpretation of the play. Shakespeare was not only concerned with historical accuracy, but he did his homework fairly thoroughly. His Rome was not an abstraction, but neither did he write for a naturalistic stage. Shakespeare's *Caesar* comes straight from Plutarch via an Elizabethan world view—the interpretation of events and characters are Shakespeare's own, but the events and characters themselves are historical fact. Nemirovich-Danchenko had few archeological corrections to make. That Shakespeare's focus was not on archeological verity is clear, but it does not necessarily shift, therefore, exclusively to Brutus. Rome and Caesar are much more than props. Shakespeare was roundly condemned by 17th and 18th century classicist writers for rooting his ideas so firmly in earthly reality—Efros need not blame this on the Art theater. But there still remains the question of whether the Art Theater's naturalistic approach went too far.

To summarize, then, Nemirovich-Danchenko saw Rome itself at the center of the tragedy, not the spirit of Caesar-superman. The main character of the play was, he said, the Roman people. This vision is as old as Pushkin, who placed the Russian people at the center of *Boris Godunov,* with all specific leaders dependent on the masses for their power and even their existence. Insofar as he could, Nemirovich-Danchenko presented the Rome of Caesar's time on the Art Theater stage. That Rome was, he determined, far more modest in appearance than the Imperial Rome usually presented on the stage. He tried not only to keep the more human scale of Julian Rome, but to present the action in its proper setting in such a way that the set never dominated the actors and the action. The set was to be lived in by the Roman people, the main character. This very naturalistic approach was not new for the theater which had just produced *Lower Depths,* nor surprising in an era when the urban masses were just beginning to flex their muscle.

Julius Caesar in Chekhovian Tones

Nemirovich-Danchenko's promptbook, of which the first four acts (I, i through III, iii of Shakespeare's play) still survive and are published, provides a concrete basis for the reconstruction of the actual production which Efros saw. Journalistic criticism can verify its information, so that we know how much of Nemirovich-Danchenko's intention was realized on the stage, but the director's notes are complete in themselves. Every detail is thoroughly worked out, with only a few decisions put off until rehearsal. Whatever improvements were discovered later, in rehearsal, were added to the promptbook. As Leonidov (Cassius) remembered, "it tells you not only what and where Julius Caesar, Brutus, or Antony does and says, but also what the twenty-eighth legionnaire does in the last act, what he shouts and to whom."[95] But its value lies beyond its preservation of the ephemeral theatrical event. The comments it contains reflect Nemirovich-Danchenko's views on certain problems of acting and directing, of dealing with the script, and of applied scenic naturalism. And there are mini-tracts throughout, in which Nemirovich-Danchenko interprets the play and its characters. The approach is derived from Stanislavski's, and the results were ultimately instructive to both men.

To begin with, Nemirovich-Danchenko is particularly careful with the script. He instructs the actor to pay close attention to the verse qualities of the lines, and he makes minor changes in Mikhailovski's translation to make the Russian version less stilted. He instructs the actors to pay close attention to Shakespeare's poetry—any lack of understanding of its rhythms could reduce it to prose. (*Plan,* p. 363) There are many notes to individual actors concerning their reading of a line, and several more general discussions. Throughout the promptbook, he quibbles with Shakespeare on minor points, usually historical. "Shakespeare was evidently little informed as to the details of a Senate session, the place of Caesar's assassination, etc." (*Plan,* p. 291)—this because Shakespeare places the Senate and the dying Caesar "on the Capitol" (I, iii, 36). The line is, therefore, reluctantly changed. Some cuts reflect a lack of perception on the part of Nemirovich-Danchenko. Thus, when Caesar says, "Mark Antony shall say I am not well,/ And for thy humour I will stay at home" (II, ii, 55-56), Nemirovich-Danchenko changes the line to "So be it./ For thy humour I will stay at home" because "I cannot undersand the contradiction between this line and the later 'Shall Caesar send a lie?'" (*Plan,* p. 359). But the contradiction is highly indicative in terms of Caesar's character, and Nemirovich-Danchenko has destroyed a valuable piece of evidence. A few very minor changes are made without any explanation whatsoever: Decius

Figure 6.   1903 *Julius Caesar*. I. Roman street, during Caesar's procession.

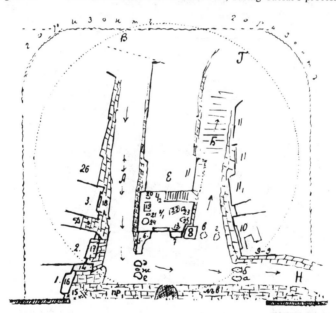

Figure 7.   Ground plan for the Roman street set. Street A rises
               from the Forum, past a butcher shop (26), fruit store
               (3), alley (D), armorer (2), and bookstore (1). A
               barbershop with rooftop patio (4) and fountain (8)
               are center, and street Б (almost a stairway) ascends
               to the Palatine Hill past a tavern (10) and citizens'
               houses (11). Sidewalks border the streets and the
               footlights; Russian letters a–e indicate stepping
               stones in the streets.

Figure 8.   1903 *Julius Caesar*. II, i. Brutus' garden, during the
                conspiracy scene.

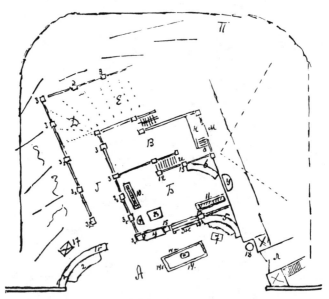

Figure 9.   Ground plan for Brutus' garden set. The forestage
                (A), framed by Brutus' house (right), marble benches
                and a balustrade, has a small fish pond with a
                fountain (14), center. A raised garden (Б), behind
                the balustrade, and a grape arbor (Г) are backed by
                various passageways, with a panoramic view of Rome
                as backdrop (Nemirovich-Danchenko presumed that
                Brutus lived on the Palatine Hill).

Figure 10.   1903 *Julius Caesar*. II, ii. Caesar's study; Calpurnia
              (N.S. Butova), right, pleads with Caesar (Kachalov),
              center.

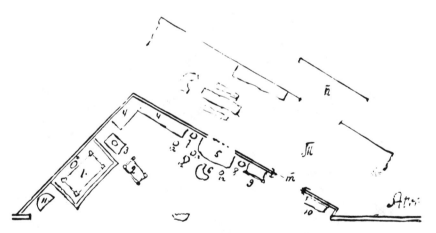

Figure 11.   Ground plan for Caesar's study set. This room is off
              the tablinium (*Jil*), decorated with mosaics and
              frescoes, and furnished with a couch (1), bookshelves
              (4) a worktable (5), chairs, statues (8 is Victory), and
              a small altar (3). The room was inspired by
              reconstructions of Roman villas seen in Italy, and
              everything in it was taken from specific drawings in
              the research albums compiled in Moscow and
              abroad.

Figure 12.   1903 *Julius Caesar*. III, i. Curia of Pompey, Senate
              session; Brutus (Stanislavski) stabs Caesar
              (Kachalov).

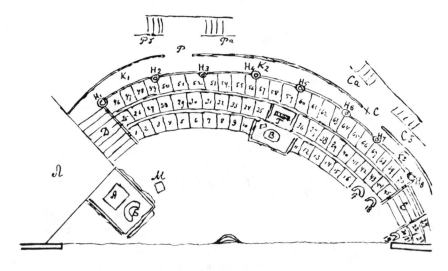

Figure 13.   Ground plan for III, i. A colossal statue of Pompey
              (A) dominates the set; a bronze statue of a female
              wolf (Γ) watches over the altar (B) in the center of
              the curved rows of seating. Each senator's place is
              assigned. With this set, Nemirovich-Danchenko
              corrects Shakespeare, who has Caesar assassinated
              on a street before the Capitol.

Figure 14.   1903 *Julius Caesar*. III, ii. The Forum, during the
mimed funeral of Caesar.

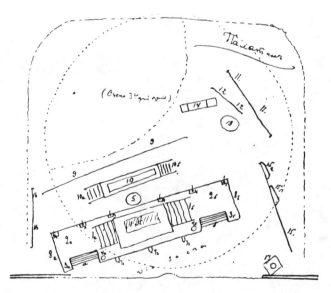

Figure 15.   Ground plan for the Forum set. The Rostra Julia
occupies most of the forestage. Caesar's corpse was
burned on a pyre (10) behind it and in front of the
Regia (9). To the right are the Basilica Julia (15),
and Aedes Vestae (13), the Atrium Vestae (12), the
arch of Fabian (14) and the temple of Castor and
Pollux (11), with a backdrop of a the Palatine Hill.

Figure 16.   1903 *Julius Caesar*. IV. The camp near Sardis; Brutus' tent.

Figure 17.   Detail of IV, Brutus' tent, showing Brutus (Stanislavski) and Cassius (Leonidov).

Figure 18. 1903 *Julius Caesar.* V, i. A field near Philippi. The trap was opened to create a ravine, down front, through which the soldiers could march. Only their helmets and spears were visible to the audience. By recycling soldiers, the directors could make an endless file of them march through the ravine and create the impression of a massive army.

simply becomes Decimus, for example. All in all, however, the play is tampered with very little, and was staged with a minimum of textual alteration.

For the naturalistic director, however, there is a strong temptation to tamper with the Shakespearean monologue because this convention clashes with the given production style. The director must help his actors find a way to talk to themselves out loud without seeming eccentric or even ridiculous. Nemirovich-Danchenko first tackled this problem in the notes for act II concerning Brutus' speeches:

> I think the actor should try to seem as though he is playing a pause with words, and so work out a diction and expression which imply that the words are spoken without his intending or noticing them.
>
> (*Plan,* p. 311)

In the given situation, he adds, Brutus is so wrapt in thought that this is easily achieved. The actor need only plunge himself into Brutus' mood and become absorbed in his thoughts. Then those thoughts must project themselves in soft speech (rather like the impression given by Olivier in his film portrayal of Hamlet).

Certain Shakespearean monologues, however, have the added difficulty of being generally well known. "When the actor is primarily concerned with giving these masterpieces some fresh and original approach, he is very far from the real task of art" (*Plan,* p. 455). The attitude of the public fosters this tendency, to the detriment of the art of the theater.

> There is nothing more dangerous for an actor than a famous monologue. The actor is chained down by those parts of a monologue which made his reputation. And the greater the reputation, the more he will try for even greater virtuosity....
>
> (*Plan,* p. 455)

Nemirovich-Danchenko suggests that "it would be best if he make himself forget about the fame of these passages" and deal with them as with the rest of his lines, honestly and without pretension (*Plan,* p. 455). But the actor must never forget that he is performing for an audience:

> A superb actor masters his audiences because he is, simultaneously, sincere to the point of self-oblivion, and always in total possession of his critical and observational faculties. He serves the audience and, at the same time, does not let it know his fear of it.
>
> (*Plan,* p. 457)

When Antony's servant enters in act III, another acting problem crops up: reported speech and the messenger. The speech itself is not the servant's, but Antony's; the servant, however, is a separate character with his own individual relationship to the others, and his own reaction to the assassination of Caesar. The directions read:

> ... Slowly choosing his words, but bravely. Almost without intonation (this is a special art— to transmit someone else's words, maneuvering adroitly between the intonation of him who originally spoke them, and of him who reports them), yet evincing the deepest devotion to Antony and to Caesar. By a successful use of pauses, rises, and drops. The monologue provides material for a superb and inspired performance, since this ostensibly simple retelling of another's speech is warmed by a flame hot and deep within the soul of this mere slave—and which he conceals only with difficulty. The actor can make the pauses easier for himself by having the slave seem almost unable to control his own turbulent emotions.
>
> (*Plan*, p. 415)

Addressing yet another acting issue, Nemirovich-Danchenko warned the actor playing Ligarius against making too much of the illness mentioned in his lines. "By forgetting what the main point is, and overplaying Ligarius' illness, the actor can drag out the scene...." The secondary must not overshadow the principal direction of a speech, scene, or act, nor should it interfere with its movement. "Everyone knows that the tempo of each section is completely subject to the staging of the act as a whole. And the act only becomes a harmonic whole when its 'central nerve' is clear throughout." In II, i, for example, the central nerve is given as "Brutus' psychology as it relates to the conspiracy. It runs a whole gamut of moods, from vacillation and the torment of doubt, to unswervable determination." It involves a gradual transition from agony at the thought of murder to the final decision which is carried out in the next act by one blow of the dagger. "Anything which impedes the development of this basic theme by creating secondary interests, as ... by being hashed up into unnecessary details, will harm the harmonic whole" (*Plan*, pp. 343, 345).

Visual detail, on the other hand, was not perceived as creating a secondary interest, but as providing a necessary stage environment for the actors. So, great attention was paid to visual accuracy, as is evident in the pains taken in the preparation of this production. Nemirovich-Danchenko was concerned by any divergence between scenic resolution and historical verity. Thus he writes in regard to the set for Caesar's house (II, ii);

> In view of the fact that Caesar receives the senators in this scene, a tablinium would seem obligatory (in the still-extant "house of Livy," this is the middle of three rooms facing onto the atrium). But the temptation to provide a more intimate setting for Caesar is too great, especially since it would be difficult, with a tablinium, to avoid the banalities usually endemic to productions of classical plays. Besides, having the reception of senators in a more intimate room, without grandiose props, will enhance the severe simplicity which I find so enticing here.
>
> (*Plan*, p. 351)

While his apologia may seem somewhat superfluous, Shakespeare himself being supremely unconcerned as to which room of a Roman house was involved, his option for historical accuracy left him no choice but to be extremely thorough. Otherwise, the production would seem inept, especially now that the wonders of the Meininger had raised the standards of theatrical archeology so high.

Nor was accuracy the only consideration. As we have seen, in dealing with the forum scene Nemirovich-Danchenko wrestled with the problem which had defeated the Meininger: how to create a necessarily impressive set without its overwhelming the actor:

> ... to present the Forum and still keep the audience's attention focused on those who speak on this Forum—here, Antony and Brutus—this problem is completely unsolved....
> The topography of the Forum, which we studied on location, imposes very definite limits on the director. The dilemma is manifest: either you shrug off the whole of historical Rome, already overstudied, and dream up something convenient, anything your heart desires—for example, the rostrum in the middle of a square, and surrounded by people—or you retain all the facts of history, but make the stage more comfortable for the actors; i.e. regard the locale with the actor's convenience in mind, and resist the yearning for a striking impression of a huge square. We preferred to do the latter.
>
> (*Plan*, p. 435)

The Forum set would be accurate, but it lacked the unforgettable scale of the Meininger Forum, which filled the stage with magnificent Roman temples.

The Forum scene presented other problems. While it is obvious from III, i, that Shakespeare knew that Antony spoke at Caesar's funeral, the lines indicate that the action of III, ii, takes place immediately after the murder. And there is no indication in III, ii, of any funeral rite, save in one brief line late in the scene. ("We'll burn his body in the holy place.")

> Meanwhile, according to most of the sources, the funeral took place seven days after the death—and, according to others, even later. And it was performed with the highest degree of ceremony. There are extremely detailed descriptions of Caesar's funeral, including Antony's oration.
>
> (*Plan*, pp. 438-9)

Nemirovich-Danchenko defends Shakespeare's omission of the interval between the murder and the funeral. There is the event, and stunned silence until the inevitable reaction:

> If newspapers and the telegraph had existed in Caesar's time, Cinna would have proclaimed to the world: "Yesterday, during a session of the Senate in the curia of Pompey, the dictator Julius Caesar was killed by Marcus Brutus. Tyranny is conquered. The people proclaim 'Peace, freedom, and liberty!'"
> And only a week later, this murder would give so resounding a belch.
>
> (*Plan,*, p. 440)

Of course, it is the belch that interests us, and not the waiting period.

Nevertheless, the time lapse and the question of a funeral made it difficult to combine accuracy with fidelity to Shakespeare's text. Elizabethan stage conventions accepted leaps and bounds through sequential time, and did not bother with archeological truth. But "the demands for realistic production have grown too much since Shakespeare's time.... We could not ignore the fact that [Antony's] speech was given during a funeral" (*Plan*, p. 439). And so a funeral was staged as a mimed background. Since the time interval clashed with the dramatic movement of the play, Nemirovich-Danchenko had to choose one or the other. He decided to cut the intermission between the acts to the barest minimum, using the revolving stage to facilitate the change of scenery; so he opted to preserve the dramatic movement. He writes in his notes: "As regards the seven-day interval, the license of stage convention will absorb it" (*Plan*, p. 440). Just to make sure that it did, he changes the lines to omit all references to any immediate removal of the corpse to the marketplace, and introduces the word "funeral" wherever mention is made of a coming oration. Nor does he bring in Caesar's corpse in the next scene; it is already on the stage. The initial lines of III, ii, are cut, and the mimed funeral, with Antony present, is in full swing when Brutus makes his entrance.

But the most important and controversial decision Nemirovich-Danchenko made in his approach to *Julius Caesar* was to establish the Roman people as the main character of the play.[96] They are treated as an active force which bursts into the flow of history with great energy and power. The people are unpredictable and hard to read, and a leader's inability to deal with them leads directly to his destruction.

Nemirovich-Danchenko used over two hundred extras in the production, most of whom were part of the crowd. Each extra had a specific character to play; Nemirovich-Danchenko wrote a background for each and demanded that the actors fill in those outlines so as to bring a lifelike persona onto the stage. Here we have Jewish booksellers, Roman armorers and petty merchants, a whole barbershop full of sundry Romans, an inn full of people, street urchins, whole Roman families, and so on to senators, and legionnaires for the last act. In this way, Nemirovich-Danchenko, and Stanislavski as director, created an entire population of real people. But when Nemirovich-Danchenko first told Stanislavski that he wanted a lively, gay, tumultuous city crowd in the first act, and no stagey hubbub and bustle, Stanislavski (whose theory proposed exactly this) scoffed at the idea as too "utopian": "Don't waste time and energy on what can't be done." Nemirovich-Danchenko refused to give up, and it was done.[97]

The people of Rome begin the play, and in the Art Theater production, their presence is felt almost constantly. Before the curtain goes up on the first act, "the pungent, vital bubbling of southern voices" (*Plan*, p. 226) is heard faintly, at first, then increases until it fills the whole house. The curtain rises on a holiday crowd on a southern street corner, by busy shops and an inn. "Of course, all the participants must examine the set carefully, and get used to it; they must understand the Lupercalia well, and feel at home on these streets" (*Plan*, p. 228). There is a sense of ceaseless motion towards the Circus Maximus where Caesar is to speak.

Nemirovich-Danchenko's plan for this scene treats the crowd both as individuals and as a collective unit. Each of the 150 members of the crowd is characterized and described, one by one or in small homogenous groups, in the first pages of the promptbook. Each one is blocked individually or in small groups from the moment the curtain rises:

> The second and third Roman women (characters 61 and 62) enter as soon as slaves 1 and 2 and the wineseller cross to the barbershop. The tenth citizen (character 20) should decide to follow, and when he sees that the wineseller and the slaves are upstairs, he speaks to the second and third Roman women who are waiting for him below.
>
> (*Plan*, p. 227)

But what the tenth citizen says, or any one citizen says at this point, is not spelled out in the promptbook. Nemirovich-Danchenko wrote lines and scraps of lines which were to function symphonically. Crucial words are emphasized, and the audience was meant to hear them clearly.

> Themes for speech: *holiday of Faun; Lupercalia; Julius Caesar should pass by soon on his way to the Circus*;... it's mobbed *in the Forum* (point to it)—you can't even squeeze through; it will be a *triumphal* procession; everyone's already gone to the *Circus Maximus* (point to it); if Julius Caesar takes the *crown*, it's *the end of the Republic*—this must be stopped...; it's humid, there'll be a thunderstorm; "Buy my flowers—you must have flowers today, it's the feast of *Faun*, buy my flowers, this little flower is pretty on you, only two *sestercii*"; "Alms for a poor beggar on the *feast of Faun*! Just a sestercius!"... *Cinna* is reciting! Are the poems any good? No, *terrible*! *He praises Caesar* and his triumphs!...
>
> (*Plan*, pp. 227-28)

And so forth. Specifically who said what was worked out at rehearsal.

When the crowd begins to break up, however, lines are assigned more frequently: "... citizens 1, 2, 3 and 5, who pays the fruitseller, shout 'Let's get to the Circus! It's time!'" (*Plan*, p. 228). When Marullus and Flavius speak their first lines, "street noises slowly quiet down" (*Plan*, p. 231). But the extras still on stage have prescribed business:

> The Jewish shopkeeper comes from the corner behind the shelves. The rabbi stands up on the edge of the sidewalk. Boy 1 climbs onto bench 14. The armorer clambers all the way out of his shop to peer through the crowd. Same for the fruitseller and the poulterer. The barber and fop 2 emerge and loiter by the doorhangings. The Numidian is busy trying to catch his donkey. The Syrian girl (39) climbs onto the fountain and leans on the shoulder of her friend (40) standing next to her....
>
> (*Plan*, p. 231)

Eventually there is a distinct hum of voices coming from the Forum, where a large crowd awaits Caesar. The power of the crowd is conveyed by the alarm of Cinna and Artemidorus at the impact Flavius and Marcellus have on the crowd. Their horror at the crowd's reaction is echoed by Flavius and Marcellus when they recognize the power of the crowd they have just stirred up against Caesar.

During Brutus' scene with Cassius, there are powerful roars from the distant crowds. Brutus and Cassius react with anxiety not only lest Caesar be crowned, but also at the strength of the popular voice should it be in support of crowning Caesar. When the crowd returns to the stage, it is obviously divided in its opinion on the events of the day. Some are clearly overjoyed that they prevented any coronation; others (the largest group) are concerned by the evidence of Caesar's illness and show great curiosity when he enters; a third group just hurries home. As in the first crowd scene, Nemirovich-Danchenko assigns some individual lines and some symphonic "themes for speech" for groups. The blocking continues to be very specific. All this is planned in detail, with each character's reaction carefully suited to his role. The stage is crowded until the beginning of the storm indicated in the play as "thunder and lightning." The crowd melts, followed by the shopkeepers as they lock up their stores.

The force of nature represented by the storm seems to parallel the power of the people. It begins with strong winds, which eventually blow objects about on the stage, breaking pots and beating at people. As it assumes hurricane force, lightning and thunder are heard—the sky has been overcast from much earlier on. The sounds of wind and thunder, shrieks of buffeted people and the metallic clanking of bolts being closed cry warning of a horrible darkness filled with thunder created in front, then over and around the audience, then fading out in back of the house. With this effect, the audience is forcibly included in the action. Flashes of lightning and a fiery rain are projected by the magic lantern. At the very end of the act, a group of Vestals and their lictors return toward the Palatine—a reminder that Shakespeare's main characters do not comprise all of Rome.

During the second and third acts, Rome and her people are often mentioned but rarely seen, save in a brief street scene which was cut during the dress rehearsals. The building of support for Cimber's cause by the conspirators in the Senate recalls some of the tumult of the crowd, but—unlike the Meininger, who staged the Senate scene outside the Senate building, with the populace present—there is only a general hubbub heard from offstage to indicate the Roman people's reaction to news of Caesar's assassination. This is repeated several times, whenever the doors open—as when the senators flee, when Antony enters, and when:

> Cinna, going behind the wings, proclaims "Peace, liberty, and freedom."
> The people meet the conspirators with *complete silence.* And when their shouts recede, a
> *low roar* is heard *from the people*—as though directed at the murderers.
>
> *(Plan,* p. 429)

When Antony's gladiators bear Caesar off, the audience sees a crush of wailing people held back at the doors by the lictors, tribunes and viators. "The people, with horror on their faces, crowd around the exits, . . . and seek the corpse with their eyes" (*Plan,* p. 433).

In act III, in the Senate scene, Nemirovich-Danchenko treats the crowd somewhat differently. The senators were divided into subgroups headed by various experienced actors, and the same was done with the crowd in the Forum.

> Each group will have its leader, who is responsible to know every movement of his group
> precisely, how many are in it and the composition of its cast for each performance. He will
> communicate with the assistant director for his group, and will be responsible for its
> costumes, make up, etc., etc. . . .
>
> *(Plan,* p. 389)

Usually, themes and lines for speech were allocated to each actor, as were definite bits of action. In the Senate scene, though, Nemirovich-Danchenko broke the whole crowd of senators and observers into five main groups, indicating the general attitudes of each, and suggesting various possibilities for its members in terms of lines and action. Further individualization was left to the actor, and expected of him. In his directions to the extras for this scene, Nemirovich-Danchenko sums up his approach:

> Each group . . . must do more than react to what happens to the principals; it must also live a
> life of its own. When a crowd only responds to the action of the play; it will always remain
> theatrical. It will only be alive when it develops its own interests.
> . . . Every actor in every group must get used to this, so that a group-division will be
> organic rather than mechanical. Then the scene will come alive. Each actor must know how
> and to whom he relates, and must use this all the time he is on stage. . . . No actor should relate
> to the others without making any distinction among them. . . .
>
> *(Plan,* pp. 391-2)

Shakespeare's Forum scene is a masterly portrayal of the inconstancy of the mob, and it turned out to be the glory of the Art Theater production. Noting that Antony's speech is given during Caesar's funeral which, historically, took place at least seven days after his death, Nemirovich-Danchenko writes:

> . . . Shakespeare omitted the interval of time, and the events which might fill it, between the
> murder and the funeral. This is completely legitimate, because it was a period of vague, silent,

agonized waiting for what would happen next—for what would blaze up at the funeral. It would be naïve to suppose that Caesar's murder was immediately followed by rebellion or investigations. First of all, the mere fact of the murder would have resulted in great mass terror, from which the people would not recover easily. Then—even more important— Brutus, Cassius, Casca, Decimus (especially the first of these) had such immense popularity among the citizens that for the crowd, as for Antony, the foremost question would be: why?

(*Plan*, p. 439)

It is this tension which informs the Forum scene. Nemirovich-Danchenko divided his extras into participators in the funeral procession, and curious onlookers. The curtain rises when the procession is well onto the stage, and it becomes evident that the set has added another dimension to the crowd:

The Forum would be where the house is, and the audience itself would replace the citizens of Rome.

(Plan, p. 437)

The inclusion of the audience into the play, begun with the storm scene, is made complete. Brutus and Antony would address the audience as much as those on stage, and the shifting moods of the crowd would be imposed on the audience. At one point in the promptbook, Nemirovich-Danchenko tells Antony to let 'er rip and work on the emotions of the audience, "Let the whole audience weep" (*Plan*, p. 469). Nothing on stage is to interfere with Antony's relationship with the audience. After Antony's speeches, when stage crowd and audience are whipped to the proper emotional peak, Nemirovich-Danchenko has the stage crowd begin to riot ("revolt"). This is followed by the burning, on stage, of Caesar's corpse (historically inaccurate, the promptbook laments, but Caesar had to be burned in the Forum to satisfy the needs of the production).

Everything seemed anticlimactic after the emotional Forum scene. The Art Theater audience, never before so brazenly included into the action, was exhausted by the experience. The rest of the production merely served to tie up dramatic threads and bring the whole to a suitable aesthetic conclusion. The army replaces the people, and is treated in the same detail, but is at an emotional distance from the audience.

So detailed a treatment of crowd scenes was entirely new, even in the Art Theater. The Meininger, for all the external naturalism of their mass scenes, never thought to bring them to this kind of life.

Nemirovich-Danchenko's vivid presentation of the Roman crowd is not inimical to the spirit of Shakespeare's early work—let us recall the teeming vitality of Cheapside and the picture of the soldiery in *Henry V*. But Nemirovich-Danchenko has shifted the emphasis of the play from Shakespeare's political interplay between nobles, generals, and kings to the power and vitality of "the rabblement" (I, ii, 243) and "rag-tag people" (I, ii, 2). The shift is not surprising; not only does it reflect the literary tradition established by Pushkin's *Boris Godunov,* but the picture Nemirovich-Danchenko gives of a nation undergoing the turmoil of political change speaks directly to the contemporary Russian situation—so much so that Soviet scholars have underscored the "progressive" nature of this approach. While there is no hard evidence that Nemirovich-Danchenko intended making a political statement with his production, its timeliness lends a certain validity to his interpretation. A play is written in a given time, but a production of it, if performed decades or centuries later, must answer not to that earlier day, but to its own time—or risk being dismissed as a period piece.

The major characters are thoroughly explored in the promptbook, but Nemirovich-Danchenko's perception of them does not differ so radically from generally accepted interpretations as does his view of the Roman crowd. The political struggle of individuals is overshadowed by the portrayal of Rome and her people, but Nemirovich-Danchenko creates parallels between crowd and main characters. Brutus' inner struggle, for example, is linked thematically with the pull of diverse influences on the crowd.

In Caesar, Nemirovich-Danchenko attempted to reunite the Julius of the Gallic Wars with Shakespeare's Julius. In the first act, he is Pontifex Maximus; in the second he is a family man; in the third, a ruler (*Plan,* p. 241).

> Caesar is high priest. Caesar is a general of genius. Caesar is used to a severe army life in which he knew how to devote every minute to the furtherance of his grandios · plans. Caesar is a wise leader who dreams of extending Rome's domination over the whole world.... Caesar thirsts for power,... is convinced of his great calling, and thinks himself greater than any other man.
>
> (*Plan,* p. 350)

Kachalov, playing Shakespeare's Caesar, was to offset the written image of a weak Caesar by force of Caesar's pride, reputation, and great ambitions. This Caesar disdains the common people, but performs for it: "he speaks beautifully, seriously, solemnly, so that every word is heard" (*Plan,* p. 241), in I, ii, asking that Antony touch Calpurnia as he runs the holy race. The people are meant to be touched by his devotion to tradition. The same delivery is used for other lines—"What touches ourself shall last be served" (III, i), for example. After he has been forced to refuse the crown, he is

> furious to the nth degree. For the past two years he has lived with the idea of monarchy. He is busy with his notes on the Gallic wars in which he praises himself throughout—thus leaving a monument to himself which will endure for thousands of generations. Thus he is used to great, even religious, homage (his statues and busts are revered almost equally with those of Jupiter). Everything had been readied for today,... and suddenly the crowd behaved itself in such a way that it was impossible to accept the crown....
>
> (*Plan,* p. 263)

He is furious, but too much the subtle politician to give his emotions away. He's had an embarrassing seizure, so he walks home on foot to prove his strength. His expression is to show that he fears no one, but that everything is as he would have it.

> But with all his soul he despises the crowd, the mob, whom he has courted all his life because only through the mob could he obtain provinces, the consulate, the high priesthood. He despises the crowd because he is a convinced elitist, and despises it all the more because it has torn the crown from his hands.
>
> *(Plan,* p. 263-64)

In act II, Caesar's arrogance is developed further. He speaks strongly and haughtily with those who are not only his equals, but until recently his superiors. "This is what makes him unbearable in the eyes of these men, who were brought up on principles of freedom and equality" (*Plan,* p. 361).

In act III, his dominant mood is one of arrogance. The more he is opposed, and the more he scents danger, the more arrogant he becomes. This is intolerable to his equals in the Senate—and, when threatened, this defense of his ensures his death. The conspirators move slowly upon him as he speaks, accompanied by growing muttered tension in the room. No one moves to save Caesar—and he is brutally and bloodily murdered in full view of everyone.

Kachalov managed to play Caesar as astute leader, and was universally praised for his performance. Nemirovich-Danchenko had had trouble getting any of his principal actors to accept the role he thought so highly of, but finally persuaded Kachalov. Stanislavski had been offered the role and later repented his refusal.[98] Kachalov played an ambitious man with an iron will, as well as human deficiencies, and was largely faithful to Nemirovich-Danchenko's interpretation. He displayed enough greatness to make Caesar's victory after death totally believable. Kachalov's Caesar became ranked with Chaliapin's Boris Godunov as a classic of the Russian stage.

Antony is read both as egotist able to turn events to his own benefit, and as a man of passionate temperament genuinely devoted to Caesar. Nemirovich-Danchenko devoted long passages to the study of this complex character.

> Historical sources about Antony are no more inconsistent than they are about any of the others. However, they all agree that he was extremely two-faced, probably incapable of an ardent love for Caesar.... But even though Shakespeare tries to preserve these traits, appropriate to a far-sighted and adroit egotist, his talent and craving for striking dramatic contrast demanded idealization of Antony. To the credit of Shakespeare's great mastery, this idealization does not result in stereotype, assigning all virtue to Antony, but in a complex portrait of an ebullient nature, flexible in its spiritual transitions.... In no work, it would seem, does Shakespeare so succeed in the realistic portrayal of a human soul, both poeticizing it and maintaining a balance of human merit and fault.
>
> *(Plan,* p. 419)

Antony's very duplicity of character is seen as an interesting comment on the character of the times. The task of the actor is most difficult: he must embrace the whole of this "supple expansive nature" (*Plan*, p. 419), expressing all its variations without losing its unity of conception. Antony can be made neither hero nor villain, nor simply a mosaic of conflicting traits.

Nemirovich-Danchenko sets up contrasts to other characters. Antony is earthy, has an inexhaustible energy: "His kind of life would be enough for several more ordinary people (*Plan*, p. 264). He acts on impulse, and is no thinker or bookworm, "both of which Brutus, and especially Cassius, might be" (*Plan*, p. 264). If the conspirators are cool intellectual men, Antony is hot-blooded:

> He has such a pliant, many-sided, stormy temperament that he is capable of anything. When everyone around him is happy, he is as merry as a little boy; when everyone is sad, he cries. He is flesh of the flesh and bone of the bone of his hot-blooded nation, and enthusiastically gives himself to life and all its phenomena—religious, political, social.
>
> (*Plan*, p. 238)

After Caesar is forced to refuse the crown, Antony shares Caesar's emotions, and violently: "if Caesar would but give him the word, he would leap on the crowd like a tiger and tear it to shreds" (*Plan*, p. 264). His grief at Caesar's death is shown as genuine and overpowering, almost frightening in its intensity. Its force overwhelms the conspirators, mainly because "at their head stands too gentle and delicate a man" (*Plan*, p. 425). So, then, that other side of Antony is given an opportunity to manipulate. The humility and grief he displays beside Caesar are repeated in the early part of his Forum speech. Turning the crowd from supporting Brutus to opposing Brutus is a task comparable to Richard III's winning of Anne. He begins quietly to get the crowd's attention, then support; not content with sympathy, he incites a riot and then a rebellion. "The stronger the roars of the people, the louder Antony declaims—like pouring oil onto flame" (*Plan*, p. 473). The emotional Antony of the early part of the play has become a calculating, capable politician. He learned from Caesar how to win a crowd and applies the lesson well.

Vishnevski played Antony, and seems to have conveyed both the duplicity and the temperament Nemirovich-Danchenko wanted. But as to internalizing the figure and unifying the conflicting traits, he was apparently unsuccessful. Gurevich wrote the harshest review:

> Instead of the brilliant Mark Antony, the fiery speeches were heard from a very fine and able actor named Vishnevski. He acted intelligently, spoke his lines with emotion and genuine inspiration, was notably enthusiastic. Nevertheless, the brilliant Mark Antony was not in evidence.[99]

Brutus presented far fewer difficulties to the director, but Stanislavski had great trouble coming to grips with Nemirovich-Danchenko's interpretation. Stanislavski saw Brutus as decisive and strong-willed, a man who finally sees the path he must follow, and then takes it. A stoic and a man of great moral purity, Brutus is doomed to failure because of his credulous belief that other men are as pure and honest as himself. There is a clear connection here to Stanislavski's interpretations of Othello and Dr. Stockmann.

Nemirovich-Danchenko saw Brutus as the moral center of the conspiracy, its head, and the reason for its ultimate failure. Brutus is not the hero of the play, but one of several main characters. Brutus himself, apart from his place in history and in this play, is perceived as akin to Hamlet. Like Hamlet, Brutus has taken on the superhuman task of cleansing his world of evil, of restoring past purity to a dirty age. The necessary decision to act is a foregone conclusion but, just as Shakespeare prolongs and attenuates it in *Hamlet,* so Nemirovich-Danchenko uses the scene in Brutus' garden to draw out the inner conflicts involved in the agonizing process of decision. The need to act is clear, but the personal cost of action is shown while Brutus reconciles himself to his own conscience.

"All the other conspirators, of course, are inspired by their republicanism, but... each brings something personal to the whole" (*Plan,* p. 319). Only Brutus has no personal motive for the murder of Caesar. Casca, too, has no personal axe to grind, but takes part in the affair almost flippantly—it strikes him as a valiant cause. In general, Casca is seen here as indifferent to life, and therefore shallow. Cassius' motive is clear: "not ambition... but burning, piercing envy" (*Plan,* p. 319). Cassius is a hot-head, violently temperamental. He loves Brutus, but realizes how impractical are Brutus' pure politics. "In truth, Brutus' gentleness and unsullied integrity are the ruin of the republican cause." If Cassius, or even Trebonius, were at the head of the conspiracy, it would have stood a better chance (*Plan,* p. 425). Trebonius "looks on Brutus with suspicion; he has little confidence in such soft-hearted types" (*Plan,* p. 321). Nemirovich-Danchenko sees Trebonius as a "straight-arrow" politician, "sly, cautious, but capable of murder" and with a certain element of blood lust (*Plan,* p. 320). Decius Brutus is a rich young power-hungry careerist. Without conscience, he is cold-blooded and, in his own way, far-sighted. Cimber is motivated by grief over the fate of his brother, and Cinna is a slow-witted, dogged hanger-on—one of the most dangerous weapons of a political party.

After the murder, when Brutus speaks on the Forum, he appears "as a formidable, merciless judge. He is fierce and awe-inspiring. He renders account of the republic itself and is literally ready to destroy any lawbreakers. Were Caesar to live again, he would murder him again—so convinced is he that he is right" (*Plan,* p. 449). Brutus is trusting. He addresses the crowd in a spirit of reason to calm it, not because he is totally ignorant of mob psychology but because he believes that Antony "will help calm the crowd, and... later they will begin together the restoration of the republic" (*Plan,* p. 445). It is not his trust, however, but his failure to assess the times that destroys him. The people want to be led; they need a Caesar—there is no strength left in them to support the weight of a republic. Caesar did not disregard the crowd, and Antony reads it well, but Brutus ignores it. He is blinded by the light of his political ideals—and the people ultimately destroy him.

Nemirovich-Danchenko pictured Brutus as a silent thoughtful type, speaking only when there is something important to say. Brutus sees in Caesar the end of the republic, while knowing the genuine greatness and genius of the man. "His thoughts whirl in a vicious circle: the great Julius Caesar—is ruinous for the republic, and therefore must perish. Somewhat simplistic, he thinks these thoughts bother him alone" (*Plan,* p. 251). It becomes apparent that he is not alone, but his conscience balks at the murder of his friend and Rome's great leader.

The mood of II, i, is that of a nightmare. "Thoughts like monsters nail themselves to his brain, pierce his soul" (*Plan,* p. 311). It is best seen in the speech:

> Between the acting of a dreadful thing
> And the first motion, all the interim is
> Like a phantasma or a hideous dream,
> The genius and the mortal instruments
> Are then in council, and the state of a man
> Like to a little kingdom, suffers then
> The nature of an insurrection.
>
> II, i, 63-69

This is reinforced by the unnatural meteor showers and falling stars. Brutus is tormented by two visions—one of Caesar bloodied and dead, and the other of Caesar crowned and all-powerful. He groans with pain. Brutus' last speech before the entrance of the conspirators comprises the death throes of conscience, and the decision to murder. "From now on, it [conscience] will be quiet, but Brutus' nature, drawn into a game foreign to it, will sicken and suffer..." (*Plan,* p. 318). This last paroxysm of spiritual discord renders Brutus no longer hesitant, but strong and energetic in carrying out his judgment. "He is completely seized by the final, irrevocable progress of his fate" (*Plan,* p. 337). There is one moment of hesitation before his dagger is used: the plea for Cimber's brother is a plea for Caesar "to save himself, ... to act with less arrogance" (*Plan,* p. 403). But Caesar does not and Brutus will "carefully" (*Plan,* p. 403) strike the last and most deliberate blow. This scene is powerfully blocked, moving from tumultuous cries, to hushed horror as the first blow, and then a frenzy of blows, is struck; Caesar finally reels from among his murderers to look for protection from the nearby Brutus. Brutus strikes him with the dagger as though offering sacred sacrifice. Caesar speaks his most famous single line, and as the conspirators surround him once more with their daggers plunging, the senators silently flee.

In distinction to the approach of most productions, Brutus was shown to be part of the world he lived in; Rome was no mere backdrop for Brutus the tragic hero. Nemirovich-Danchenko strove for a delicate balance between the heroic and the ordinary, the tragic and the typical. In no way wishing to diminish Shakespeare's poetry, he did not want to remove it too far from the prose of his audience's experience either. Stanislavski did not manage to achieve that balance until the production had been performed many times.

From the first, Stanislavski was able to create the physical impression that he wanted, but the complex personality of Nemirovich-Danchenko's Brutus had not yet been absorbed and consolidated. Not only had Stanislavski seen Brutus differently than Nemirovich-Danchenko, but he was playing to audiences which expected—as Efros evidently did—to see Brutus the romantic hero and raison d'être of the play. Stanislavski was in despair. He wrote to Chekhov: "I have just recovered after my devastating failure as Brutus. It...confused me to such an extent that I no longer understand what's good and what's bad in the theater.... Life has become slave labor...."[100] "You act, and you think: who needs this?"[101] He explained to Chekhov that he hated the play because his Brutus was unsuccessful and therefore onerous.[102] Everything he had learned to date had been tried on Brutus, and he felt that he was still hiding behind externals. Yet there were as many raves in the press about his Brutus as there were complaints. Ermolova of the Maly Theater "was in ecstasy": "I met Konstantin Sergeevich and told him that I had seen his Brutus and thought it excellent. And he replied, 'If you find my acting good, it must mean that it's really not bad.'"[103] As he continued to work, the role jelled. During the last performances of *Julius Caesar* in Petersburg, he responded to rave notices with his usual deprecatory self-criticism: "My make-up was all right, and my acting wasn't bad."[104]

Stanislavski worked constantly on the production, often reluctantly as though performing an onerous chore, but sometimes enthusiastically as when directing the student actors. He watched his partner apply the Art Theater's Chekhovian discoveries to Shakespeare, and saw his own work from a new perspective. By and large, it depressed him—because he admired his partner's work, but did not find the method effective in staging Shakespeare.

The Fate of the 1903 *Julius Caesar*

The critics concentrated on praising the picture of Rome and its people, and many, like Efros, took issue with Nemirovich-Danchenko's interpretation of the play. However, there were many others who agreed with the interpretation and found it exciting, even revelatory. There was also some talk of imitating the Meininger *Julius Caesar*. Nemirovich-Danchenko must have expected that;

Julius Caesar had been the pride of the Meininger and the strongest statement of its theatrical principles. The storm it created on its two Russian tours had not been forgotten.

Many critics disagreed with the relevance of Nemirovich-Danchenko's stated goal of developing the historical atmosphere of Shakespeare's play. Varneke thought Shakespeare would be better served by a study of the Elizabethan era and its visualizations of Rome. In Nemirovich-Danchenko's approach he saw "much zeal and not enough taste," "many archeologists, but no specialists in aesthetics."[105] Andrei Bely went to see it reluctantly, fearful of another unthinking worshipful rendition of the English "genius," but as least assured that the acting would not rely on tragic temperament. He wrote that "out of this somewhat mechanistic, but conscientious and thoughtful, performance—as though emerging from a frame—stepped Shakespeare nonetheless, not *in toto* but at least in part."[106] He found the sets talented and clever, the crowd well directed, certain acts (II, ii, III and IV) harmonious, and—in general—an honest approach to a good play. He declined to debate the director's premise which had annoyed Efros and Varneke. Enough that there was no pretension.

Several critics yearned for great tragedians, and did not care about the production elements—in short, they missed the good old days. "Brutus must walk differently than other men, talk differently, because he is a hero. That is Shakespeare."[107] Actually, that's Racine, or Sumarokov. Shakespeare was careful to keep his heroes human, if on a larger scale. That Brutus thinks differently than other men need not affect his gait.

Sergei Diaghilev was one of the more outspoken critics in favor of the Art Theater's production. He was vexed by a general attitude among critics that the Art Theater should stay on its own turf (Chekhov and Gorky and Maeterlinck), and not presume to tread holy ground, under option to the feu sacré and academic orthodoxy. He praised the Art Theater's attempt to stage Shakespeare with a new reading, and was impressed by the talent with which it was done. Artistically, he said, the production had unity, freshness, and conviction. That interest lagged after the Forum scene he blamed, quite rightly, on the play, and not the production.

> It is such a delight that the Moscow artists have shown, with *Caesar,* that they can perform the classics properly, and with exactly the approach to classic theater that appeals to a contemporary—very contemporary—spectator.[108]

Diaghilev's article raises some good questions: how can a critic rave about a production, and simultaneously cluck that it isn't Shakespeare? Can one damn a production style as no good for the classics, but find it perfect for the contemporary plays that might well become classics? Is every play doomed to be permanently frozen into the first suitable production style found for it?

Theater is an ephemeral art, if literature is not—and like all ephemera, it is part and parcel of its day.

While Nemirovich-Danchenko's interpretation of *Julius Caesar,* had it been written as critical essay, would be highly debatable, on the stage it passed the supreme test. It worked. In one year, it was shown eighty-four times, as often as five times a week during its first month, and always to full houses. That is more than double the number of times any Shakespeare production was shown on the Russian stage over a twenty year period, from 1890/91 through 1910/11. Normally, a Shakespeare production might run ten times a year, certainly no more. Nor can this success and this public demand be attributed to curiosity concerning the technical achievements of this production. *Tsar Fyodor* is the nearest parallel, technically speaking, to *Julius Caesar,* and it ran nowhere nearly so often during its first season. In fact, no production of a Chekhov or Gorky play was quite so popular as this one.

There remains only the assumption that with this play, as Nemirovich-Danchenko interpreted and produced it, the Art Theater said something of interest to its audience, and said it well. It is pedantic to quibble over whether or not it was "Shakespeare," maybe even irrelevant. In this vein, L. Gurevich, after praising the Art Theater's "victory" and evaluating its strengths and weaknesses, writes:

> And if there are those who admit that the directors demonstrated masses of knowledge, ability, artistic ingenuity, and Kachalov was an amazing Caesar and Stanislavski a noble Brutus, but still say, "It's not Shakespeare," then I'd like to know where they saw the real Shakespeare, where you can see the genuine Shakespearean *Julius Caesar.*[109]

What would Shakespeare himself have done with the play had he produced it at the Art Theater in 1903, instead of at the Globe in 1599?[110]

Nemirovich-Danchenko admitted the duality which governed his approach: he was interested in both the *Julius Caesar* written by Shakespeare, and in the epoch of Julius Caesar recorded by history.[111] He hoped that the former would not be swallowed up by the latter. Unfortunately, his views of Shakespeare's play and of Rome were either not sufficiently well formed or not communicated clearly enough to unify those two interests. One has an undeniable sense of double vision in dealing with this production. While the play was not entirely overwhelmed by the mise-en-scène, it was in constant danger of so being. Only Kachalov's Caesar managed to achieve some unification of the two foci. Another critic wrote: "But what about Shakespeare, the spirit of Shakespeare?... True, this spirit did not reign supreme in the House of Stanislavski. His genius was made to struggle with the spirit and genius of Rome...."[112] It would have been better had the struggle been resolved during rehearsals, because it was in this clash that lay the greatest fault of the production: a dual focus, a blurring of ideas.

In spite of its success, *Julius Caesar* was removed from the repertory after the 1903/04 season. There were several reasons for so doing. Foremost was the difficulty of maintaining the high standard of technical and organizational work necessary in this extremely complex production. There were roughly two hundred extras—theater and university students, various technical workers from the Art Theater—involved in the crowd scenes. Since, if public response allowed, the play had to run often in order to defray initial production expenses, these two hundred people were working constantly. Discipline was a problem: the extras each had fully detailed roles of their own, and they were expected to give as complete attention to their work as Kachalov was to playing Caesar. At first, it was exciting, but after the novelty wore off, this work became a chore for many.

> And things we did not notice before, in the first frenzy of creation, became wearisome and oppressive: the weight of armor, shields, weapons, animal skins, headdresses, togas whose folds required constant attention, the fatiguing costume changes, the unceasing fussing over every detail, and all this now on the stage—now under the stage,—now over the stage, it was painful and sometimes unbearable.[113]

The other major reason for this decision was Stanislavski's almost pathological aversion to the whole production, which stemmed largely from his trouble with Brutus. "He was very nervous and tense, and this affected those around him."[114]

In spring of 1904, the set and costumes were sold to the Solovtsov Theater in Kiev. Nemirovich-Danchenko also lent them his promptbook—to his dismay, the last act was missing when they returned it. It has never been found. The Art Theater took *Julius Caesar* to Saint Petersburg for fifteen performances, the last of which, on April 27, 1904, was the theater's final presentation of *Julius Caesar*. The Moscow and Petersburg press mourned the loss of *Caesar* as though for a national figure. "The public, of course, lamented the disappearance of the play from our programme," Nemirovich-Danchenko wrote. "On the other hand, we behind the scenes were indifferent and even pleased."[115]

Both Nemirovich-Danchenko and Stanislavski regarded *Julius Caesar* as an important technical achievement, however. It took the naturalistic approach of the Art Theater as far as it could go. But in so doing, it both knelled the death of this approach and served as an impetus to new work. *Julius Caesar*, precisely because it was so fine a technical accomplishment, demonstrated conclusively the dangers inherent in this style: the unnecessary complexity which it imposed on production work, and the miring of larger ideas in smaller details.

It could even be said that this production style made the unification of Nemirovich-Danchenko's two themes impossible. Meyerhold noticed this when he wrote about *Julius Caesar* in 1907 that this "synthesis . . . can never be effected by kaleidoscopic 'living' scenes." He further stated that the basic conflicts of the play were lost in a welter of historicity.[116] Although this latter statement goes too far, *Caesar's* historicity certainly had a muddling effect.

When one remembers that the approach to this play was considered by the directors to be the same as that used for Chekhov, one can appreciate the significance of *Julius Caesar* to the Art Theater. They had hoped to use the selective naturalism of the Chekhov productions to achieve the same portrayal of the human soul, to elucidate the same inner truths. Unquestionably, they were right in assuming that Shakespeare had as much to say about the human soul as Chekhov, but wrong in assuming that the same method of revealing it would work for both playwrights. Not that naturalism is necessarily the best style for staging Chekhov either, but in 1898-1904 its accumulation of ordinary details presented no curious spectacle to the audience, and did create an environment which permitted the actors to convey Chekhov's nuances. When used for a play set in a remote period however, naturalism tended to distract. The greater the play, the more annoying the distraction—the critics did not complain much at being distracted from A. Tolstoy's *Tsar Fyodor*. But they objected when the brilliance of the stage environment of *Julius Caesar* kept the audience gawking at life in Julian Rome instead of following Shakespeare's play.

Naturalistic detail had often been used by Stanislavski and his actors to elicit inner truth, since it surrounded them with external likeness to truth. And Stanislavski found, in Brutus, that he could take refuge in verisimilitude when verity eluded him. But *Julius Caesar* served as ample proof that external truth did not necessarily stimulate actors to inner truth, and—by providing a refuge—could even be dangerous. The lesson of the 1896 *Othello* finally hit home. As Stanislavski later recalled, "we . . . slipped from the line of intuition to the line of history and mores."[117] The fault lay not in the style itself, but in its distraction of the actor from his real work. Had the intuition been found, the historicism would have graced it—as indeed it did in the case of Kachalov's Caesar.

The real importance of the 1903 *Julius Caesar* lies not in the success it enjoyed nor in the controversy it aroused, but in the conclusion it forced Stanislavski to draw: that selective naturalism, while it can create an effective stage environment, does not necessarily inspire the inner truth of feeling and experience found in the Art Theater's work with Chekhov. The means of expressing this truth in producing other plays—again with a Shakespeare play as the ultimate test—had to be found elsewhere. So Stanislavski renewed his search.

3

Symbolism: The 1912 *Hamlet*

But I see a loophole by which in time the actors can escape from the bondage they are in. They must create for themselves a new form of acting, consisting of the main part of symbolical gesture.

Craig

Search and Experimentation

Looking back on 1904, Stanislavski described the Art Theater as having come to a dead end.[1] Its method of staging Chekhov and Gorky had defined, and thus constrained, its approach to other plays; its discoveries were becoming a cliché. Stanislavski even found his own acting dry and hollow. Success had given the Art Theater a case of artistic paralysis.

"That exploratory stage in which the new becomes an end in itself began again—novelty for novelty's sake."[2] At this point in his artistic development, Stanislavski's path crossed that of his former student, Vsevolod Meyerhold. For several years, Meyerhold had sought new means of theatrical expression. He was bursting with ideas, but needed money and capable actors. "Thus I found the very man I so desperately needed at that time. I decided to help Meyerhold in his new efforts, which then seemed to coincide so nearly with my own."[3] Together they established a studio, and experimented with some of these ideas. The credo of the new studio was that realism had outlived its day, and that the business of theater was the depiction not of life itself, but of life as it should be and as it exists only in dreams. Poetry, painting, music were all rallying to this new standard. Art was to devise intricate suggestion, to hint at visions which it would then compel its audiences to complete for themselves. This could not but attract Stanislavski, whose ruling idea as a director had always been to involve the emotions of the audience in the life presented on the stage. (The thunderstorm in *Julius Caesar* is a blatant example; subtler are his countless references to acting devices which ensure an audience's full attention.)

As he watched the dress rehearsal of the studio's first efforts, Stanislavski was disappointed. The young actors, playing in various one-act plays, as well as Maeterlinck's *Death of Tintagiles* and Hauptmann's *Schluck and Jau,* succeeded in presenting the new methods only in a few scenes. Wherever these nonrealistic plays contained some profundity of thought or delicacy of characterization, no amount of directorial devising could mask the actor's incompetence.

> ...Given the lack of acting technique of his cast, the director could only demonstrate his ideas, his principles and experiments—but he could in no way make them live. And therefore the interesting inventions of the studio turned into dry theory and formula. Once more, I became convinced that there was a huge gap between a director's dreams and their realization, and that the theater belongs especially to the actor and cannot exist without him. New theaters need new actors, with a completely new technique.[4]

Stanislavski decided to close the studio because of financial problems, and because "a good idea badly shown will die."[5] He returned his attention to the ever successful activity of the Art Theater, while doubts about his work continued to assail him.

Until this time, Stanislavski had been dictatorial as a director. His promptbooks, written before the rehearsals of a play and revised during them, give evidence of an iron hand. He prepared thoroughly not only the interpretation of each role, but even its gestural details—leaving very little scope for the actor. He taught his actors as well as directed them, which inhibited as well as benefited the actor. In working with the studio, however, Stanislavski came to realize that "neither the set, nor the director, nor the designer can carry the play—it is in the hands of the actor".[6] The actor must be an independent cocreator of the production and the main creator of his role. The director had to limit himself to supporting and leading the actor. By the early 1920s, Stanislavki would take an even stronger stand, writing that twenty-five years of work and experimentation had proved to him "that the principal creator on the stage is the actor. All the strength and searching of our theater are centered on him...."[7]

After the Art Theater's first foreign tour, in 1906, Stanislavki went off to Finland to rest, and to reassess his work as an actor and his theories on theater in general.

> As the result of my artistic activity, I had collected a bagful of every sort of material on the techniques of theater. But it was all thrown together indiscriminately, making it impossible for me to use the artistic wealth I had accumulated. I had to put it all in order, analyzing and classifying it. I had, as it were, to lay my material out on the shelves of my mind. What was rough had to be smoothed out and laid, like foundation stones, at the base of my art. What had become tattered had to be repaired. Without this, any further progress was impossible.[8]

Stanislavski's own acting deficiencies disturbed him as much as his directorial quandary. He forced himself to recall and analyze the parts he had played, squeezing out all he had learned from each one. In so doing, he explored the interaction between the inner life of a character and its outward expression, and came to recognize the importance of an actor's work of the details and emotions remembered from analogous personal experience. His ideas were written down as notes for "An Experimental Guide to Dramatic Art."[9]

The discoveries he made during these months were not entirely new. New or old, however, they would comprise the foundation for his "system" of acting. He noted that the actor's state of mind on the stage before an audience is unnatural, "theatrical" in fact, and seriously impedes good acting. Rather than resort to stage gimmickry to portray emotions which he does not feel, the actor must develop a different condition of mind and body for the stage. Stanislavski called it the "creative state of mind." This state is marked by complete freedom of the body and relaxation of the muscles. It requires the actor's complete attention to the life on the stage. This concentration on the stage, he noted, draws the attention of the audience and arouses its curiosity as to what the actors "find so interesting there."[10] All the physical and spiritual being of the actor must be centered on what is happening in the soul of the character he is playing. In order to prepare himself for this complete a concentration, he must arrive at the theater early enough to prepare the inner design of his role, to prepare his soul as well as he does his body.

Crucial to the success of a role is the actor's belief in it. He must develop an artistic sensitivity to truth so as to arrive at an inner creative truth. Stanislavski found the root of this sensitivity, as today's acting students know well, in a rule of childhood play. Translated into theater terms, it is: "If everything around me on the stage were true, then this is what I would do, and this is how I would react to this or that."[11] "If" is the keystone of Stanislavski's approach; he called it "the magic if" and discovered that it enabled the actor to make the pretense of theater become tangible reality. This alchemy is achieved by a childlike ability to believe in the unbelievable—a faith born of imagination and possessed of immense creative power.

The resultant sense of truth could, he found, be acquired and developed by exercises—as could concentration and muscular relaxation. Moreover, it had to be so completely developed that "absolutely nothing be said, done, or percieved on the stage without first having been filtered through the artistic sense of truth."[12] The sense of truth had to become a habit.

It is notable that these new definitions of the work essential to acting all concern the actor's inner self. Until this summer of meditation, Stanislavski had relied on external truth to awaken the inner one. That was fine, more or less, if the outward characteristics of the part came easily—but if they did not, the actor got bogged down and was lost. This early tendency toward the external resulted in the extraordinarily naturalistic productions of *Tsar Fyodor* and *Julius Caesar,* not to mention Gorky, who didn't object to it, and Chekhov, who did. Stanislavski's artistic crisis of 1904-1906 was caused by his recognition of the essential poverty of an external approach. The summer of 1906 marked the beginning of a new understanding of theater, and new answers to the old questions. But it would be at least a decade before the ideas had been refined and extensively explored.

Upon his return to Moscow, Stanislavski tested his new concepts in new productions and roles. There were many setbacks, some mockery, and a fair bit of resistance from his veteran actors. Although his emphasis was plainly on acting, there were other elements to be considered in producing a play. Freed from the strictures of naturalism, anything seemed possible. There was plenty of new dramatic literature to work with, and Stanislavski found ample material in Maeterlinck, Hamsun, and Andreev. Exhilarated, he set about redefining stage space, experimenting with sets, lighting, and the new abstractions accepted in the visual arts. Actors who could pretend did not need re-creations of reality, and could create their own. "Creative" actors could perform in any setting, thus allowing a Meyerhold to design and direct with no limits put on his imagination, and without sacrificing vitality or credibility of performance. But it was hard for Stanislavski to convince his colleagues.

The Invitation to Gordon Craig

In 1907, Stanislavski went by chance to a performance by Isadora Duncan during her second tour of Russia. He was impressed by her talent and her revolutionary approach to dance, and attended every performance she gave. She was feted by the Art Theater and saw a great deal of Stanislavski. The two discussed their respective arts, and found that they held many ideas in common. Stanislavski would later quote her as saying:

> Before going on stage, I have to put a motor in my soul; it begins to work within, and then my legs, my arms, my body begin to move by themselves, independent of my will. But if I am not given time to put the motor in my soul, I cannot dance.[13]

He added that "at that time I, too, was looking for this creative motor, which the actor must be able to place in his soul before going on stage."[14] Recalling their conversations, he realized how much they were both moving in the same direction, each in his own field. It seems to have been a tonic to him; he wrote to her in January, 1908:

> Do you know what you have done for me—I still haven't told you this.
> In spite of the great success and many supporters our theater has, I have always felt alone (only my wife has consistently supported me in my moments of doubt and disillusion). You are the first to tell me, in a few simple and convincing sentences, basic and significant things about the art which I want to create. This has given me new energy at a moment when I was preparing to give up my career in the theater.[15]

It was during these talks that Duncan spoke of Gordon Craig, "whom she considered a genius and one of the greatest men in contemporary theater. 'He belongs not only to his own country, but to the whole world!' she said, 'and he must be wherever his talent can best express itself, where the working conditions and general atmosphere suit him best. His place is in your Art Theater.'"[16] Stanislavski, still wrestling with his barely nascent "system," was excited by the idea that there were, in various corners of the world, different people in varied fields all reaching toward the same creative principles. The idea of working with one of them was very attractive.

Edward Gordon Craig was the son of the great English actress, Ellen Terry. He had served his theatrical apprenticeship under Henry Irving at the Lyceum, but gave up acting in order to direct, design, and study the great writers and theorists on the art of the theater. He developed a mystical attitude toward Art and ideal Beauty, not atypical of the turn of the century. He saw Art as the outcome of conscious effort which was firmly disciplined but free to seek what truth it would. Art, in his view, is expression for the inexpressible. Artistic activity is completely absorbing and requires a state of ecstasy which commands the entire being of the artist. Craig was absolutely uncompromising as to the degree of committment demanded of any real artist.

Constantly experimenting, Craig worked to free the stage of its decorative clutter, and to unite all the components of theatrical production into a perfect harmony. He directed his attention to theater as it should be—the "theater of the future," of which he saw himself as the prophet.

In 1905, at thirty-three, he published his first theoretical work, *The Art of the Theater,* which appeared in Russian the following year.[17] He began by defining:

> ... the Art of the Theater is neither acting nor the play, it is not scene or dance, but it consists of all the elements of which these things are composed: action, which is the very spirit of acting; words, which are the body of the play; line and color, which are the very heart of the scene; rhythm, which is the very essence of the dance.[18]

Unity of all these elements, but not their fusion, is essential to a vital performance. A piece for the theater is meant to be seen rather than heard. (Stanislavski saw it as meant to be experienced rather than watched.) Theatrical renaissance depended on the upgrading of the stage director. The ideal director must be a master craftsman, with all aspects of theater technique at his fingertips. He is inspired by the play, and demands obedience from all the workers of the theater as he creates the production. He designs scenery, costumes, lighting, and instructs the players on their every gesture—all this in the interests of unity. Unity can only be achieved when one man is responsible for every aspect of the production. This artist of the theater creates with "ACTION, SCENE, and VOICE"[19] as the material for his masterpieces:

"Then... the Art of the Theater would have won back its rights, and its work would stand self-reliant as a creative art, and no longer as an interpretative craft."[20]

The kind of disciplined teamwork, under a masterful director, which Craig describes, already existed to a certain extent at the Art Theater and elsewhere. In fact, Stanislavski was beginning to move away from this Craigian vision. What of the actor, for example? He, too, is to obey the director. In 1908, in the second issue of his new journal, *The Mask,* Craig discusses this further in one of his best-known essays, "The Actor and the *Über-Marionette.*" Here his statements sound, at first completely outrageous—particularly from a man who began his theatrical career as an actor: "The actor must go, and in his place comes the inanimate figure—the *Über-marionette....*"[21] If the purpose of the journal, as stated in its preliminary prospectus, was to restore theater by creating it anew, the purpose of this article was to replace the actor with a new kind of performer—it being too late to reform either the theater or the actor. The actor, according to Craig, is no artist, but a slave to transient emotion and to someone else's written word. He is at best a medium. The actor must move away from realism, from impersonation, and control his part from the outside. He must use his intelligence and imagination to retain complete mastery of his emotions and instinct. Thence, the *Über-marionette*—the actor who has incorporated some of the virtues of the marionette, and freed himself from egotism and passion. The new actor controls himself and his art, is conscious of his gestures and movements. To summarize, this concept of the actor and his role implies a new acting technique. The actor must no longer express himself, but something else; he must no longer imitate, but indicate. This impersonal technique is directed toward a symbolical acting style, "based on the power of creative imagination" and on the ability to use voice and body as instruments rather than as personal attributes.[22]

As the unnatural and controlled movements of the marionette are preferable to the too natural and uncontrolled movements of the actor's body, so the rigidity and depersonalization of the mask are superior to the grimaces and verisimilitude of the actor's face.[23] By requiring the actor to strip himself of all egotism, and achieve the discipline of nonrealistic theater modes, Craig demanded of him the same discipline which he demanded of the theater as a whole. The actor is to use himself as an instrument, and to be used as such by the director. Without this, no production could have the unity necessary to a work of art, as Craig saw it.

One cannot imagine a vision more at odds with Stanislavski's new perceptions. Craig's line of thought is much closer to Meyerhold's. But Stanislavski seems to have been unaware of the specifics of Craig's drive for a renewed theater, at the same time that he was attracted by the drive itself. While Duncan praised Craig to Stanislavski: "you should find him interesting. He has been generally repudiated and misunderstood, because he is too great and original an artist,"[24] she wrote to Craig about Stanislavski and the Art Theater, persuading him to come to Russia. In April of 1908, Stanislavski convinced the Art Theater's administration to invite Craig, and to set aside a large sum of money to finance the project. Craig answered on May second with the announcement that it would give him great pleasure to produce *Hamlet* for the Art Theater.[25]

Preparations for *Hamlet*

Craig had been making designs for *Hamlet* since 1901. He claimed in 1908, however, that "to represent *Hamlet* rightly is an impossibility."[26] Stanislavski, after his attempts at staging Shakespeare, doubted that the "Chekhovian principles" on which his theater based its art were suitable for Shakespeare. In 1908, he stated in his "Report on Ten Years of Work by the Moscow Art Theater" that the "Chekhovian style" did not prepare the actors "to experience, genuinely and simply, the strong emotions and noble ideas" of Shakespeare.[27] Nevertheless, in 1908, these two men were contemplating a *Hamlet*.

Craig later explained why he chose *Hamlet:*

> ... it is of all modern plays the most inspired, the most literary, the most picturesque. As a mixture of literature, drama and picture represents our modern idea of the Art of the Theatre it is therefore the most representative example of *modern* theatrical art.[28]

Stanislavski agreed to stage *Hamlet* not only to accede to the wish of an honored guest of his theater, but also because it was tempting to test his new system of acting in one of theater's most demanding plays.

Craig arrived in Moscow on October 26, wearing a light coat, a long scarf and a wide-brimmed hat. Winter, however, had preceded him, and he was bustled off to the theater and bundled into a fur coat and hat from among the costumes, and big felt boots. He was charmed. That night he saw Maeterlinck's *The Blue Bird,* one of the Art Theater's newest productions. He thought it lovely, if too cluttered, and particularly liked Ilya Sats's music. But the next night he was disappointed by the nonrealistic production of Andreev's *Life of Man,* a symbolist drama staged entirely in black velvet; he left before the first intermission and wrote in his Daybook that when the Art Theater tries to avoid realism it fails entirely and manages only to be clever.[29]

From the very first, he seems to have been comfortable in the Art Theater, and was warmly received by everyone in it. He spent long hours discussing the art of the stage with Stanislavski. Certain ideas they held in common: they both regarded theater as sacred, deplored false theatricality whether in actors or in scenery, and demanded dedication and perfection from themselves and their colleagues. Stanislavski was not dismayed by Craig's avowed preference for puppets over actors, claiming that Craig appreciated fine actors—and only "when he saw lack of talent, he would become furious and dream of his puppets again."[30] Craig was an idealist, a visionary, flamboyant and impassioned. Stanislavski, with more perspicacity than most of his contemporaries, was able to distinguish between Craig's extravagances of manner and the essence of his ideas.

The Directorate of the Art Theater discussed various plays that Craig might be invited to direct, but finally settled on *Hamlet* since he had already requested it. Indeed, *Hamlet* had been vaguely decided on earlier, and Egorov had been asked to design the sets. Egorov had already researched his ideas in Denmark and Germany, and begun his sketches and floor plans, but Craig rejected his work as having too realistic an approach. Egorov's designs were as firmly archeological as Simov's had been for *Tsar Fyodor* and *Julius Caesar*. Craig, therefore, took on set and costume design as well. The theater hired him on his terms, gave him everything he asked for, and the pick of actors and technicians. Stanislavski and L.A. Sulerzhitski were to be his assistants. On November 25, he returned to Florence to work on his production plan.

In general, Craig had already decided on his visual approach to the play. He had discussed it, in theory, with Stanislavski and secured his approval. There would be no traditional scenery, but a fluid architectural set. Earlier, in 1907 and early 1908, he had conceived the idea of movable cubes and screens, the screens reaching all the way up into the flies. The painter Piot saw Craig's design in 1910, and was intrigued that Craig had devised a way to make stage space infinitely variable. As Piot described it, the simplified scenery acquired expressiveness mainly from the lighting and achieved a kind of musical ebb and flow which would heighten and refine the movement of a play.[31] Craig's scenery was abstract rather than symbolic. It consisted of lines, planes, light and shadow, and could move from one design to another without any need to lower a curtain and interrupt the action. "The scene stands by itself—and is monotone. All the colour used is produced by light, and I use a very great deal of colour..., such colour as no palette can ever produce."[32] In 1911, he designed a portable version of his concept and showed it in London, where it seems to have been well received. At that time, of course, his designs were about to be used for two plays at the Abbey Theater in Dublin and for *Hamlet* at the Moscow Art Theater. After seeing the screens used for his *The Hour Glass*, Yeats was so pleased with the possibilities offered by this new concept in singing, that he wrote to Craig: "Your work was always a great inspiration to me. Indeed, I cannot imagine myself writing any play for the stage now, which I did not write for your screens."[33]

Stanislavski was not looking so much for an ideal scenic solution as he was for a valid experiment in nonrealistic dramatic presentation. He and his actors were happy and successful with modern Russian drama, but found the most recent symbolic plays difficult. Stylized scenery was used in Hamsun's *Drama of Life* and Andreev's *The Life of Man,* among others, and the public responded well, but Stanislavski saw this work as facile. Craig's new scenery, on the other hand, was a real innovation that could put his actors and his method to a valid test. The new scene provided complete freedom from familiar detail: the actor would have to rely on his own powers and could not use the set as a crutch. Stanislavski was in no way abandoning his realist principles, but looking for ways to make realism subtler, more psychological in orientation, and more generally applicable. "That is why we have invited Gordon Craig," he wrote to the critic Gurevich. "We are questing once more, and we shall enrich our realism again. I have no doubt that every abstraction on the stage, stylized or impressionistic, can be achieved by a more refined and more profound realism."[34] By realism Stanislavski obviously did not mean a style of visual presentation, but a spiritual realism to be communicated by the actor to the audience.

Stanislavski began rehearsing *Hamlet* in early March, without Craig. While one or two of Craig's ideas were prefigured in this early work, most of Stanislavski's interpretation had its roots in his earlier work and reflected Egorov's archeological naturalism: Elsinore as a stone military bastion of a brutal early middle ages, Fortinbras as a Viking in iron armor and fur pelts. At least some of the actors still thought that Craig was invited to work only on the visual aspects of the production, as a consultant, and so accepted Stanislavski's early direction as definitive. They would be astounded and bewildered when Stanislavski announced, on May 21, 1909, that Craig was to direct *Hamlet*.

Craig returned to Russia in April, 1909, and stayed until mid-June. During this stage of the preparation of *Hamlet,* the directors were to determine the interpretation of the play. Craig had brought a whole library with him, for reference. In discussing the play, he found many errors in Kroneberg's translation, and they were corrected. Later, certain of the Russian critics would note with disapproval the changes in the familiar text.

Transcripts of some of the Craig-Stanislavski discussions of *Hamlet* are in the archives of the Moscow Art Theater; English notes on some of these discussions are in the Gordon Craig Collection in the Bibliothèque de l'Arsenal. From these one can learn Craig's initial interpretation of the play and Stanislavski's reactions to it. These conversations do not represent more than the first phase of the work on the play, and they do not give us the final interpretation used in the production itself. But they do present some of the basic ideas underlying that interpretation, and reveal some of the early differences of opinion between the two directors and the spirit thereof. The conversations recorded were held with the assistance of two interpreters, Ursula Cox and Mikhail Lykiardopoulo. Cox and Sulerzhitski recorded some of the conversations, sometimes word for word and sometimes as running commentary. Other conversations were written down in notes by Stanislavski, and Craig embellished some others with illustrations and blocking notes.

Hamlet was given a preeminently mystical interpretation by Craig. He would stage the struggle between good (Hamlet) and evil (the court, or the entire world—whichever the spectator might prefer). Hamlet is the best of men, different from other men because he has seen that future world in which his father suffers. In order to lighten his father's agony, he must act: not merely must he kill the usurper, he must also cleanse the court of evil and repudiate the corrupt Rosencrantz and Guildenstern and their ilk. His struggle is to understand Truth, and to purify the world in its name. But Truth is glimpsed only partially, half-truths at a time, in each new idea and revelation. Inevitably, Hamlet is forced to proceed slowly, and seems therefore to hesitate.[35]

The general tone was "to be in no way realistic," said Craig. "In the staging of this we must speak not so much of what *to do* as of what *not to do*. I think it is possible for the actors, without getting into stiff and unnatural poses, and without speaking with unnatural pauses and emphases, quietly to convey the thought and feeling."[36] Stanislavski described his understanding of Craig's intentions in his notes for act I, i. Craig, he said, saw three tones for the actors in *Hamlet:* 1. abstract, for Hamlet's inner life; 2. semi-realistic, wherever the tragedy has its roots and impetus, as in the first scenes of the play; 3. realistic, wherever comedy edges in—and here Craig would allow a Chekhovian realism, as for the gravediggers' scene or Hamlet's scene with Polonius.[37] Craig felt obliged to utter warnings against too much Chekhovian realism, obviously worried that it might spread to too much of the production. In his notes for I, ii, he warns Stanislavski that if this scene is done as the theater does Chekhov, there may be too many irrelevant details.[38] He saw his entire approach as laconic: the scenery would be elemental, the actors were to move as simply and rarely as possible, and only the most important lines were to be given any emphasis at all. In Hamlet's monologue in I, ii, for example, Craig considered only the first two lines and the last two lines important, and wanted the rest of the monologue to be projected more as music so that the audience loses the thought in following the sound of the words. While the individual style of the actor would determine precisely how this was to be done, Craig said, the main point was to keep the important from being swamped by the unimportant.[39] But he would not cut the play. He felt strongly that a fine play should not be cut. He did, however, once propose to Stanislavski that they might stage the play entirely without words, using only music, light and movement. It must be noted that Craig's was a quicksilver mind, and that lapses into self-contradiction were typical of an impetuous and continual creativity. Stanislavski seems to have taken the mental fireworks in stride.

Craig's interpretation of the play smacked more of the current Russian avant-garde than of Chekhov. His mystical trend of thought was not far from Merezhkovski's brand of symbolism, and his creative daring akin to that of Meyerhold. While Stanislavski admired Craig's audacity, he was also somewhat disconcerted by it. Craig emphasized that, in *Hamlet* (and elsewhere), Shakespeare colors his characters in broad strokes. He cautioned Stanislavski against too much detail:

> All the tragedy of Hamlet is his isolation. And the background of this isolation is the court, a world of pretence....
>
> And in this golden court, this world of show, there must not be various different individualities as there would be in a realistic play. No, here everything melts into a single mass. Separate faces, as in the old masters of painting, must be coloured with one brush, with one paint.[40]

To express his ideas, Craig was willing to use a wide range of devices from Commedia dell'Arte to Stanislavski's "delicate"[41] naturalism. Stanislavski, on the other hand, was cautious, and, for all his talk of new directions, not really eager to wander too far afield.

In dealing with the isolation of Hamlet, Craig distilled the play into abstract thought and tried to describe how those abstractions might be physically represented. He wanted the actors to understand that Hamlet is spirit and all that surrounds and even engulfs him is matter, that there is no point of agreement between Hamlet and his surroundings—nor any hope of a reconciliation.

> ...the chief, ruling idea must be the collision of two antagonistic objects—spirit against material. And our problem on the stage is to find the tone, first of the material then of the spirit....[41]

To incarnate these concepts, Craig began by placing Hamlet even more center stage, by treating the play as a monodrama. Stanislavski spelled the notion out: the audience must understand that it sees everything through Hamlet's eyes, so that nothing is shown as it might really be but only as Hamlet sees it. He had no difficulty envisioning this approach in the scenes when Hamlet is on stage. But Craig wanted Hamlet somewhere on the stage in every scene; whenever Hamlet was not directly involved in a scene, Craig wanted him in the distance, to the side of the other actors or behind them, and so on. The audiences must never lose sight of him, must be constantly reminded of the connection between Hamlet and the action, must be moved by the horror of Hamlet's situation. Stanislavski demurred, and there was yet another quiet conflict about realism on the stage.[43] Hamlet was not continually onstage in the final version, but many of the scenes with Hamlet did present themselves to the audience from Hamlet's point of view. In III, ii, for example, the stage audience faced the real audience, so that the players performed with their backs to the house. As Hamlet's main interest is in the reactions of the stage audience, or at least certain members of it, so the real audience was compelled to share his interest.

Hamlet was perceived as a force, and his strength was central to Craig's interpretation of the play. Craig called him one of the strongest characters ever created by Shakespeare.[44] Hamlet's problem, and the cause of his long inaction, was to decide how to avenge himself justly and for the good of Denmark. His tragedy was that he was impersonal and reasonable. This understanding of Hamlet so impressed Stanislavski that at the end of his life he still saw Hamlet as strong and active: he must seize his sword "and cleanse the palace from top to bottom. Like a Messiah, Hamlet must purify the world."[45] The comparison with the Messiah parallels Craig's description of Hamlet as the first Christian in a barbarian world, a description reminiscent of Dalmatov's unconventional 1891 Hamlet.

Craig saw all the other denizens of Elsinore as depraved, vicious, stupid— a crowd of spies, plotters and murderers—with the exception of Horatio, the ghost, and sometimes Gertrude. Ophelia was interpreted as stupid and bourgeois, thoroughly uninteresting except as Hamlet saw her—a projection of his mental vision of all that is good, beautiful and feminine. Craig labels Hamlet naïve because of this tendency to credit the rest of the world with virtues it should have.

Craig's interpretation was also laced with the bohemian mysticism then fashionable in artistic circles. In fact, he told the cast that the production would be abstract and "supernatural."[46] At one point in the early stages of preparing the production, he envisioned a figure of great beauty, representing Death, who would lure Hamlet to abandon the imperfect world of the living; he would have her appear for the first time during the monologue "to be or not to be." Stanislavski muttered, not for the first time, that Craig was digressing, and the idea was dropped for the moment.[47] But Craig sketched this idea for Stanislavski, and the drawing still hangs in Stanislavski's house, now a museum. Stanislavski even considered the notion, but decided that no one but Duncan could play the role and so the idea was finally rejected.

To judge from letters and memoirs, the two men held more or less continual discussions. Only a small number of them were actually recorded. One finds traces of these other conversations in material such as the letter Stanislavski wrote to the composer Ilya Sats at the end of April, 1909. Stanislavski complained that, between watching Duncan perform until early morning and holding long dialogues with Craig "about the convolutions of Hamlet's psyche" from noon until seven, "you can imagine what a headache I've had all week!"[48] Their conversations were apparently held in a mind-bending mix of English, pidgin German, and the occasional French phrase.

It was during one of these unrecorded conversations that Craig spoke to Stanislavski about the music he wanted for the production. He often referred to *Hamlet* as symphonic, and "in his ponderings hears trumpets, the ringing of bells—sometimes sonorous and festive, sometimes cracked and funereal. Echoes of funeral themes are mixed in with this. In the scene with his father, Hamlet also hears these trumpets and hymns, together with the howling of the wind, the sounds of the sea, and otherworldly dirges. . . ."[49] Later he would talk of music that had the quality of Bach, with bright and valiant tones.[50] After attending rehearsals and becoming thoroughly acquainted with the production, Sats would compose along these lines. Later, some of the production music was recorded and has survived.[51]

In May, the Art Theater began to experiment with Craig's screens on the stage, testing prototypes in iron, oak, tulle, plywood, reed and bamboo. None of these were practical, however, and some were entirely too heavy for the stagehands to maneuver safely. Finally the directors settled on canvas, which proved remarkably receptive to an imaginative lighting plan. Both Craig and Stanislavski hoped to change sets without using a curtain, in full view of the audience, by having ten stagehands, dressed in dark grey, move the screens and props. In June, lighting rehearsals began, using plain screens made of pale grey canvas stretched over wooden frames.

With Sulerzhitski, and occasionally with Kachalov who would play Hamlet, Stanislavski and Craig outlined the rest of the play in discussion and rehearsal. Some of the concepts generated at this point would be evident in the production: the set, but not the blocking, for Polonius' scene with Hamlet, and the vision of Ophelia as victim, bait set out for the hunt in III, i. But many did not survive: the set for "Hamlet's room" in act II, Ophelia's mad scene, the graveyard set, and the projection of Osric's grotesque decadence by having a smell of perfume in the house. The work was intense. Sulerzhitski collapsed with nephritis in early June. Stanislavski, after working with Craig so closely and so long, began to speak to his actors half in Russian and half in German.

By the end of Craig's second visit, rumors of a split with Stanislavski had spread throughout Russian theater circles. Despite the heat of some of their discussions, there was mutual affection and admiration between the two men—though they may not have fully understood one another. They were very different personalities. Craig was eccentric, emotional and impractical; Stanislavski was conservative, calm and sensible. Craig was content to generate ideas; Stanislavski could not rest until they were realized on the stage. But Craig's intellectual and artistic daring was stimulating to the comparatively stolid Stanislavski: "Craig has proved so talented and has so unpredictable an imagination that it seems to me he will soon metastasize something in me that will open up new horizons."[52] For his part, Craig wrote to a friend:

I have been here three weeks—Rehearsals have begun—in a most *orderly* fashion, and nice through and through owing to the really sweet nature of the manager—"Hamlet" the play— The entire company, taking their lead from the manager, do *everything* I say. It may be a dream, dear old chap, but my God, it's like Heaven after years of Hell.[53]

And in response to rumors he had heard, Stanislavski wrote to Gurevich:

As to Craig—it's all nonsense. . . . The theater, Nemirovich-Danchenko, and I are not only not disillusioned with him, but to the contrary—we are convinced he is a genius. Because of this, he is not accepted in his homeland. He creates amazing things, and the theater has been placed at his disposal, and as his closest assistant, I have put myself completely at his command, and count myself proud and happy in this role. If we manage to do justice to Craig's talent, we will perform a great service to art. It will be a long time before many people begin to understand Craig, for he is half a century ahead of us. He is a superb poet, a remarkable artist, and a director of the most refined taste and knowledge. I don't hide any of this from the public, even though they might take it as an advertisement for Craig.[54]

Craig sang the praises of Stanislavski and his theater throughout Europe. He would later write:

It is quite enough to say that what these Russians do they do to perfection. They waste time, money, labour, brains and patience like emperors. . . .
They give hundreds of rehearsals to a play, they change and rechange a scene until it balances to their thought: they rehearse and rehearse and rehearse, inventing detail upon detail with consummate care and patience and always with vivid intelligence—Russian intelligence.
Seriousness, character, these two qualities will guide the Moscow Art Theater to unending success. . . . [55]

He praised Stanislavski's acting for its intelligence and grace, obviously supportive of psychological realism that commanded his artistic respect.

Through 1909 and 1910, their multi-lingual correspondence was friendly, even jovial. An embarrassing exception was Craig's constant begging for more money to found a theater school. Stanislavski was not put off by this, though he did not take the school plans very seriously. Otherwise, they relayed family news, discussed the play, and poked mutual fun at their none-too-fluent German.[56]

The money issue, however, was to alter their relationship. Without losing respect for Craig's genius, Stanislavski began to lose faith in his reliability, and to sense that *Hamlet* was far less important to him than finding money to begin his school. Stanislavski, not without some justification, began to feel used.[57] Craig began to write to the administration of the Art Theater to badger it for money; he seems to have been completely muddled about the real terms of his contract. He apparently thought that anyone with money, including the Art Theater treasury, should support the projects of a penniless genius. The administration began to feel unjustly harassed.[58] By 1911, Stanislavski was trying to act as peacemaker, as anonymously as possible. Still professing great admiration for one another as artists, the two men would finally be relieved to see the completion of their joint venture.

"Craig worked with exhilaration in Florence" (where he had his home and workshops), writes Craig's biographer Denis Bablet, adding, however, that he had moved beyond *Hamlet* and felt that work on this production was a waste of time, a rehash of old ideas. He was obsessed by the idea of establishing a theater school. "But, perhaps, *Hamlet* would be a stepping stone towards the art of his dreams. He went on working."[59]

In February 1910, Craig went to Moscow with his plans, and the work on *Hamlet* was soon in full swing. Alisa Koonen, then a student actress at the Art Theater,[60] recalls that Stanislavski had prescribed Craig as "new blood" to shake the theater out of its success-induced lethargy. No sooner had Craig arrived to work in the theater, she writes, than it was jogged from its measured pace of life: people even walked faster.[61]

His plan for the set was based on his screens. There would definitely be no curtain, and the audience would have time before the house lights went down to get used to the general idea of an abstract, architectural set. Before the beginning of the play, the lines of the set would be in harmony with those of the house, so that the stage would seem to be an extension of the auditorium. When the lights went down, the screens would begin to move and then gradually settle into position for the first scene. And so on throughout the play: a fluid set would rearrange itself for each new scene. There would be twenty-four such rearrangements in the final production. The screens, some plain and others covered in gold paper, were to be on trolleys, and move as propelled by the concealed stagehands. A few props were envisioned, to help establish the place of action.

Lighting would assume the major task of creating atmosphere. Craig used it two ways:

> ... by the use of moving projectors to pick out a surface, round an angle, or create a kind of tragic shuddering at moments of climax; and in diffused splashes to colour certain bright or sombre portions of the scene.... Sometimes it fell from above, sometimes it seemed to spring up from the stage, at other times it swept right across it. Instead of a curtain at the end of each scene, there would be darkness.[62]

In April the theater worked to devise lighting which would mask the base of each screen with shadow and send sharp shafts of light between and behind the screens. Special apparatus had to be ordered, and K.A. Mardzhanov later went to Berlin to acquire some of it. The equipment was the best available.

In a small rehearsal room, a large model of the stage was erected. On Craig's instructions, it was electrically lit and fully equipped as though for a miniature production. From Florence, Craig brought models of the screens, steps, platforms and props, and he made models of the actors while in Moscow. He used all this to experiment and to demonstrate, moving the figures "on stage" with a long crook. Sometimes Alisa Koonen, who worked closely with Craig, would be asked to move about the real set to verify experiments done on the model. Too often, though, Craig would shut himself up in his laboratory to maipulate his figures and screens, and leave the cast to wonder what his next demands on them might be. In general, he kept himself aloof from most of the actors and even avoided showing them concretely what he wanted them to do. He dealt mostly with his fellow directors and assistants; Stanislavski, Sulerzhitski and Mardzhanov would be invited in and shown, with the models, how given scenes were to be directed.

In April, all the screens ready so far were set up on the stage, and Mardzhanov worked with Sulerzhitski and Egorov to make them stand without listing or losing their smooth taut grandeur. The technical rehearsals seemed endless, but finally the stagehands mastered the art of shifting the screens gracefully, without any undue revelations of backstage activity or backside of stagehand. This task was not made easier by Craig's occasional decisions to redo a scene arrangement, only to have it prove impractical and be scrapped.

The costumes were to be designed according to Craig's concepts. They were to give a general impression of the middle ages without being tied to any specific period. The court was to be in gold, with the cloth for their costumes specially woven at the textile factory owned by Stanislavski's family. Ophelia, some of the ladies-in-waiting and Fortinbras were in white. Hamlet and Horatio were meant to wear black, though Hamlet's costume was eventually changed to deep blue-grey. The ghost, the gravediggers and a few others were dressed in neutral grey. The color choices were intended to underscore Craig's interpretation of the play. But Craig was reluctant to design anything definitive until he had seen the actors move in rehearsal because he wanted each costume to reveal and complement the form under it.

Discussions of the play's interpretation continued daily, as did the reading rehearsals (eventually, these would total an unprecedented 159). Craig generated ideas and spoke to the actors of the need for monumental gesture; the stenographers took constant notes, and the actors tried to reconcile all this with Stanislavski's close analysis and his emphasis on the physical expression of psychological fact. As a whole the Art Theater struggled earnestly to bring Craig's ideas to life, but Craig did not recognize his concept in their results. After one read-through, he commented, "All very fine, except for one thing: no Shakespeare."[63]

Rehearsals on the stage were usually conducted by Stanislavski and Sulerzhitski. Although they made every effort to understand Craig's intentions, both they and the actors were hampered by the old Art Theater tradition of acting. Stanislavski had not communicated his new discoveries successfully enough to find any help there, and the actors resented his attempts to tamper with the psychological approach that had worked so well in Chekhov and Gorky.[64] Craig wanted stylized acting, neither contrived and theatrical nor intimate and psychological. He described it as a musical sonority, beauty in sound and movement, simplicity, restraint and a sense of splendor. Together, Sats's music and Craig's lighting would create a symphony, moving in waves without beginning or end; the actors were to become part of this pattern. This was all too vague for a theater used to a precise statement of how to proceed, and Stanislavski was still too excited by his own discoveries to translate it properly if he actually understood it.

Indeed, Stanislavski was sure that his own method, which he had discussed with Craig, would really meet Craig's needs. During rehearsals, Craig seemed to approve of the naturalistic acting of the Art Theater, calling it theatrical in the best sense of that word.[65] But he felt that Stanislavski reduced his actors to servitude, condemning them to fulfill only his wishes. While he saw some sense in this approach, Craig—the formulator of the "Über-marionette"—was clearly appalled. Later, in June, Stanislavski would write to Craig via a translator that he and Kachalov had gone over his whole part and marked it according to Craig's indications and "to my system that you do not yet like, but that answers better than anything to your purpose."[66] Sulerzhitski was under no such delusions; if Craig was to have the actors perform in a style so alien to them, he said, he would have to found his own Craigian Art Theater.[67]

Early in April, Stanislavski had written to Isadora Duncan to announce the beginning of work with the actors, and set out the timetable for *Hamlet:* once Craig was pleased with the progress of rehearsals, he would return to Florence and leave the Art Theater to continue without him; rehearsals until August, the return of Craig to affirm and revise work to date, and an opening in November.[68] Craig returned to Florence on April 28, confident that the theater could proceed with the material he had left behind.

In fact, the screens and props were ready and the lights nearly so. But Stanislavski's timetable met its first delay when he and Mardzhanov tried to cope with the problem of costumes. Stanislavski wrote a detailed letter to Craig chronicling the difficulties they were having in understanding what Craig wanted. Craig had left his drawings and cut-out figures, but not designs, and a library of books on period costuming. Stanislavski and Mardzhanov concentrated on reproducing the sculpturesque lines and folds they saw in Craig's sketches, but found it too expensive to experiment on the fabrics already selected by Sulerzhitski and which Craig had approved. So they used cheaper cloth, and were at a double disadvantage: the cheap substitutes didn't hang well enough to test their designs, and they were none too sure that they saw in Craig's sketches what Craig saw.

Other than this, the schedule went smoothly enough through June and July. Mardzhanov and Sulerzhitski were to return to Moscow from vacation on August 2 to work with the lights, test the screens and rehearse the stagehands. The company would gather on August 14 to hear Mardzhanov read the notes Craig and Stanislavski had written, and he and Sulerzhitski would demonstrate the set and the lighting. Craig and Stanislavski were due on September 3, Craig to work on costumes and Stanislavski to help him and to rehearse the cast.[69] But when Sulerzhitski arrived in Moscow according to this schedule, the theater's administration insisted that he first overhaul the lighting and sets for the other plays in the repertory, so that technical work on *Hamlet* was postponed until August 16.[70] The delay was disconcerting, but not disastrous.

Then, on August 17, the theater received a telegram from Lilina in the Caucasus: Stanislavski had fallen seriously ill with typhus. The doctors prescribed weeks of complete bedrest, and forbade any exertion for the next few months. On August 19, the theater administrators met and decided to delay further work on *Hamlet* until Stanislavski was well enough to participate.[71] Lykiardopoulo wired Craig, who wired his condolences to Lilina and grumbled privately in his Daybook.[72]

Stanislavski did not return to Moscow from the Caucasus until December 20, and by January had so overworked himself that "the doctors seized on that and now they're chasing me out of Moscow."[73] On January 25, he left for Berlin and Rome with his daughter Kira.

Once in Rome, he wrote at length to Sulerzhitski, in Paris with the Art Theater's production of *The Blue Bird* to prepare it for a March opening at the Théâtre Réjane. Craig was in Paris, and Stanislavski wanted to arrange a meeting with him or, failing that, arrange for the future of *Hamlet*. He wanted to clarify several issues: whether the Art Theater could make final plans for the placement of screens on the stage with only general reference to Craig's many models, and whether he could present Craig's interpretation "in a slightly different form, i.e. subtler and therefore less naïve."[74] While not disturbed by Craig's approach to Hamlet, he was afraid that the caricaturization of the other roles, and Craig's puppet-like devices, would alienate the Moscow audience—a fear he had had since 1909. And Stanislavski wanted to know when Craig would prefer to come to Moscow to work on the production.

Sulerzhitski contacted Craig and wrote back to Stanislavski that Craig trusted Stanislavski's judgment as to the staging and the treatment of individual roles, and that he would prefer to come to Moscow in May. Craig wrote directly to Stanislavski, but only to ask for money and complain about the Art Theater administration. Probably to avoid more of the same, Stanislavski persisted in contacting Craig through Sulerzhitski. Despite Sulerzhitski's best efforts at diplomacy, tension between the two directors built to the point that Craig balked at any further work on *Hamlet* and Stanislavski decided to proceed without him.[75]

Before leaving Moscow Stanislavski told O.V. Gzovskaia, who would play Ophelia, and Muratova to organize readings of his notes on the system for members of the cast of *Hamlet*. He reminded her in a letter from Rome on February 27, warning her that he would be in Moscow during the first week in Lent and *Hamlet* rehearsals would start right up; if the actors were not well acquainted with his notes, "we will be completely unable to understand one another."[76] Clearly, Stanislavski planned to test his system during these rehearsals. No doubt he believed that Craig would approve; during conversations with Craig in 1909 and 1910, the system had seemed to evoke Craig's interest. Craig recorded one such discussion in his Daybook and concluded, "it is interesting—it is a theory of acting, arrived at through practicing acting, and therefore demands respectful attention."[77] Even so, while Craig and Stanislavski constantly reiterated the commonality of their artistic goals during their 1909 discussions, they also recognized how different were their approaches. "The only question is," probed Craig according to a Russian transcription, "by whose system we will quest—mine or yours."[78] At one point during those same conversations, Stanislavski thought he had converted Craig to his system, but Craig's reaction to the 1910 rehearsals must have demolished those illusions. Nevertheless, in 1911 Stanislavski would have to work without Craig. It was no time to work without his own system as well.

In January of 1910, Stanislavski had announced to the Art Theater administration that he intended to continue his experiments and research into the art of acting. "Maybe I am overly enthusiastic, but that's my forte. Maybe I make mistakes, but that's the only way to make progress. I am now, more than ever, convinced that I am on the right track."[79] After the success of his production of Turgenev's *A Month in the Country,* Stanislavski wrote to Duncan that he had put his theories into practice "and I must admit, the results exceeded all my expectations."[80]

Six months of illness and recuperation had him straining at the leash. In March of 1911, he lectured the cast on the new approach to shaping their roles, based on his system. The young student director, E.B. Vakhtangov, took notes so energetically that Stanislavski immediately collared him to work as rehearsal stenographer; later he would ask him to guide the actors through experiments with the system. Throughout the spring, Stanislavski took the cast through the play scene by scene, dividing each scene into sections and assigning "inner desires" for each speech. The actors were to write the assignments next to their lines and memorize their part as so defined.

In Stanislavski's promptbook for *Hamlet* II, i and ii, housed in the Art Theater archives, "inner desires" are written next to various lines, and eight objectives are listed for scene ii. The approach used in this fragment is similar to that evolved in early work on the system as seen in the promptbooks for Gogol's *Inspector General* (1908) and *A Month in the Country* (1909).[81] All three promptbooks bear no resemblance to earlier detailed expositions like that for *Julius Caesar,* contain few or no general essays on interpretation, and concentrate on identifying psychological units and objectives for each actor and developing inner technique.

Similar terminology, derived from Stanislavski's notes on the system, was used during rehearsals. According to one rehearsal diary, Massalitinov (Claudius) was advised to "find the truth in outer sensation—then you can also speak to inner truth,"[82] and Kachalov was told to focus on the spirit of the objective rather than its superficial aspect.[83] Indeed, 1911 saw increased use of the system as Stanislavski persuaded members of the theater administration, Nemirovich-Danchenko and various members of the troupe, one by one, of its advantages. Not all of the actors, especially the charter members of the company, were converts, but "in 1911 the Art Theater laid the first stones of the foundation of Stanislavski's 'system.' The whole theater was in motion."[84] *Hamlet* was the first production to experiment with the system so openly and so wholeheartedly.

During rehearsals and the accompanying analyses of scenes and characters, Stanislavski's remarks indicated that he intended to be faithful to Craig's interpretation. But either he did not understand it or was deluding himself, because Craig's ideas were steadily altered as Stanislavski dissected the play. Hamlet, he said, could not be both a neurotic and the best of men; therefore Stanislavski returned to a pre-Craig vision of Hamlet as a Christ figure purifying a barbaric court of its depravity; Ophelia became more a tragic beauty than Craig's little fool. (Later, Nemirovich-Danchenko would return to the Viking analogy associated with Egorov's designs.) No mention was made of mystical confrontations with Death. Stanislavski openly parted company with Craig, predictably, on the interpretation of Claudius, Polonius and the Court, claiming that Craig's exaggerations were beyond the acting capabilities of the Art Theater.[85]

In April, Mardzhanov was put in charge of the theater workshops, told to resolve specific problems concerning scenery and costumes, and to have the screens, their placement, the lighting, the costumes and the stagehands ready by May 28. On June 2, Sulerzhitski demonstrated the scene changes and the lighting; Stanislavski judged the results "superb."[86] When the troupe returned from vacation in August, Stanislavski approved costumes. After the visual side of the production had been assembled, it was shown to the company. Their reaction must have been enthusiastic, because Stanislavski exclaimed, "For the first time, our dunderheads understood the genius of Craig."[87]

Rehearsals were scheduled daily. Kachalov moved in with Stanislavski to rehearse with him at home in their free time, until the family returned from vacation. The entire cast and crew were approaching exhaustion, particularly since they were performing every day as well. Partial run-throughs began in November; complete run-throughs and dress rehearsals were scheduled from December 26 to January 4. In order to facilitate this final work, the theater administration cancelled all performances from December 25 until the opening of *Hamlet* so that the cast and crew could work on the main stage day and night.

The theater's administrators also decided not to invite Craig to return to Moscow until the last rehearsals, because they felt that his presence would invite new complications. The view that Mardzhanov expresses in his memoirs, that Craig was unable to stop generating new ideas long enough to stage a given concept,[88] was widely held at the Art Theater; the administration claimed that Craig's participation would inevitably delay the opening of *Hamlet.*[89] Stanislavski insisted that "Craig at the present moment is the greatest talent in our art"[90] and that the theater would make a sad mistake were it to break off relations with him; he also requested that the theater subsidize Craig's trip.

Craig arrived in Moscow on December 26. The first run-through was in progress on the main stage. According to Gzovskaia[91] Craig went uninvited to the theater, annoyed that rehearsal had begun without him, and was not noticed until the Mousetrap scene when he shouted "stupid!" in English—at which point he was escorted politely but firmly from the theater. The run-through continued uninterrupted on the main stage, and resumed after a brief dinner break, this time on the rehearsal stage. Kachalov finally pleaded exhaustion at 2:30 in the morning and Stanislavski, who had lost track of the time, ended the rehearsal. Craig arrived at the theater the next day, but was discouraged from attending any more rehearsals until the first dress on January 1.

When Craig finally saw the results of the Art Theater's ten months of work, he was shocked. The costumes, blocking and lighting were not, he affirmed, his. He insisted that he had left forty or fifty costume sketches with fabric swatches attached—probably the sketches Stanislavski and Mardzhanov struggled with in 1910. Sulerzhitski had designed the positioning and shifting of the screens in 1910 and again in 1911. The blocking was clearly not Craig's because it had been evolved in 1911 in accordance with the demands of the system. After the first dress, Craig spoke with Kachalov about speeding up his pace in the Mousetrap scene ("Hamlet's crosses should be like bolts of lightning slashing across the stage") and about his restrained tone in that scene ("The actor's temperament should emerge in full force here: stormy bursts of rage, despair, irony and, finally, triumph").[92] Stanislavski had broken Hamlet's performance in this scene into eleven units, to create tragic power from the "simplest mechanical objectives."[93]

It was the lighting that most infuriated Craig. His patience, fragile as it was, crumbled completely during the Mousetrap scene. The lighting was diffused, whereas Craig had specified shafts of light and a sharply defined chiaroscuro to emphasize the height and massiveness of the palace. The two directors argued vehemently in French, and Craig ended by storming out of the stalls. The rehearsal was abruptly ended.[94]

Stanislavski then summoned Craig, Sulerzhitski, Moskvin and Kachalov to an evening meeting in the theater to discuss possible changes. Alisa Koonen caught wind of this and hoped to find out what was happening. Locked out, she waited in the bitter winter cold:

> The conference dragged on forever, and I . . . had just decided to go home, when Craig suddenly bounded out of the office. Coatless and with muffler flapping, he dashed up the street. Sulerzhitski ran after him, holding the coat and shouting, "Wait, Mr. Craig, wait!"

> Shortly thereafter, Stanislavski, Kachalov and Moskvin emerged from the theater. By their gait and their nervous chatter, I knew something unpleasant had happened. The next day, when I asked Vasili Ivanovich [Kachalov] what had happened, he answered darkly: "They destroyed Craig. At first he sat there gritting his teeth and restraining himself, but when they got to the 'Mousetrap,' he threw his inkwell at the stage and shouted that he wanted his name off the program."

She saw Craig somewhat later:

> He was depressed and foul-tempered. He said that nothing of his remained in the play, that there were only three scenes to which he could put his name: "the Throne room," "the Mousetrap," and the finale. With grim humor he added, "If Stanislavski wanted to turn Shakespeare into Gorki, why did he invite me and use my screens?"[95]

Sulerzhitski predicted that it would all blow over, and for a while it did, more or less.

But Sulerzhitski was to take the brunt of Craig's anger. Even though Stanislavski had altered the interpretation of many of the roles and rehearsed the actors exclusively by his new system, Craig's objections were directed mainly at Sulerzhitski whom he blamed for the changes in costumes and lighting. He insisted that Sulerzhitski's name be taken off the program, and that Stanislavski be named codirector. (Sulerzhitski was named, finally, as regisseur on the program for opening night, and later Stanislavski changed the programs to give Craig top billing as director with Stanislavski and Sulerzhitski as his assistants.)[96]

The lighting was changed to meet Craig's demands, although Sulerzhitski was incensed by the last-minute revisions. When he heard a rumor that Stanislavski had agreed to remove his name from the program, Sulerzhitski refused to return to the theater. Stanislavski pleaded with him to forget his anger and overlook Craig's behavior in the interests of art. He defended the lighting changes, both because he thought the revised lighting more effective and because *Hamlet*'s design was Craig's and he had a perfect right to insist on his vision of it. On the day of the premiere, Sulerzhitski relented and worked in the theater with Stanislavski, trying to perfect the lighting for the closet scene.

Meanwhile, Craig holed up in his hotel suite and refused to see anyone. He carved a medallion for Kachalov to wear in the performance, encased it in thin copper foil, and inscribed it to Vasili Kachalov from Gordon Craig, adding "readiness is all."[97]

The Moscow press was delighted. For two years it had been publishing rumors of a Craig-Stanislavski split, and now it had a real story to report and embellish. Sulerzhitski's departure was blown up into a first-rate scandal. Even after Stanislavski effected a reconciliation, the dissension continued to be featured in the press.

The theater's mood was dismal, but rehearsals had to continue. Koonen compared what she saw on stage with the ideas Craig had shown her in his workshop and was struck by the dissimilarity: "All the time I saw two different plans, sensed Stanislavski's endless debate with Craig."[98] Kachalov was convincing in the lyrical scenes, but too muted in the dramatic ones and knew it. "Tell me honestly," he asked Koonen, "am I a very boring Hamlet?"[99]

On the day of the premiere, an hour before the curtain, there was one last catastrophe. After a rehearsal of scene changes, during a tea break when the stage was deserted and the whole theater silent, Stanislavski saw that

> suddenly one screen began to list, and leaned further and further until it fell onto a second, and they toppled a third, and so on until the entire set collapsed like a house of cards. The wood frames cracked and I heard the sound of ripping canvas. The stage was covered with a formless mass that looked like the aftermath of an earthquake.[100]

The audience was already filtering into the house while the screens were hastily repaired behind the curtain. For safety, Stanislavski abandoned the idea of moving the screens in full view of the audience, and scene changes would be made more traditionally, behind closed curtains. Craig's fluid continuity was chopped up into twenty-four little bits, and his screens reduced to a well-designed background. Much of the intended theatrical magic was lost.

The Production

The 1912 *Hamlet* cannot be reconstructed by the same methods as used for *Julius Caesar*. There was no definitive promptbook, for example; Stanislavski's notes in the partial promptbook housed at the Moscow Art Theater Museum are extremely sketchy, and Gordon Craig's annotated copy of *Hamlet* kept at the Bibliothèque de l'Arsenal dates from 1909. The stenograms of conversations between the two directors date back to 1909 and 1910. Notes on rehearsal proceedings, however, cover the entire span of work on the production. There could even be said to be two productions, from these written records: the Craig version of 1909 and 1910 and the Stanislavski version of 1911. What emerged onto the stage in January of 1912 is probably best gauged from the many critical reviews and discussions; the merits of the production were so long debated in the press that an unusual amount of material exists there. Many of the memoir accounts, on the other hand, were written decades later, and one must allow for a certain blurring of facts and sequence. There is only one production photograph, but there are sketches of several scenes, a recording of Sats's music, studio portraits of some of the actors in costume, and Sulerzhitski's ground plans for the arrangements of screens and cubes. From all these sources, one can reconstruct the ephemeral event to some extent.[101]

Even before the curtain rose, the audience heard music which seemed to come from underground: choruses in various tonalities, merging with subterranean blows and the howling and whistling of winds, pierced by a wierd far-off cry. This effect was created by a women's choir singing a very chromatic wordless hymn; into this was blended sound effects, the faint accompaniment of a first and second viola, cello, bass viol and the infrequent "sorrowful"[102] sound of a gong. An unusual piece of music, it has the wave-like effect Craig wanted. The curtain rose on Craig's screens as arranged for the first scene. The grey tone of the plain screens gave the impression of an odd complex of corners and passages. There were areas in deep shadow and moonlit patches. While the screens suggested the walls of a castle, the shadow hid the entrances and exits and obscured the intervals between the screens. In *Russkoe Slovo (The Russian Word),* one critic described the impact made on the audience:

> One senses...that all this is happening in some evil place,...In a place like this, the appearance of a ghost does not seem quite so fantastic. The mystical mood of the characters becomes fully understandable....[103]

The ghost, quietly searching, entered from among the screens, appearing and disappearing in the shadows and half-lights. His face was set in a mask of unbearable pain. His costume was the neutral color of the screens, and he was wrapped in a long cloak and apparently not in armor. A spot illumined him for a moment, and then he vanished as though frightened off by the opening lines of Francisco and Bernardo.

In the court scene (I, ii), sound again preceded the opening of the curtains, this time sinister trumpet fanfares. The set was as aggressive as the music. It was done in gold, the color of power and wealth, a color which represented the despotic rule of a brutish and ambitious man. The king, queen and courtiers were dressed in gold and further layered in it by an unforgettable visual device of Craig's: the royal couple sat on a high golden throne upstage center, and from their shoulders seemed to spread a huge golden cloak which widened until it covered the entire stage. (Although the original concept required a single cloak with holes cut in it through which the heads of the smiling courtiers would be thrust, it was too impractical. In the production, the individual courtiers wore mantles which flowed out to give the impression of Craig's monolithic golden pyramid.) The courtiers were arranged in graduated levels on broad steps, and all faced Claudius and Gertrude upstage. Spots shot a beam of light over the gold, making it glitter ominously—the more so as the "cloak" undulated with every movement of the actors. In front of this glaring golden morass Hamlet reclined, alone in his somber deep blue-grey and cut off from the court by a physical barrier made of cubes. His back was toward the court, and he faced the audience. Hamlet was clearly a stranger to this world, Craig's civilized man of the future living among the barbarians of the present.

Claudius snapped out his opening lines like a robot. Hamlet glanced at him and the queen only occasionally, and responded to Gertrude with his back half-turned to her, as though speaking to himself.

The court scene was planned as a grotesque; the place, people and events were to be seen by the audience as though through the eyes of Hamlet. Apparently, the scene was presented according to Craig's directions. Many of the major characters were conceived in terms of the animal world, as beasts from a somehow prehuman era. The king was reptilian, the queen a she-wolf who fiercely protects her young but otherwise adapts to anything. Polonius was a fox, an aged and sometimes very feeble fox, but one who survives by dint of his craft. (Another of Craig's references to Polonius makes him a frog.) Laertes was not only a younger version of his father, somewhat lacking in the latter's sly intelligence, but was also an ordinary lad of the times and was presented in contrast to Hamlet. Because of the comparison between the two, Hamlet's character was revealed more clearly. Ophelia was not placed in a Craigian bestiary, but was classified merely as a moral and intellectual infant, albeit beautiful. As a whole, many in the audience found this scene confusing. Others, however, understood it to be Hamlet's nightmare world, a world in which he lives but of which he is not part.

After Claudius' last lines, the upstage lights dimmed until the court dissolved into darkness and was finally blacked out by a dark tulle curtain which fell between it and Hamlet. Thus, as Hamlet began his monologue, "O, that this too too solid flesh' (I, ii), he seemed to wake from an exteriorized nightmare to his own inner hell. Not an emotional Hamlet, Kachalov spoke his lines drily, with what the critics described as deep-rooted bitterness. The monologue was accompanied softly by Sats's "Hamlet's solitude" theme, a wordless chorus of male and female voices which would recur in I, v.

The scenes in Polonius' chambers (I, iii and II, i) were done with grey screens and were brightly lit. Craig saw the whole tribe of Polonius as stupid but crafty, with Polonius the brightest and Ophelia the least intelligent. In the production, Craig's harsh view of Ophelia was softened by emphasizing a childlike quality.

The next scene was reminiscent of the first, with similar lighting but a different placement of screens. Hamlet and Horatio waited in an embrasure for the ghost to appear. It moved close to the walls, taking on their coloration and sliding in and out of view. The audience and the actors saw the ghost simultaneously, when the lighting picked him out. In this scene, Kachalov's Hamlet began to lose his monkish introspection and take fire.

According to memoirs, Hamlet's father was understood by the cast to have been morally strong, an enlightened ruler in a rough and primitive world. As such, he brought peace and kindness to his country and his court. Hamlet inherited his father's nature, and was trained in his virtuous way of life, his world view. This was reinforced by his university experience. When the king died, his brother-successor returned to older, more warlike behavior, and both court and country reverted to the ways of a cruder past. Hamlet's world was thus destroyed, and he was unable to accept his uncle's world or to reconcile himself to his mother's acceptance of it. It was at this point that he heard of the ghost.

> The scene with his father [I, v] took place at the highest point of the castle walls, against a clear moonlit sky which would later redden with the approach of dawn. . . . The transparent fabrics which covered the dead body of the former king were ethereal and other-worldly against the night skies. In contrast, the black figure of Hamlet, in its heavy fur cloak, bore strong witness to the fact that he was bound to this rank material world, this vale of suffering from which he vainly struggles upward, vainly tries to guess the secrets of earthly existence and of the the world from which his father's spirit came. This scene, and many others, were imbued with terrifying mysticism.[104]

However, the harsh lighting from sharply focused spotlights blinded Kachalov and made intimacy with the ghost an impossibility—especially since the symbolism of the scene required Kachalov to stare up into the lights. But the critics stressed Kachalov's development of his character and noted that it was in this scene that Hamlet assumed a dual personality: Hamlet the man and Hamlet the actor and feigner of madness.

For the second scene of act II, after the king's line "We will try it," Craig built, in a curve from left front to upstage center, a long corridor of gold screens, juxtaposed with plain canvas ones down right. The lighting was designed to make it look endless, buried in the labyrinth of palace passages. The dark figure of Hamlet moved about in it as though caged; to a modern audience the scene might hold some of the claustrophobic impact of a fun house mirror maze. It is difficult to determine whether this arrangement was used only for the latter part of scene ii or for the whole scene. According to the ground plans the former seems indicated; according to reviews and memoirs, the latter. One reads that Hamlet is watched on this golden set by the golden king and his golden spies, and that the golden court passes through this corridor, past Hamlet in his mourning. According to rehearsal notes, Hamlet went offstage before the golden parade and reentered after it had passed, looking around suspiciously to see whether the king has left his spies behind.

In his scene with Polonius, Kachalov's Hamlet used his book as an evasion. Respectfully but doggedly, he tried to avoid Polonius by using long pauses before and during his responses to Polonius' questioning, and to deflect his curiosity with jokes. Hamlet's attitude to Rosencrantz and Guildenstern was different. These two, caricatures of sycophancy and suspicion (chameleons, in Craig's bestiary description), entered shoulder to shoulder glancing around nervously. Hamlet welcomed them warmly at first, and then, as their behavior made him doubt their motives, his affection became clearly feigned and he began to move brusquely, to speak sternly. Critics wrote of his intensification of suppressed emotion, saying that his eyes blazed and his voice was edged with angry malice. He began to play cat to his former friends' mice. "At this moment in Kachalov's Hamlet, one sensed a kind of madness, a sort of quiet inner frenzy...."[105] Sitting beside Rosencrantz and Guildenstern, his back to them, looking upward, Hamlet proceeded toward inner monologue as he delivered "What a piece of work is man!" almost in a whisper.

Apparently the visual presentation evoked a strong sense of imprisonment, desperation and alienation—and the golden walls remained oppressive until the arrival of the players. Since this corridor was so powerful a visual statement, the arrival of the players must have been incredibly bright and active to overwhelm the set as it reputedly did..

> A crowd of actors entered, in brilliant and very stagey costumes, wearing long feathers like Indians. They walked gracefully, consciously performing even "offstage." Their arrival took place to the sound of their flutes, cymbals, oboes, piccolos and drums. In the procession, they bore their brightly painted costume trunks and bits of gaudy painted scenery—for example, trees done in a naïve medieval style wih its inaccurate perspective. Some actors carried theatrical banners, weapons and halberds; others brought rugs and fabrics; still others were draped head to foot with tragic and comic masks; still more carried all sorts of ancient musical instruments on their shoulders and backs and in their hands. Taken all together, these actors personified the beautiful and joyful art of the theater.[106]

Hamlet's heart lightened. For a moment he became the young enthusiast he had been before his father's death. It was a moment of spiritual release from his golden prison. The audience was meant to see the actors as Hamlet saw them, as a bright respite from crippling pain. And so, apparently, it was in the performance, because witnesses agree that the actors' entrance made the shimmering gold walls pale into insignificance.

The same set, lit yellow and with the addition of a flight of steps, was used to begin act III. There was no trace of Craig's vision of death. Instead, Kachalov entered pensively and spoke the "to be or not to be" monologue with a quiet intelligence; critics attest to the disappointment of the audience at the lack of thespian fireworks. The scene with Ophelia was also poorly received, because the audience expected Hamlet to be passionate and not gentle or pitying. Ophelia, who was at the top of the stairs at the opening of the scene, was pushed down a few steps by Polonius during the soliloquy and stopped in a spotlight which showed the tears streaming down her face. She continued down the steps into the shadow and stepped back into the light on the last lines of the soliloquy, still weeping. Between the tears and the distracting blocking, Kachalov's subdued reading must have been neatly upstaged.

Hamlet's later scene with the actors was played in much the same lively spirit as the earlier one, and was seen by many critics as one of Kachalov's best scenes. Hamlet addressed the actors as they were getting into costume and make-up, warming up and fooling around with their instruments. Craig identified Hamlet with the life of the spirit, synonymous with art; Hamlet was at home with the actors. Stanislavski used a great deal of backstage detail in this scene, but it seems to have met with Craig's approval.

The Mousetrap scene was performed as Craig wanted. Two "columns" on the forestage marked the proscenium of the stage within a stage. Between that and the stage audience, the huge Art Theater trap was opened, with stairs leading up to the forestage and more stairs leading up to the throne upstage center. The scene opened with the entrance of the king and his court to a march by Sats called "Power." The king and queen faced the real audience, and the courtiers were ranged in rows on either side of the throne and on the stairs. The actors, brightly decked out, mounted their stage from the house side and played to Claudius and Gertrude, that is, with their backs to the real audience. Horatio was downstage, and Hamlet crossed brusquely between him and Ophelia and the queen and the throne and the trap. The actors, and Horatio, were brightly lit; the stage audience was in partial darkness, with lavender and greenish lights playing over their golden costumes and focusing the real audience's attention where the direcctor wanted it. When Hamlet was downstage, in the trap, he was well-lit from the waist up so that the audience could see his face and hands, but he was nearly invisible when he sat upstage. Since Hamlet had his back to Claudius and because he could not see beyond the shaft of light in which he stood, he could only learn of Claudius' reactions to the play from Horatio, whom Hamlet had overtly placed on the forestage behind a column to observe the king. (To emphasize his connection to Hamlet, Horatio held Hamlet's sword in his arms.) When the play within a play reached its climax, according to Stanislavski in *My Life in Art,* Hamlet was downstage and, at the first sign of alarm from Claudius, leapt into the trap toward the king.[107] Senelick's reconstruction has Hamlet behind the throne at this point, his hands on its back, his face close to Claudius'.[108] All accounts agree that his voice began to rise to a shout as the scene mounted to the king's "give me some light. Away!" The king showed his panic, and pandemonium broke out in the upstage shadows. The king leapt awkwardly through the bright swatch of light on the forestage, with Hamlet following him like a hound after the fox. As the king disappeared offstage, Hamlet stopped short on the forestage, where he enveloped himself in the yellow cloak left behind by the player king, and cavorted and pranced in hysterical triumph. This moment was noted by nearly all the critics as the peak of Kachalov's performances, electrifying and horrifying the audience with its psychological force.

Here Kachalov seems to have pulled out all the emotional stops. Craig did not want a theatrical "inspired" Hamlet, but did want moments of deliberate emotional intensity. At first, Kachalov found it difficult to play a nontheatrical Hamlet with emotional peaks. Late in 1911, he remarked to a colleague that his was a boring Hamlet, too Chekhovian and understated. (The critics leveled precisely this accusation at his performance in the next scene, the closet scene.)

By the night of the premiere, apparently, he had managed to build to occasional explosions of temperament without having it spill over to spoil the general tone of restraint his directors wanted of him.

Three later scenes were noted consistently by the critics. The first of these was IV, v: Ophelia's madness. The screens represented the Queen's chamber, with the gold of the court set into a semi-circle upstage. The Queen's throne was set between two "columns" of neutral screens and the whole was lit startlingly white. The queen was in the company of a number of white-clad ladies in waiting, some singing madrigals. They were interrupted in this, one at a time, by the entrance of Ophelia whose songs were made more incongruous and more touching by their contrast with the music which began the scene. She was in distress not at her father's death, but at the absence of Hamlet, and many of her lines were addressed to an invisible Hamlet as though he stood next to her. She was shown predominantly as a child who was completely overwhelmed by the mysteries and complexities of adult life. She was never really absent from the stage during this scene, except during Laertes' short-lived uprising. When not onstage, she was heard offstage, still singing—either being led away, or meandering back to Gertrude and Claudius.

Laertes' rebellion broke into this gentle setting with all the realism at Stanislavski's command. A medieval petty king was shown as threatened by those whom he has terrorized and who had rallied under the leadership of an ambitious noble, himself wronged. It was, however, a brief moment. Even so, the naturalism of its staging intruded as much into Craig's production as did Laertes' rebellion itself into the peace of a court just then singing madrigals. It was perhaps the most extreme example of the clash between the theater styles of Craig and Stanislavski.

Another such intrusion was, predictably enough, the gravediggers' scene. Two superb actors played naturalistically a scene always treated naturalistically in order to underscore its humor. But the graveyard itself was composed of a few stylized cubes and tall rectangular columns. The realism of the acting on the abstract and visually impressive set was jarring to most critics.

The last scene was one of the most successful. The stage was broken up into many different heights by using a number of platforms. The king and queen sat, as usual, up center, on their great throne, and the duellists were ranged on the forestage below. The duel was well and excitingly fought. At is end, everything seems to have been resolved visually. Sats's solemn and triumphal funeral march reinforced the final visual statement. Hamlet's body was stretched out on a black cloak, lying on the stairs which led up to the throne. His face was smiling, as though content with the accomplishment of all that had had to be done. The spirit has triumphed. There was a pause, for the audience to take that in. Then a forest of spears entered, while an intrusive march, tonal and crude in a dark minor, blared out with the energy of a full military band. Fortinbras mounted the top platform like an avenging angel, in white. A brass ensemble played an ominous slow march, almost a dirge, as giant banners were lowered slowly over Hamlet's body. The drama was ended in a reverent solemnity.

The Aftermath

Hamlet began at 7:30 and ended somewhat after one in the morning. Little was cut, except for the scene of Claudius at prayer and the first three scenes of act IV. The length of the performance would not, however, deter an audience whose curiosity had been piqued by the continual attention given *Hamlet* in the press. Russian audiences were accustomed to longish evenings at the theater, and five hours did not seem so lengthy there as they might elsewhere.

Gossip about a rift between Craig and Stanislavski, rumors about innovation in production style, speculation about "decadent" art taking hold in the Art Theater, all tantalized Moscow theatergoers, and brought them to the theater, albeit with a predictable array of preconceptions. Some were surprised by this *Hamlet,* and others found it proof of their prejudices for better or for worse.

To the nervous cast and crew, the audience seemed cold. The Art Theater actors were used, as they still are, to an emotional response from the house to their "theater of experience." With a more intellectual and abstract approach, which summoned a different audience reaction, they had lost their old sense of the audience and were rattled. Nevertheless, the applause seems to have been so long and stormy that after the third act, for example, that Craig, Stanislavski and Sulerzhitski took a curtain call; they were called forth again at the end of the performance as was Kachalov.

> After the end of the performance, there was even louder applause. The audience would not go home, and determinedly called for V.I. Kachalov. The calls were so loud and so insistent that the theater finally decided to break its rule that actors do not respond to such calls, and Kachalov took a bow. A real storm of appreciation resounded through the house.... The applause did not diminish, and the actor who had so thrilled the house with his noble portrayal of the Danish prince, came out again together with Gordon Craig.[249]

Yet Koonen remembers the applause on opening night as scanty, the audience cold; she fled the theater immediately after the curtain, upset by *Hamlet's* poor reception.[250]

The press responded in every conceivable way: *Hamlet* was brilliant; it was awful. The production represented a bold new concept which would revolutionize modern theater; how could the Art Theater allow itself so to be duped by a talentless foreigner? The screens were magnificent, evoking every possible mood; they were too garish and blinded the audience to the rest of the production; they were boring—after you'd seen one, you'd seen them all; they were appropriately subtle—once you'd gotten used to so new a scenic idea, they permitted the actor to take full command of the stage. The lighting was superb; it was too impressionistic, putting important scenes in the dark when the audience needed a clear view of the actors. There was only one point of consensus: that the screens and lighting could not, between them, create a small intimate chamber.[251]

As for Kachalov, he was either brilliant and presented Russian theater with a new Hamlet, or out of his depth in such a great role because he lacked the temperament needed to play a tragic hero.[252] It must be remembered that Moscow was used to a sentimental Hamlet, played in ringing tones with grand gestures. Kachalov gave Moscow an intellectual Hamlet, low-keyed and thoroughly believable. Instead of the usual melancholy Dane, Kachalov played a determined man of principle, dignified and princely, extremely demanding of himself—a doer, albeit one who thought things out first. He was still a tormented man, but in terms too realistic for the romantic. Many of the critics missed their old Hamlet, and could not forgive Kachalov for the new interpretation. Others recognized it for what it was: a brilliant achievement by a master actor. In the history of Russian theater, it is remembered as one of the great Hamlets, and one of Kachalov's greatest roles. Except for Michael Chekhov's (1924) and Goriunov's (1931) Hamlets, all modern Russian stage interpretations of the role stem from Kachalov's. It was no accident that the audience called for Craig and Kachalov.

Even after *Hamlet* was no longer in the Art Theater's repertory, Kachalov continued to read the role in "concert-performances." All traces of Craig's mysticism disappeared as Kachalov continued to develop the role, but his Hamlet remained a cross between Craig's innovations and Stanislavski's psychological truth. There is a recording of his reading of the Hecuba speech (II, ii) taken during one of these performances; it is now in the State Theater Museum in Leningrad. Kachalov speaks simply and naturally, using peaks of intensity (but not emotionality) to underscore key lines. It is a musical reading, and can easily be imagined among Craig's screens.

Only Kachalov, among the actors, was able to add anything to Craig. The other actors received mixed reviews, except Knipper-Chekhova who reluctantly played Gertrude. She was certain that she did not suit the role, and the critics agreed. Stanislavski, who gave it to her at Craig's insistence and against his own better judgment, thought later to remove it from her, but did not. The production ran forty-seven times, over three years. The case remained the same, and their performances developed further—although only Kachalov was to achieve anything major.

Both Stanislavski and Nemirovich-Danchenko were to work with *Hamlet* again, although in theory only. Nemirovich-Danchenko was preparing to stage it again, in the 1940s, but his plan was never realized. Both men retained the basic interpretation of the 1911 production, stripped of its "mysteries" and otherworldliness. *Hamlet* remained for them the tragedy of the principled

Figure 19.   A sampling of costumes from the 1912 *Hamlet*
illustrates the visual distinctions between groups of
characters. Ophelia (Gzovskaia) in white, and
Polonius (V.V. Luzhski) in the gold costume and
exaggerated make-up typical of the grotesque court.

Figure 20.   Hamlet (Kachalov) in his long blue-grey costume
with dark geometric embellishments, and his lank
center-parted dark wig. To a Russian audience, this
made him look like a monk.

Figure 21.   1912 *Hamlet*. One of Craig's model sets for act IV, 1910.

Figure 22.   1912 *Hamlet*. One of Craig's model sets for act V, 1910.

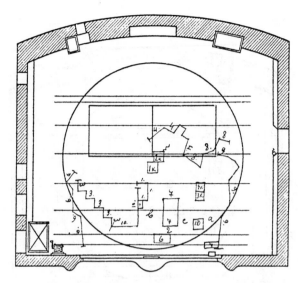

Figure 23.   1912 *Hamlet*. Sulerzhitski's ground plan for I, i, 1910.

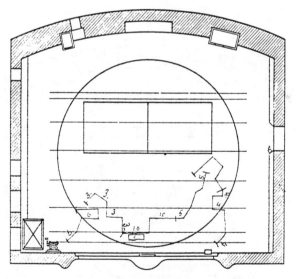

Figure 24.   1912 *Hamlet*. Sulerzhitski's ground plan for I, iii, 1910. These ground plans give some indication of the extent of the screen shifting expected of the stagehands. Presumably, the final arrangements of screens in 1912 differed little from those indicated by the ground plans Sulerzhitski developed during the late spring and summer of 1910.

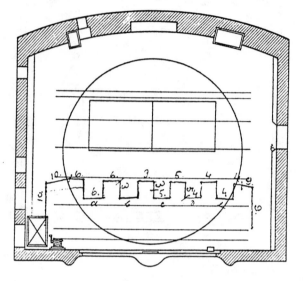

Figure 25.   1912 *Hamlet*. Sulerzhitski's ground plan for I, iv, 1910.

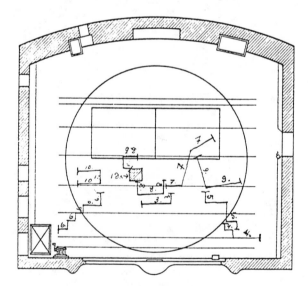

Figure 26.   1912 *Hamlet*. Sulerzhitski's ground plan for I, v, 1910.

Figure 27.   1912 *Hamlet*. I, i. Sketch by A. Lyubimov, photographed from the original.
Lyubimov's sketches, some of which were published in *Teatr i Iskusstvo* in 1912, give
us some notion of the visual effect of Craig's sets for *Hamlet*. Here, the ghost of
Hamlet's father approaches from the left, startling Bernardo, Marcellus and Horatio,
on the right.

Figure 28. 1912 *Hamlet*. I, ii. Gordon Craig's preliminary sketch is the only pictorial demonstration of his concept for the court scene. The court is a massive pyramid of gold topped by the king and queen, with Hamlet, in profile, reclining down left against the barrier which separates him from the glittering court.

Figure 29.   1912 *Hamlet*. I, v. Sketch by A. Lyubimov. This drawing shows the blocking which had Kachalov's Hamlet looking straight into the blinding lights so that he was unable to establish any intimacy with the ghost of his father.

Figure 30.   1912 *Hamlet*. II. Sketch by N. Istomina.

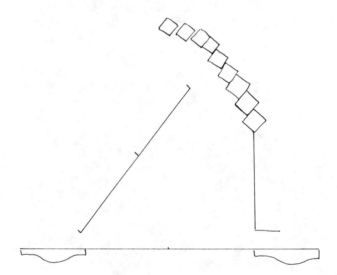

Figure 31.   Detail from Sulerzhitski's rough ground plan for this
scene, showing that the golden wall was probably
not intended to be smooth as in Istomina's sketch,
but irregular—so that Claudius's "golden spies"
might indeed hide in its angles.

Figure 32.   1912 *Hamlet*. III, iv. The queen's closet, set in plain canvas screens. Sketch by A. Lyubimov.

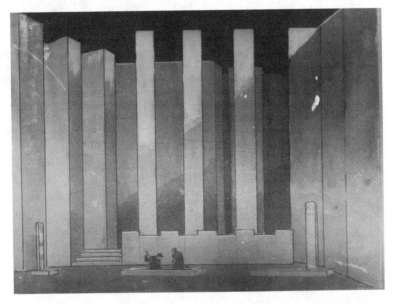

Figure 33.   1912 *Hamlet*. V, i. A churchyard, with plain canvas screens and the gravediggers in the trap, downstage center. Craig had had an entirely different concept for this set, and found Stanislavski's version banal.

Figure 34. 1912 *Hamlet.* V, ii. Final tableau, in the only photograph of the production extant. The forest of spears, up center, belongs to the army of Fortinbras, and was criticized by more than one reviewer as overly gimmicky.

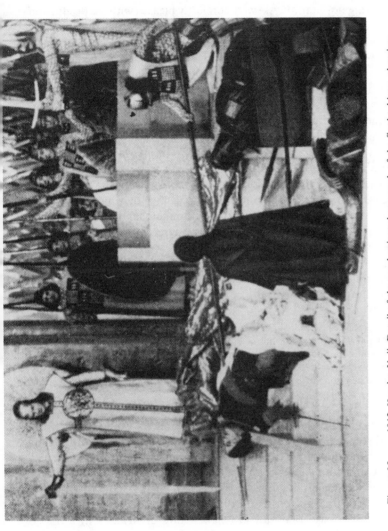

Figure 35.   1912 *Hamlet*. V, ii. Detail of the production photograph of the final tableau, showing Hamlet's body on the steps, his arms extended, a half-smile on his face, and banners draped over his lower body. Horatio kneels at his feet, upstage of Laertes's corpse; Gertrude's body is at Hamlet's head, and Claudius lies dead at the foot of the throne. In a white costume emblazoned with a golden cross and with a round golden shield strapped high on his back, Fortinbras stands with his sword like an avenging archangel.

intellectual who cleanses his kingdom at the behest of a better past, in hope of a better future. Russian theater would never return to the emotional version, starring a doomed and helpless prince, that had once dominated European stages.

Neither Craig nor Stanislavski were comletely pleased with the production itself. It was a box office success, gratifyingly controversial and patently innovative. But it did not fulfill their own hopes. In their desire to create a new theater, they both chose the wrong man to work with. Craig's theater of the future was to be a highly stylized merging of the various arts, in which the depersonalized actor was merely a part. Profound truths would be stated abstractly. Stanislavski's new theater was increasingly based on the actor, who would use the poetic possibilities of his own personality, emotions and experience to create a real-seeming theatrical character. The rest of the production was to be subordinated to his immediate and human communication of truth. Craig wanted to separate the actor from the man and base performance on symbolic gesture and movement. Stanislavski's actors, directed according to two conflicting methods neither of which were quite jelled, were hard put to hold center stage. Craig thought that theater was meant to be seen, and indeed the strongest and most effective statements of this *Hamlet* were made visually.

The attempt by Craig and Stanislavski to realize their ideals on one stage at the same time resulted in a dual focus that made their production schizophrenic. Briusov complained,

> A non-naturalistic production style demands non-naturalistic acting: this is what the Art Theater did not grasp in its production of *Hamlet*. The actors kept trying to *live* on the stage. But then *life* must be shown on the stage. As soon as the director moves away from that task, as soon as he exchanges life for artifice—then the actors must follow suit. Instead of a palace, there was the suggestion of a palace; correspondingly, instead of a shout, there must be the suggestion of a shout. . . . [253]

Later directors, such as Meyerhold and Vakhtangov would resolve the dilemma, and reconcile Stanislavski's and Craig's ideas of artistic truth. But in 1911, this confrontation of the two styles was unresolved on the one stage, and it confused actors and audiences alike. It also diminished the very real accomplishments of the production: the trial of a totally new concept of scene, the attempt to take a classic off its dusty shelf and present it afresh, the Art Theater's attempt to use Stanislavski's new acting discoveries in a major foreign classic—and the partial success of this effort, notably with Kachalov.

Stanislavski later wrote that, in trying to analyze *Hamlet,* the Art Theater had merely chopped it up. Methods of interpretation and acting that worked in modern plays did not transfer easily to "plays in the heroic and grand style."[254] In all of this, he was concerned that the Art Theater had let Craig down. In

1910, while he was sick, he wrote to Nemirovich-Danchenko "You know what's beginning to worry me: whether Craig's genius will be understood, or whether he'll simply be taken for a freak."[255] By 1912, he was sure that his theater had not done justice to Craig's ideas, and blamed himself. Yet Craig placed no such blame at the time, and remained a staunch supporter of the Art Theater. As his departure from Moscow approached, he bade the theater farewell as follows:

> Dear friends, I thank you with all my heart and, believe me, you have made me a thousand times happier if the little that I brought you proves to be really valuable for our Art, which I believe you love as devotedly as I do.
> In your theater there are many people blessed with great talent, and you have such a remarkable literary director as Mr. Nemirovich-Danchenko, and also an ideal artist such as one could not find in any other theater in Europe, Stanislavski.
> He has laid the cornerstone of international theater. And that is an excellent, a great thing.[256]

However, Craig was disappointed in the production too. The acting was not what he wanted, and in spite of extraordinary efforts on the part of the Art Theater, his set did not operate as planned. He had come to agree with Sulerzhitski on one thing at least: he needed his own theater. In 1926, he would write, "The experience in Moscow decided me to wait [to produce a play] until I should possess my own theater."[257] He turned his attention to his projected school. It is interesting that Stanislavski should initiate the First Studio of the Art Theater in 1911, very possibly spurred on by Craig's insistence on training facilities for young theater artists.

Gordon Craig was more than a symbolist designer; his ideas constituted a whole theatrical revolution. If Stanislavski saw him as a catalyst which might open new possibilities in theater, younger artists were even more profoundly influenced by Craig's vision. Several young theater artists involved in the Craig-Stanislavski *Hamlet* heard the English director's ideas with particular interest. Evgeny Vakhtangov was to become a major innovator in Russian theater during the next decade. Serafima Birman, who played a courtier, would be an outstanding actress of the new "leftist" theater. As they matured artistically, their work grew away from the Art Theater realism in which they had been trained, and closer to Craig's ideal theater. Alisa Koonen later became the leading actress in Tairov's theater of artistic synthesis. She never lost her admiration for Craig. His ideas travelled beyond the walls of the Art Theater to reach other young innovators. By the time he returned to Moscow in 1935, Russian theater had produced a veritable fireworks of new ideas. Meyerhold, Tairov and Eisenstein joined Craig's Art Theater acquaintances in welcoming him, and acknowledged their debt to his ideas. He saw, among other outstanding productions in that year's repertories, a new Shakespeare production: *King Lear* at the Jewish State Theater, the Habima. The director-translator S.E. Radlov and S.M. Mikhoels, the actor whose Lear was to become a landmark in Russian theater history, both acclaimed Craig as their master.

Stanislavski's collaboration with Craig gave him the opportunity to talk and work with one of the great theorists and designers of this century. Though working with Craig was never guaranteed to develop Stanislavski's own theories, the Soviet scholar M.N. Stroeva notes that it did affect his approach to theoretical work: before 1909 his quest had been instinctive and uncoordinated; under Craig's influence it acquired concentration and clarity of purpose.[118] Looking back at the history of the production, Stanislavski seems to have worked almost as Craig's disciple in 1909 and 1910, whereas in 1911 he had defined his system and wanted to test it. This change in Stanislavski may well have been the main cause of *Hamlet*'s dualism.

With *Hamlet,* then, Stanislavski began to concentrate more completely on acting and, at last, began to free himself from his long preoccupation with the external. From the *Hamlet* years on, his promptbooks reflect a diminished concern with the set, while detailing the psychological development of the characters and the action. He had had to teach himself the hard way to eliminate the inessential to focus on the heart of the matter. For him, that was the art of the actor.

Two Later Productions

*We shall reach to Shakespeare some day. Then we shall at the same time reach our ideal—
and so The Theater!*

Craig

After *Julius Caesar* and *Hamlet,* the Art Theater was plagued by the myth that it was incapable of producing Shakespeare and, by extension, any of the great classics. It is surprising that the accusation should be made: *Hamlet* and *Julius Caesar* were both highly successful productions, no matter how controversial. Both played to full houses for the length of time they were in the repertory, and both were landmark productions—one realizing the full potential of a theatrical style, and the other radically innovative in style. Controversy does not imply failure, but the contrary. But the charge found some basis in the directors' discontent with their accomplishment in these two ambitious undertakings. More successful in the eyes of Stanislavski and Nemirovich-Danchenko were two later meetings with Shakespeare: one in an experimental studio, and one which had no box-office success but whose promptbook was published, and translated into several languages, as Stanislavski's definitive approach to Shakespeare.

In 1917/1918, the most exciting production of the season was acknowledged to be *Twelfth Night* at the First Studio of the Moscow Art Theater, directed by Stanislavski and B.M. Sushkevich. "Stanislavski worked on *Twelfth Night* like a poet of life and of the theater. Together with Shakespeare, he fired everyone's enthusiasm, and the performance rang with the joy of living."[1]

Only memoirs, a few photographs, and reviews sketch the event. The sets were simple and evocative, fixing the locale by a bit of furniture or tapestry, or a garden well in one corner. The rest of the stage was hung in unobtrusive curtains. To make the action continuous, other curtains bissected the stage diagonally and swung alternately left and right to mark the change of scene. Pivoting the curtain, or only its back half from a central point, created right-angled triangles to the left or right, or a shallow isosceles triangle down front.

In the area behind the curtains, stagehands quietly arranged the set for the next scene, and there was almost no break in the action on stage.[2]

The studio was a low-budget affair. Stanislavski could only afford to rent for it three low-ceilinged rooms on the top floor of the Komissarzhevskaia Theater. One of the rooms was large, but too low to have a raised stage, and the other rooms were very small. There was no place to store elaborate sets even if they could be afforded, and no way to haul them up to the top floor rooms. The stage was not set off by platforms or footlights, but went right up to the first row of seats. Only a carpet marked the edge of the acting area. It was closed off during intermissions by a simple curtain. The seating was raised on a gradient, so that everyone in the audience had a clear view of the stage. The audience felt so incorporated into the play physically that Stanislavski had no need to resort to gimmickry to include the spectators into the action; the action was all but in their laps. All this created an atmosphere which S.V. Giatsintova, who played Maria, called "not intimate chamber theater, but one which drew the entire house into the performance. This was something new."[3] Birman remembered that "a merry bridge of mutual understanding and reciprocity sprang up like a rainbow between the stage and the audience."[4] Here, Stanislavski was forcibly freed from all the elaborate and perfectionistic visual resolutions which had seemed so necessary to him on the Art Theater's main stage.

The approach used for *Twelfth Night* was new even to Stanislavski. He had recently had difficulties with his own acting, and a new book, *The Actor's Creative Work and Stanislavski's Theory,* distorted his as yet unpublished method into a pure spiritual naturalism devoid of any artistic imagination.[5] So Stanislavski decided to approach acting from a new angle. As Stroeva defines it, he moved from "the cult of *feeling*" to "the cult of *action,*" looking to physical tasks for a key to theatrical creativity.[6] He stressed theatricality, broad comedy, crisp verbal duels and improvisation. To speed up the pace of the performance he manipulated the text so that nothing interfered with the forward thrust of the play—taking more liberties in this regard than he ever had. The simplicity of the staging made it possible to use most of the text without making the performance overlong (a little over three hours), but there were frequent displacements of scenes. The play was divided into thirteen episodes, each with its own setting.[7]

"The play," Stanislavski wrote to Gurevich, "was successful in spite of the fact that we had to make it up out of all sorts of odds and ends."[8] Its freshness, vivacity and originality made it an instant hit with the public. The production itself, and its success, reveals a great deal about Stanislavski. First, it is another indication that he was much more comfortable with Shakespearean comedy than with the tragedies; the comedies gave him the down-to-earth qualities he could work with. Secondly, and more importantly, he did not need the nearly unlimited resources of the Art Theater, and may well have been hampered by them.

In the studio, he was dealing with student actors training at the Art Theater, who had chosen to study Stanislavski's system. His discoveries had been explained to all the senior Art Theater actors and had not always met with acceptance. The students, having no artistic methods of their own to reconcile, were much more eager as a group to learn from Stanislavski. Here Stanislavski's ability to teach was as welcome as his ability to direct, and he could work free of the human tensions that had clouded his past decade at the Art Theater.

Like the 1897 version, the production linked the lyrical to the musical—but in 1918, the lyrical also gave way to stylized buffoonery, reclaimed the stage, and then yielded again. The pace was fast, and the constant transitions kept the performance lively. Viola and Sebastian were played by one actress with two costumes, since the two never meet on the stage until the last scene; at that point another actress appeared as Viola and kept her back to the audience throughout. The trick was simple. The audience saw through it and enjoyed it immensely. The mise-en-scène was the closest Stanislavski ever came to staging Shakespeare on an Elizabethan stage, and the production seems to have had a suitably Elizabethan sense of beauty and merrymaking. The critics raved, and those who were young in the audience then still rave about it now in their old age.

The production was transferred to the Art Theater's main stage soon after its premiere. Later, when the First Studio became the Second Moscow Art Theater, this *Twelfth Night* was part of its regular repertory. (By this point, though, it had acquired new sets, a more glamorous adaptation of the first.) For Stanislavski, the production began a whole series of experiments with the system based on physical technique.

In 1926, under the direction of Sudakov, the Moscow Art Theater began work on *Othello*. In March of 1927, Stanislavski also began to work on it, returning to the play after thirty-one years. He was pleased by what he saw at rehearsals, most particularly by Leonidov's portrayal of Othello. Gurevich remembers him saying, "it surpasses Salvini's" and noted that Stanislavski had never praised a lead actor so highly.[9] But rehearsals stopped early the next year. Rumor had it in the western press that the new Soviet government was not interested in having Shakespeare staged at the Art Theater and had put a stop to *Othello*. Certainly, Stanislavski and his theater were under constant fire from the Soviet press, implying government disapproval, for being old-fashioned and not sufficiently Revolutionary.

But the real reason for cutting short work on *Othello* seems to have been less political. In February of 1928, Stanislavski fell ill. In May, concerned about his continued poor health, he began to write to friends either that he considered his career over, or that he would have to limit his activities severely. (He was now sixty-five years old.) He went abroad to recuperate, and returned to work in Moscow in October. On October 29, as he was playing Vershinin in

Three Sisters on the thirtieth anniversary of the Art Theater, he felt sick. After the first act, he suffered an attack of angina pectoris. He was bed-ridden for months in Moscow, and left for a rest cure in Badenweiler and Nice in May of 1929. The London *Daily Telegraph* spoke of a "breakdown of Stanislavski's health" caused by clashes with "Bolshevist obscurantism," and reported that "he has come to the conclusion that 'in existing circumstances it is impossible for him to go on working in Russia.'"[10] Stanislavski was evidently concerned that reports like this might be read in high places back home, because on September 27, 1929, he wrote to the administrator of the Sovnarkom (Council of People's Commissars), "If you hear that I am a runaway and a fake, don't believe it," adding that he was indeed seriously ill and that his doctors would not permit him to return to Moscow in his condition.[11] He would stay a year and a half in western Europe, and the rumors would persist. In May of 1930 he wrote to the theater, "It still worries me that again they say I won't return.... How could I not return?"[12]

Rehearsals for *Othello* resumed in January of 1929, under the direction of Sudakov again, since Stanislavski was ill. In June, from Badenweiler, Stanislavski began to correspond with Leonidov concerning the production: "During my absence I beg you to take over the rehearsals for *Othello* if such there will be. It's very important that, from the beginning, no one veers from the straight 'through-line.'"[13] Leonidov kept him informed of progress on the play, and Stanislavski wrote that he hoped to return in time to work on *Othello* in the fall. In the meantime, he did his best to direct from abroad. His letters are full of technical suggestions and solutions, advice on casting and working with the foibles of the individuals in the cast, and so on. As Leonidov's work progressed, Stanislavski discussed the interpretation of the play and of his role. Since Stanislavski was also working on a nearly final version of the three-part *An Actor's Work on Himself* (*An Actor Prepares, Building a Character,* and *Creating a Role*), the letters are full of descriptions of his system of acting. Leonidov read installments of the current draft as Stanislavski forwarded them to him, offered his opinions and contributed an idea or two.[14]

Later that year, in Nice, Stanislavski began dictating the mise en scène to his son Igor. "Maybe I can take some part in [the work on *Othello*] from a distance," he wrote to Nemirovich-Danchenko, and suggested that he could send an approximate idea of the production to Leonidov and the cast. "Of course by correspondence, as I now work, the mise en scène—done without any preliminary test with the actors on the stage—cannot be precise or free of mistakes. It would only give some ideas to those who are staging the play."[15] The promptbook was written from December of 1929 through March of 1930. Since *Othello* opened on March 14, it seems clear why Stanislavski discontinued his work at that point. In 1945, it was published in Russian and has been accepted as Stanislavski's definitive approach to Shakespeare. The assumption is understandable: Stanislavski was in the throes of putting his system into near-final written form at the same time that he was dictating the *Othello* notes. Stanislavski himself never felt that he had arrived at anything definitive, theoretically or practically. He preferred to state merely that he had made certain discoveries. The promptbook for the 1930 *Othello,* like the published promptbook for *The Seagull,* reveals some of these discoveries. They both serve as practical examples for the lessons given in *An Actor's Work on Himself,* the more so because neither promptbook was written for publication but for use in preparing a production. Furthermore, because the 1929/30 promptbook was Stanislavski's only contact with the cast of *Othello* other than individual letters, it may well contain passages which would normally be communicated verbally during rehearsal. Stanislavski's letter of February 10, 1930, to Leonidov mentions parenthetically that "it's very difficult to *write* a mise-en-scène; besides I'm at a distance from everyone and . . . only imagining what is coming of all this."[16]

The promptbook treats the first three acts of the play (I, i through IV, i, 210 of Shakespeare's play) with diagrams of the sets and blocking and a detailed analysis of the action and characters. Although Golovin was designing the sets with his usual luxurious touch, Stanislavski wanted to keep the set changes simple enough that the play would run almost continuously. Some of the sets were almost identical with those of the 1896 *Othello*; others were completely reworked. Othello himself was conceived as the more traditional African, rather than as an Arab. There was no extraordinary research nor any ultra-perfectionism in historical detail. The sets were to be designed for the revolving stage, with set changes being made backstage while the actors were performing in front, a device deliberately revived from the studio *Twelfth Night.*

> There is yet another important condition. While the stage is revolving and as the actors in the previous scene continue to act, the new scene is appearing and its actors are beginning to perform. In this way, the action of the play is not only uninterrupted by entr'actes, but its effect is doubled as it takes place on two sets simultaneously. The spectator is torn between the two, trying to watch them both and afraid of missing something. This effort stimulates his energy and attention, instead of killing them as would an entr'acte with its little conversations and candy nibbling.[17]

The promptbook is, however, remarkable for its minimal attention to external resolution. Stanislavski toned down not only his concern for the visual, but also those scenes which had been showpieces in 1896 and which had distracted from the main drive of the play. The full-fledged rebellion on Cyprus was almost totally excised, for example, and nothing is left of the naturalistic street scene with a cross-section of Cypriot life under the Venetian yoke.

The emphasis of the promptbook is on the psychological interpretation of the play and the characters, and on the technical aspects of performing them according to his "system." The interpretation of the play does not differ radically from that of 1896; it is the detail in which it is studied that is so changed. Stanislavski devotes whole pages to analyzing each character's psychological state and development before the action begins and all through the play. *Othello* becomes a study of an honorable man hideously deceived by an envious one. The audience is invited to watch the destruction of Othello by Iago. Desdemona is secondary. A vulnerable young woman of considerable character, she is the means of Othello's destruction chosen by Iago for its effectiveness; she is not a focal character in herself.

All this is not to say that the historicism of the 1896 *Othello* was absent from this *Othello;* it was not. But Stanislavski's use of history is completely transformed.[18] He no longer equates historical truth with archeological detail, and now uses it to construct a psychological environment. In 1930, Stanislavski's Venice is a world of arrogant calculation, where only expedience is more important than ossified social norms. Othello is accepted only insofar as his military ability makes it expedient to do so; he is forgiven his abduction of Desdemona because a military crisis makes it expedient to favor the outsider general. He is neither part of this environment nor merely surrounded by it, but lives in spite of it and in opposition to it. Desdemona also opposes Venetian society by flouting its conventions and eloping with Othello, and she is therefore a worthy mate for him. All the other characters are part and parcel of Venice and represent some aspect of its worldview: Brabantio the powerful aristocrat, Cassio the well-born scholar-soldier, Roderigo the weak offspring of wealthy merchants. Iago personifies the dark underside of this society, and Stanislavski makes him almost schizophrenic in his treachery; in public he is a good-natured diamond-in-the-rough soldier, and in private he is vicious to the point of pure evil. As Stanislavski establishes the position of each character in Renaissance Venice, the seeds of the tragedy are visible even before the play begins.

The use of history as a psychological determinant permits Stanislavski to elevate some characters to the heroic. He can thus make Othello more than an ordinary man, draw him to the larger scale used by Shakespeare. Stanislavski's focus remains on the play's characters, and he stressed to Leonidov the intimacy of the play's action, but he also insisted in his letters that the historical background is crucial if the theater is to present the scope and significance of Shakespeare's ideas. However, the historical must emanate from the characters, not from the props. The crowd scenes are diminished in order not to distract the audience's attention but they are still seen as more than incidental.

Clearly, Stanislavski had learned from his own mistakes. Equally clear is the influence of previous productions, including that of the 1912 *Hamlet* with its emphasis on Hamlet's isolation and his opposition to his environment. But Stanislavski does not resort to abstraction. He keeps the tragedy where he perceives it to be, in a solid real world.

A large part of the promptbook is dedicated to teaching the actor how to convey the interpretation of the whole, and the psychological truth of his own part. It is broken down for each actor into a series of tasks which must be done at each stage of the development of his role during the play. Stanislavski discusses the through line of each scene and breaks it into its physical, emotional, psychological and technical elements. He presents the notions of rhythm and tempo, of "piano" and "forte." One section concentrates on the relationship of temperament to technique, clearly earmarked for Leonidov whose acting was based on temperament and who worried about his tendency to uneven performances. From the first pages of the promptbook, Stanislavski fleshes in the prehistory of events and characters, and throughout the text he fills in the action which he presumes to have taken place in the intervals between scenes. The terminology is that of *An Actor's Work on Himself.* As it stands on the printed page, the promptbook is a masterful presentation of Stanislavski's system at work.

But what of the production itself? It premiered on March 14, 1930, and was labeled a failure. After ten performances, *Othello* was removed from the repertory. "I am horrified," wrote Stanislavski on hearing news of the disaster. He was upset that the production had not been faithful to his mise-en-scène, that all his efforts had been wasted, that his name was on the program. "I blush when I think of it."[19]

The date for *Othello*'s opening was set back in February of 1930 by the administration of the theater. Leonidov wrote to Stanislavski then that it would be difficult to have the production ready by that date, but possible. Two days later, he wrote, "Now begin the worst days in preparing *Othello.* The work itself is going as it should, but they are rushing us so that we can't possibly make it."[20] Five plays were being prepared at the same time, and the theater was not able to juggle them all. Two weeks before opening night, Leonidov wrote, "In a word, a lot of it is good, but a lot is bad."[21] Sudakov did not follow Stanislavski's promptbook faithfully, and several of the actors ignored its interpretation of their roles. The sets designed by Golovin, also seriously ill and unable to work at the theater, were poorly realized. The crowd scenes were even sloppily rehearsed, so hurried was the work on the production. The administration was not particularly supportive, and Leonidov expected bad reviews for anything classical. Everyone involved in the production sensed a general public apathy toward their work on *Othello.* The dress rehearsals went well, however, and the production was passed by the Soviet censors.

"Yesterday, on the 14th, the Kremlin sat in the director's box," wrote Leonidov. "It's a good thing your name was on the program. It's very important for you, and for us."[22] There were many hints of difficulties with the government, and of Party interference in the theater and with the play. New union regulations created ridiculous complications, like rotating obligatory days off so that the cast was never able to rehearse all together. The Party wanted Communist-oriented productions, not Shakespeare. And in general, the Art Theater and its leadership seem to have been suspect.

Nevertheless everything went smoothly until late March. According to those who were present during the dress rehearsals and final run-throughs, and at the premiere, the production was superb. More accurately, Leonidov's Othello was superb, and so moving that people left the theater thoroughly shaken by his performance.[23] As an actor, Leonidov has been described as all nerves; he was capable of the kind of emotion that fired the best of the romantic actors. But he was not a well man, and suffered from a form of agoraphobia that affected him when playing to a full house. At the second performance, on March 20, the theater was crammed. Leonidov made his first entrance and, to the amazement of the cast and crew, played the whole scene far upstage, holding onto the nearest chair for support during his longer speeches. The next scene went no better. Beginning with the third act, he "began to warm up gradually, although almost the entire time he sought something to hold onto (a table, a chair, and sometimes even the frame of a fellow actor)."[24] In the last act, he played beautifully. There were twenty-two curtain calls.

Since Leonidov had collapsed once before and spent a long time recovering in a sanatorium in 1925, the pressures of so demanding and emotional a role as Othello would seem dangerous for him. But the Soviet scholar Vinogradskaia postulates that he might have been able to overcome his problem in time and regained the intensity of the Othello people had seen in rehearsal.[25] However, on May 28, the promising young actor playing Iago died, and further work on the production was abandoned.

So the 1930 *Othello* was labeled a failure. It was more a victim of circumstance than an example of any inability of the Art Theater or of Stanislavski to come to grips with Shakespeare. In fact, had the extraneous obstructions—illness, government and administrative pressures—been absent, the Art Theater would most certainly have triumphed with this *Othello*. Stanislavski had finally found a way to make his system and his historicity compatible with Shakespeare; Golovin had designed sets which, in spite of their magnificence, could create a sense of time and place without overwhelming the performances; in Leonidov the Art Theater had a tragedian of sufficient power and maturity to take on Othello. Everything necessary was there—and is still visible in the shards that remain.

5

Conclusion

At the beginning of his career, Stanislavski defined the ideal theater in terms of what it was not, and rebelled against the bureaucracy and cliché of the Imperial theater system. By the time he joined forces with Nemirovich-Danchenko, he had identified many of the elements of theater as it should be, and the two men established a cooperative artistic venture which chose well-written plays and prepared their production carefully to interest and educate the public. These basic reforms were not difficult to effect in the new Art Theater, but no sooner did Stanislavski introduce the conditions which could foster ideal theater than he was plagued by a more basic question: how does the performer, individual or collective, create good theater?

From his own experience as a member of the audience, Stanislavski could identify master performers: the star-actors Lenski, Ermolova, Fedotova, Rossi, Salvini, and the ensemble troupe of the Duke of Saxe-Meiningen. Various of the masters had tried to analyze their art and to teach it in books and articles, schools and consultations, but they were unable to identify its core elements. Stanislavski was determined to seize that core and dissect it.

His early attempts at consciously shaping a role were naïve; playing Othello by mimicking the masculine grace of a young Arab is a good example. It must be remembered that Stanislavski's early inspiration was twofold, originating both in the intangible power of individual performances and in the technical mastery of the Meininger's naturalistic production style. It is not surprising, then, that his early experiments in theatrical form had a dual focus. At this point in Stanislavski's career, Othello logically springs both from an unforgettable performance and from the striking figure of a chance acquaintance in a Paris café. Since Stanislavski found it easier to reproduce the visual effect than the performance, he began to use external naturalism as his starting point.

In his early work, he tried to use naturalistic visual presentation to activate the unidentified mainspring of acting performance. Unfortunately, naturalism became a trap. No more than one of many possible styles, it would do no more than give shape to an existing idea. Stanislavski had begun to expect naturalism to provide the idea itself.

The 1903 *Julius Caesar* was a nearly perfect naturalistic production. It was carefully designed and built, with attention to both text and historical verity. It answered every scenic demand but the one most crucial to Stanislavski: quality of performance. Stanislavski sensed this impending shortcoming during the preparation of the production, expressed acute discomfort, and announced that he would rather work on a Chekhov play.

Still fired by the performances that made Chekhov come alive on the Art Theater stage, Stanislavski was impatient to experiment further with new plays as they flowed from Chekhov's pen. However, he could not yet put his finger on the element which fueled his actors to such artistic achievement. Mistakenly, he looked toward the meticulous naturalistic detail he had developed for *The Seagull* and *Uncle Vanya*. From the actors' success with those plays, Stanislavski concluded that his realistic stage environment gave rise to the realistic acting performances. It was a comforting conclusion; he had developed considerable expertise in creating lifelike stage environments. *Julius Caesar*, therefore, brought home a bitter truth. Its stage environment could not be faulted, but it did not inspire better acting. The style, no matter how brilliantly applied, could not *be* performance. Even work on two more Chekhov plays, and three plays by Gorky, did not alleviate Stanislavski's distress. He had discovered his "theater of experience" by accident, as it were, after struggling to understand Chekhov by embedding *The Seagull* in naturalistic detail. He knew no other approach to Chekhov and Gorky but from the outside. At the same time, he recognized that the theater magic lay not in the set but in something that the set made possible. Later, he described the difficulty as it existed in 1904, during his work on *The Cherry Orchard:*

> At that time, our inner technique and ability to stimulate the actor's creative forces were as primitive as ever.... To help the actors we had to use scenic illusion and lighting and sound effects.[1]

In the same breath, however, he could laugh at his dilemma as he recorded Chekhov's gentle mockery:

> "Listen!" Chekhov said to someone, loud enough for me to overhear. "I am going to write a new play, and the first line will be, 'How wonderful—it's so quiet! No birds, no dogs, no cuckoos, no owls, no nightingales, no clocks, no sleigh bells, not even a cricket.'"[2]

Stanislavski's torment was that he did not know how to begin without the cricket.

In 1906, in Finland, Stanislavski reviewed his roles and the pain involved in their creation, remembered the advice of Chekhov and Nemirovich-Danchenko, and evaluated his experience to date. He returned to Moscow with the idea which would clear the way to a new conscious approach to acting: the creative mood—a state of freedom from artificial inhibition which allows the actor to concentrate on his performance. Having made this discovery, Stanislavski scrutinized and analyzed his work and that of other actors to understand better how the creative mood worked.

After that summer of contemplation, Stanislavski also rejected the naturalism in which he had become enmeshed. In his decision to investigate the new symbolism, however, he merely escaped from one style to another, thereby begging his central question. He perceived symbolist stage design as minimizing the visual element of a production so that the actor would be neither distracted nor overwhelmed by the set. Armed with the abstract set and with the rudiments of his nascent system of acting, Stanislavski hoped to help his actors concentrate on the inner content of a role.

When Gordon Craig brought his revolutionary new concept in scene design to the Art Theater, he rendered Stanislavski the same service that *Julius Caesar* had. A revelation in theatrical innovation, the set could not be faulted. But it merely surrounded the actor, and did nothing to improve the quality of his acting. Stanislavski lamented that his search for a simple modest set had resulted in scenery more spectacular than before. The problem lay not so much in the set itself as in the inability of the primitive "method," except as masterfully employed by Kachalov, to compete with a perfected visual resolution. The clue to future progress lay in Kachalov's triumph.

During the years he worked with Craig on *Hamlet,* Stanislavski was learning to define the motive forces of his "theater of experience." He began to understand the relationship between the actor's subconscious knowledge and the work of internalizing a role. By the end of 1911, Stanislavski had arrived at a genuine understanding of the creative process of acting. He was finally ready to reject externalism. It had taken two decades to outgrow the influence of the Meininger which had trapped Stanislavski into preoccupation with stage environment. It took the 1903 *Julius Caesar* to prod him into the beginnings of a reassessment. Exchanging style for style, he remained bogged down in external resolution even after abandoning the naturalistic approach. Not until his collaboration with Gordon Craig did he perceive the specific direction of his "theater of experience." From that point on, he could give his complete attention to acting.

For the next two decades, he would explore the spiritual core of the actor's art, unravelling its secrets and making them accessible. The overriding accomplishment of these two decades is the systematic analysis of acting preserved in *An Actor Works on Himself.* The previous two decades were more than mere prelude, however. They teach the necessity of persistence through mistake, misconception and even through public acclaim in order to reach the solid ground on which real achievement is built. The example of those two decades is as much a contribution to the art of theater as the three volumes which summarized the later accomplishment. In fact, without the process, there could be no accomplishment.

Notes

Abbreviations

MATM   Moscow Art Theater Museum (Muzei Moskovskogo Khudozhestvennogo Teatra).

N-D   Vladimir Ivanovich Nemirovich-Danchenko

O.S.   Old style, i.e. according to the Julian calendar.

SS   Stanislavskii, Konstantin Sergeevich. *Sobranie sochinenii v vos'mi tomakh.* Ed. M.N. Kedrov. 8 vols. (Moscow, 1854-1861). The eight volummes include *My Life in Art,* in vol. I (in the definitive 1926 rewrite of the 1924 version hastily composed during the Art Theater's American tour, for publication in the English language [in J.J. Robbins' translation, Boston, 1924]. The second version has been translated by G. Ivanov-Mumjiev into stiff and sometimes inaccurate British English for the Foreign Language Publishing House [Moscow, n.d.]. For this study, I have provided my own translations, rather than juggle two flawed English versions, neither of which was used in my research) and *An Actor's Work on Himself* in vols. II, III and IV (available in E.R. Hapgood's English translation as *An Actor Prepares, Building a Character and Creating a Role*). Articles, speeches, remarks, fragments and reminiscences constitute vols. V and VI, and vols. VII and VIII contain selected letters from Stanislavski's extensive correspondence.

Stan   Konstantin Alekseevich Stanislavskii.

Chapter 1

1.   Sergei Sergeevich Danilov, *Ocherki po istorii russkogo dramaticheskogo teatra* (Moscow-Leningrad, 1948), p. 218.

2.   Shakespeare's tragedies and histories seemed to make the censor nervous; quite a few of them were banned for production at one time or another. The censor much preferred lighter plays, foreign or domestic, and this preference was reflected in the allowable repertory of the 19th century.

3.   Nikolai Georgievich Zograf, *Malyi teatr vtoroi poloviny XIX veka* (Moscow, 1960), pp. 400-401.

4.   Danilov, *Ocherki po istorii,* p. 423.

5..   Prior to its reform in 1882, the benefit consisted of a weekly production put together by the actors themselves, who received a percentage of the box office receipts. Established to reward the major actors of a theater, financially and creatively, it gradually became a device for avoiding raises in salary to any regular member of the troupe. In this way, minor actors would be allowed to "share a benefit," as would, occasionally, even prompters, prop men etc. (see A.N. Ostrovskii, *Polnoe sobranie sochinenii,* vol. XII [Moscow, 1952], p. 144.) After the reform, benefits were limited to four per year per theater and were given only to the major actors; these were the so-called "half-benefits"—that is, half the receipts went to the actor, half to the theater directorate.

6.   Sheldon Cheney, *Stage Decoration* (New York, 1928), p. 31. On pages 28-30 Cheney describes the technical arrangement of such a set.

7.   The company of Duke of Saxe-Meiningen, whose disciplined, integrated naturalistic production techniques greatly impressed both Antoine and Stanislavski.

8.   *SS,* I, pp. 191-92.

9.   Lee Simonson, *The Stage Is Set* (New York, 1932), p. 295.

10.   Mordecai Gorelik, *New Theatres for Old* (New York, 1962), p. 140.

11.   L. Leonov, "Ob upravlenii moskovskimi kazennymi teatrami," *Russkaia Mysl',* 1880, XI, as cited by Zograf, *Malyi teatr,* p. 415.

12.   John Gassner, *Directions in Modern Theatre and Drama* (New York, 1965), p. 26.

13.   A. Derman, *Moskovskogo malogo teatra aktër Shchepkin* (Moscow, 1951), p. 193.

14.   Ia. Grinval'd, *Tri veka moskovskoi stseny* (Moscow, 1949), pp.. 100-101.

15.   *SS,* I, pp. 133-34.

16.   Ibid., p. 70.

17.   Cited by Iu. D. Levin in "Na putiakh k realisticheskomu istolkovaniiu Shekspira," *Shekspir i russkaia kultura,* ed. M.P. Alekseev (Moscow-Leningrad, 1965), p. 365.

18.   Ibid., p. 317. When in 1841 the censor Nikitenko demanded of the Petersburg Censorship Committee that "improper" lines be cut from a new translation of *Henry IV,* the Committee demurred, claiming that Shakespeare was too great a writer to be so treated.

19.   Cited by Grigorii Mikhailovich Kozintsev, *Shakespeare: Time and Conscience,* trans. J. Vining (New York, 1966), p. 120.

20.   Anton Pavlovich Chekhov, *Ivanov,* in *Polnoe sobranie sochinenii i pisem* (Moscow, 1944-1951), vol XI, p. 73.

21.   Cited by Kozintsev, *Shakespeare: Time and Conscience,* p. 127.

22.   Original in the Shakespeare Centre Library, Stratford-upon-Avon, England.

23.   Aleksandr Pavlovich Lenskii, *Stat'i, pis'ma, zapiski* (Moscow, 1950), p. 125.

Chapter 2

1.   *SS,* I, p. 129.

2.   Simonson, *The Stage Is Set,* p. 287.

3.   *SS,* I, p. 129.

4.   Aleksandr Nikolaevich Ostrovskii, *Polnoe sobranie sochinenii,* vol. XII (Moscow, 1952), pp. 279-80.

5. *SS,* I, p. 130.

6. Quoted by Nikolai Efros in *K.S. Stanislavskii: Opyt kharacteristiki* (Petersburg, 1918), p. 60.

7. *SS,* I, p. 162.

8. Ibid., p. 164.

9. Ibid., pp. 164-65.

10. Ibid., p. 195.

11. Cf. *Rezhissëerskii plan "Otello" (1896),* MATM, Arkhiv K.S. Stanislavskogo.

12. Cf. the reminiscences of N.A. Popov in *O Stanislavskom. Sbornik vospominanii,* ed. Liubov' Iakovlevna Gurevich (Moscow, 1948), p. 211.

13. Aleksandr Sergeevich Pushkin, *Polnoe sobranie sochinenii,* vol. V. (Moscow-Leningrad, 1938), p. 460.

14. Elena Ivanovna Poliakova, *Stanislavskii* (Moscow, 1977), p. 115.

15. Letter from Besnard to Stanislavski, MATM, Arkhiv K.S. Stanislavskogo.

16. *SS,* VII, p. 114-15.

17. Ibid., p. 115.

18. Ibid., p. 116.

19. In MATM, Arkhiv K.S. Stanislavskogo.

20. *SS,* I, pp. 170-71.

21. Ibid., p. 173.

22. Ibid.

23. Ibid.

24. Review in MATM, Collection of Press Reviews.

25. *SS,* I, p. 174.

26. Ibid.

27. I. Rudin in *Teatral,* Moscow, 1898, vol. 4, p. 60. MATM, Collection of Press Reviews.

28. S. Vasil'ev-Flerov, in *Moskovskie vedomosti,* Moscow, 1897, No. 352. MATM, Collection of Press Reviews.

29. Program for the 1897 *Twelfth Night,* MATM, Arkhiv K.S. Stanislavskogo.

30. In *O. Stanislavskom,* p. 280-81.

31. "Naturalistic Theater and Theater of Mood," in *Chekhov. A Collection of Critical Essays,* ed. R.L. Jackson (Englewood Cliffs, New Jersey, 1967), pp. 62-68.

32. Ibid., pp. 65-66.

33. *SS,* I, p. 226.

34. Stan, Notebook, 1908-1913, in MATM, Arkhiv K.S. Stanislavskogo. Quoted by Iurii Sergeevich Kalashnikov, *Esteticheskii ideal K.S. Stanislavskogo* (Moscow, 1965), p. 187.

35.   Stan, from a ms written in the early 1900's, MATM, Arkhiv K.S. Stanislavskogo. Quoted by Kalashnikov, *Esteticheskii ideal*, p. 125.

36.   Petr Petrovich Gnedich, *Kniga zhizni* (Leningrad, 1929), p. 233.

37.   Danilov, *Ocherki po istorii*, p. 483.

38.   *SS*, I, p. 262. The "coming season" is that of 1903-04.

39.   N-D, *Teatral'noe nasledie* (Moscow, 1952 and 1954), vol. II, pp. 45-58.

40.   Ostrovskii, *Polnoe sobranie*, XII, p. 279.

41.   Lenskii, *Stat'i, pis'ma, zapiski*, p. 81.

42.   *SS*, I, p. 262.

43.   Ibid.

44.   N-D, *Teatral'noe nasledie*, II, p. 110.

45.   Ibid., p. 236.

46.   Quoted by Nikolai Nikolaevich Chushkin and B. Rostotskii, "*Iulii Tsezar*' na stsene Moskovskogo khudozhestvennogo teatra," in N-D, *Rezhissërskii plan postanovki tragedii Shekspira "Iulii Tsezar'"* (Moscow, 1964), p. 31.

47.   N-D, *Teatral'noe nasledie*, I, p. 378.

48..   N-D, "Pochemu 'Iulii Tsezar' byl sniat posle pervogo zhe sezona ogromnogo uspekha?" MATM, Arkhiv Vl. I. Nemirovicha-Danchenko. Quoted by Chushkin and Rostotskii, "*Iulii Tsezar*' na stsene Moskovskogo khudozhestvennogo teatra," p. 31.

49.   N-D, *Teatral'noe nasledie*, II, p. 121.

50.   *SS*, V, p. 461.

51.   Chushkin and Rostotskii, "*Iulii Tsezar*' na stsene Moskovskogo khudozhestvennogo teatra," p. 31.

52.   N-D, *Teatral'noe nasledie*, II, pp. 217, 222-23.

53.   N-D, *Iz proshlogo* (Moscow, 1936), p. 259.

54.   Stan, "O teatre panteone," in *SS*, VI, p. 36.

55.   *SS*, I, pp. 262-63.

56.   Ibid., p. 263.

57.   *SS*, VII, p. 258.

58.   *SS*, I, p. 263.

59.   At Chekhov's insistence, a famous general came to verify the authenticity of the costumes. Chekhov did not want any of the actors to produce the usual caricatures of provincial and military life, and supported all efforts toward natural stage behavior.

60.   N-D, *Teatral'noe nasledie*, I, pp. 378-79.

61.   *Rezhissërskii plan postanovki tragedii Shekspira "Iulii Tsezar'"* (Moscow, 1964), p. 439. Subsequent references will be cited as *Plan* and will appear in the text.

62.   N-D, *Teatral'noe nasledie*, I, pp. 243-45.

63. Chushkin and Rostotskii, "*Iulii Tsezar'* na stsene Moskovskogo khudozhestvennogo teatra," p. 34.

64. Ibid., p. 63.

65. Ibid., p. 43.

66. N-D, *Teatral'noe nasledie*, II, p. 246.

67. Ibid., I, pp. 247-48.

68. Ibid., I, pp. 250-51.

69. *SS*, I, p. 264.

70. MATM, Arkhiv VI. I. Nemirovicha-Danchenko. Quoted by Chushkin and Rostotskii, "*Iulii Tsezar'* na stsene Moskovskogo khudozhestvennogo teatra," p. 73.

71. *Ezhegodnik Moskovskogo khudozhestvennogo teatra*, 1944 (Moscow, 1946), vol. I, p. 222.

72. *SS*, VII, p. 263.

73. Quoted by Chushkin and Rostotskii, "*Iulii Tsezar'* na stsene Moskovskogo khudozhestvennogo teatra," p. 493.

74. Ibid., p. 65.

75. Ibid., p. 67.

76. Chekhov, *Polnoe sobranie*, XX, pp. 189-90.

77. Quoted by Chushkin and Rostotskii, "*Iulii Tsezar'* na stsene Moskovskogo khudozhestvennogo teatra," p. 69.

78. Ibid., p. 72.

79. Ibid.

80. N-D, *Teatral'noe nasledie*, II, pp. 246-51.

81. Ibid., I, pp. 379-80.

82. *Ezhegodnik Moskovskogo khudozhestvennogo teatra*, pp. 158-59.

83. In the reminiscences of V.P. Verigina, in *O Stanislavskom*, p. 349.

84. *Moskovskii khudozhestvennyi teatr. Istoricheskii ocherk ego zhizni i deiatel'nosti* (Moscow, 1913-1914), vol. I, p. 89.

85. Quoted by Chushkin and Rostotskii, "*Iulii Tsezar'* na stsene Moskovskogo khudozhestvennogo teatra," p. 76.

86. *O Stanislavskom*, p. 90.

87. Ibid., p. 91. Stanislavski even sacrificed his magnificent moustache for *Julius Caesar;* make-up had always managed to work around it but couldn't for Brutus, so on October 11, it was shaved off. (Make-up promised to create a fake exactly like Stanislavski's own before Stanislavski would agree to the shave. [Irina Nikolaevna Vinogradskaia, *Zhizn' i tvorchestvo K.S. Stanislavskogo: Letopis.* (Moscow, 1971-1976), vol. I, p. 429.])

88. N-D, *Teatral'noe nasledie*, II, p. 252.

89.. Ibid., I, p. 380.

90. Quoted by Chushkin and Rostotskii, *"Iulii Tsezar'* na stsene Moskovskogo khudozhestvennogo teatra," p. 80.

91. *SS,* I, p. 380.

92. Quoted by Chushkin and Rostotskii, *"Iulii Tsezar'* na stsene Moskovskogo khudozhestvennogo teatra," p. 81.

93. N. Efros, "Rim," in *Novosti Dnia,* October 2 (O.S.), 1903 (Moscow), MATM, Collection of Press Reviews.

94. N-D, *Teatral'noe nasledie,* II, pp. 253-54.

95. Leonid Mironovich Leonidov, *Vospominaniia, stat'i, besedy, perepiska, zapisnye knizhki* (Moscow, 1960), p. 113.

96. N-D, *Iz proshlogo,* p. 203.

97. Nikolai Efros, *Moskovskii khudozhestvennyi teatr 1898-1923* (Moscow, 1924), pp. 177-78.

98. Chushkin and Rostotskii, *"Iulii Tsezar'* na stsene Moskovskogo khudozhestvennogo teatra," p. 200.

99. In *Obrazovanie,* 1904, No. 4, p. 82. MATM, Collection of Press Reviews.

100. (October 26, 1903) *SS,* VII, p. 264.

101. (November 20, 1903) *Ezhegodnik MKhATa,* 1944, p. 229.

102. (November 28, 1903) *Ibid.,* p. 231.

103. S.N. Durylin, *Mariia Nikolaevna Ermolova, 1853-1928* (Moscow, 1953), p. 424.

104. In a letter to his wife, Lilina, in *O Stanislavskom,* p. 92.

105. B. Varneke, "Po povodu postanovki *Iuliia Tsezaria* na stsene Mosk. khudozhestv. teatra," *Teatr i Iskusstvo,* 1903, No. 45 November 2, (O.S.), p. 839. MATM, Collection of Press Reviews.

106. A. Belyi, "Iulii Tsezar' na stsene khudozhestvennogo teatra," *Mir Iskusstva,* 1903, No. 12, p. 22. MATM, Collection of Press Reviews.

107. V. Mirovich, "Pervoe predstavlenie *Iuliia Tsezaria* v khudozhestvennom teatre," *Mir Iskusstva,* 1903, No. 12, p. 24. MATM, Collection of Press Reviews.

108. S. Diagilev, "Eshche o *Iulie Tsezare," Mir Kskusstva,* 1903, No. 12, p. 28. MATM, Collection of Press Reviews.

109. In *Obrazovanie,* 1904, No. 4, p. 87. MATM, Collection of Press Reviews.

110. Date given for *Julius Caesar* by E.K. Chambers, *Shakespeare: A Survey* (New York, 1958), p. 146.

111. L. Freidkina, *Dni i gody VI. I. Nemirovicha-Danchenko. Letopis zhizni i tvorchestva* (Moscow, 1962), p. 190.

112. Garofa, "Otkliki mimoidushchego," *Kur'er,* 1903, October 5 (O.S.), MATM, Collection of Press Reviews.

113. N-D, *Iz proshlogo,* p. 204.

114. Ibid., p. 205.

115. Ibid.

116. Vsevolod Emil'evich Meierkhol'd, *O teatre* (St. Petersburg, 1913), p. 16.

117. *SS*, I, p. 265.

Chapter 3

1. *SS*, I, p. 278.

2. Ibid..

3. Ibid., p. 281.

4. Ibid., p. 285.

5. Ibid., p. 286.

6. MATM, Arkhiv K.S. Stanislavskogo. From an unpublished fragment of *Moia zhizn' v iskusstve (My Life in Art)*, quoted by Kalashnikov, *Esteticheskii ideal*, p. 199.

7. *SS*, VI, p. 204.

8. Ibid., I, p. 295.

9. Irina Nikolaevna Vinogradskaia, *Zhizn' i tvorchestvo K.S. Stanislavskogo: Letopis.* (Moscow, 1971-1976), vol. II, p. 33.

10. *SS*, I, p. 301.

11. Ibid., p. 304.

12. Ibid., p. 305.

13. Ibid., p. 334.

14. Ibid.

15. Ibid., VII, p. 378.

16. Ibid., I, p. 334.

17. Entitled *Stsenicheskoe iskusstvo*, it was published in St. Petersburg in 1906.

18. In E. Gordon Craig, *On the Art of the Theatre* (Chicago, 1911), p. 138.

19. Ibid., p. 180.

20. Ibid., p. 178.

21. Ibid., p. 81.

22. Denis Bablet, *Edward Gordon Craig*, trans. Daphne Woodward (New York, 1966), pp. 109-10.

23. From his "Note on Masks," published in *The Mask* one month before "The Actor and the Über-marionette."

24. *Moskovskii khudozhestvennyi teatr. Istoricheskii ocherk ego zhizni i deiatel'nosti*, vol. II, p. 97.

25. MATM, Arkhiv K.S. Stanislavskogo. Published in Laurence Senelick, *Gordon Craig's Moscow "Hamlet"* (Westport, Connecticut, 1982), p. 16.

26. Craig, *On the Art of the Theater*, p. 285.

27. Stan, *Stat'i, rechi, besedy, pis'ma* (Moscow, 1953), p. 204.

28. Craig, *Catalogue of an Exhibition of Drawings and Models for "Hamlet" and Other Plays* (London, 1912), p. 6.

29. Senelick, *Gordon Craig's Moscow "Hamlet,"* p. 21.

30. *SS,* I, p. 336.

31. Bablet, *Edward Gordon Craig,* pp. 122-23.

32. Craig, *Scene* (London, 1923), p. 20.

33. Quoted by Bablet, *Edward Gordon Craig,* p. 130.

34. *SS,* VII, p. 414.

35. Marina Nikolaevna Stroeva, *Rezhissërskie iskaniia Stanislavskogo* (Moscow, 1973 and 1977), vol. I, p. 266, from MATM, Arkhiv K.S. Stanislavskogo. "Obshchie zamechaniia Kreg," Notebook 1.

36. Gordon Craig Collection, Bibliothèque de l'Arsenal, Paris. Published by Senelick, *Gordon Craig's Moscow "Hamlet,"* p. 64.

37. "Gamlet, Publikatsiia materialov k postanovke spektaklia v Moskovskom khudozhestvennom teatre—1911 g." *Ezhegodnik Moskovskogo Teatra,* p. 651.

38. Gordon Craig Collection, published in Senelick, *Gordon Craig's Moscow "Hamlet,"* p. 64.

39. Ibid.

40. Ibid.

41. Craig, *Books and Theatres* (London and Toronto, 1925), p. 148.

42. Gordon Craig Collection, published by Senelick, *Gordon Craig's Moscow "Hamlet,"* p. 75.

43. Ibid., p. 64-65.

44. "Beseda G. Krega s ispoliteliami *Gamleta,*" March 30, 1910. MATM, Arkhiv K.S. Stanislavskogo.

45. "Stanislavski on Hamlet," *Daily Worker* (New York, October 24, 1938).

46. "Beseda G. Krega s ispolniteliami *Gamleta.*"

47. Gordon Craig Collection, published by Senelick, *Gordon Craig's Moscow "Hamlet,"* pp. 68-69.

48. *SS,* VII, p. 430.

49. Ibid.

50. Senelick, *Gordon Craig's Moscow "Hamlet,"* p. 109.

51. In the Leningradskii gosudarstvennyi teatral'nyi muzei, Fond zvukozapisei.

52. *SS,* VII, p. 430.

53. Edward Craig, *Gordon Craig. The Story of His Life* (New York, 1968), p. 253.

54. *SS,* VII, p. 433.

55. Gordon Craig, *On the Art of the Theatre,* p. 133.

56. MATM, Arkhiv K.S. Stanislavskogo

57. In his letter of February 19 (i.e. March 4), 1911, to L.A. Sulerzhitski, *SS,* VII, p. 515.

58. MATM, Arkhiv K.S. Stanislavskogo.

59.. Bablet, *Edward Gordon Craig,* pp. 149-50.

60. Later to be one of Russia's most prominent actresses.

61. Alisa Koonen, "Stranitsy iz zhizni," VI in *Teatr,* Moscow, Moscow, 1967, No. 10, pp. 77-78.

62. Bablet, *Edward Gordon Craig,* p. 150.

63. Koonen, "Stranitsy iz zhizni," p. 79.

64. Stanislavski put it bluntly: "They found it hard to work with me, and I found it hard to work with them." *SS,* I, p. 348.

65. Senelick, *Gordon Craig's Moscow "Hamlet,"* p. 108.

66. MATM, Arkhiv K.S. Stanislavskogo, quoted by Senelick, *Gordon Craig's Moscow "Hamlet,"* p. 116.

67. *Moskovskii khudozhestvennyi teatr. Istoricheskii ocherk,* p. 99.

68. *SS,* VII, p. 463-64.

69. Letter from Stanislavski to Craig, July 4, 1910, MATM, Arkhiv K.S. Stanislavskogo.

70. Leopol'd Antonovich Sulerzhitskii, *Povesti i rasskazy, stat'i i zametki o teatre, perepiska, vospominaniia o L.A. Sulerzhitskom* (Moscow, 1970), p. 457.

71. Vinogradskaia, *Zhizn' i tvorchestvo,* II, pp. 248-49.

72. Senelick, *Gordon Craig's Moscow "Hamlet,"* pp. 119-20.

73. *SS,* VII, p. 495.

74. Ibid., p. 506.

75. This correspondence, from *SS,* VII, pp. 505-7, 511-12, and 515, and Sulerzhitskii, *Povesti i rasskazy,* pp. 480 and 478-79, is reproduced in translation in Senelick, *Gordon Craig's Moscow "Hamlet,"* pp. 124-29.

76. *SS,* VII, p. 516.

77. Edward Craig, *Gordon Craig,* p. 259.

78. Stroeva, *Rezhissërskie iskaniia,* I, p. 279.

79. Vinogradskaia, *Zhizn' i tvorchestvo,* II, p. 223.

80. *SS,* VII, p. 464.

81. Described by Stroeva, *Rezhissërskie iskaniia,* I, p. 245.

82. Vinogradskaia, *Zhizn' i tvorchestvo,* II, p. 307.

83. Ibid., II, p. 312.

84. Serafima Germanovna Birman, *Put' aktrisy* (Moscow, 1959), p. 47.

85. "Beseda o *Gamleta* s truppoi MKhT, 23 marta (O.S.) 1911 g.," MATM, Arkhiv K.S. Stanislavskogo.

86. *SS,* VII, p. 523.

87. Ibid., VII, p. 532.

88. K.A. Mardzhanishvili, *Tvorcheskoe nasledie: vospominaniia, stat'i i doklady* (Tbilisi, 1958), p. 57.

89. Vinogradskaia, *Zhizn' i tvorchestvo,* II, p. 310.

90. Ibid.

91. Although this story was published in the *Ezhegodnik Moskovskogo khudozhestvennogo teatra, 1948* (Moscow 1951), vol. II, pp. 476-77, no Soviet scholar has referred to it when discussing the "scandal," but rather base their discussion on Birman's and Simov's accounts of the dress rehearsal argument about lighting. Senelick cites the incident cautiously, noting that "it accords well with the barring of Craig from the theatre and his subsequent attitude." *Gordon Craig's Moscow "Hamlet,"* p. 215)

92. Koonen, "Stranitsy iz zhizni," p. 78.

93. Vinogradskaia, *Zhizn' i tvorchestvo,* II, p. 309.

94. This is the "scandal" usually discussed, as taken from Birman, *Put' aktrisy,* p. 56, and Simov (as quoted by Chushkin, *Gamlet-Kachalov: Iz stsenicheskoi istorii "Gamleta" Shekspira* [Moscow, 1966] p. 331).

95. Koonen, "Stranitsy iz zhizni," p. 79.

96. However, until Stroeva's evenhanded treatment of Craig in *Rezhissërskie iskaniia* in 1972, most Soviet theater historians, notably Chushkin, saw Craig as the source of all of *Hamlet's* problems and blamed him alone for the discord that arose as the premiere drew nearer.

97. According to Vadim Vasil'evich Shverubovich, interviewed in Moscow on April 15, 1966.

98. Koonen, "Stranitsy iz zhizni," p. 79.

99. Ibid.

100. *SS,* I, p. 345.

101. Laurence Senelick has done a masterful job in his book, *Gordon Craig's Moscow "Hamlet,"* using many of these materials.

102. *SS,* VII, p. 732.

103. MATM, Collection of Press Reviews.

104. *SS,* I, p. 342.

105. *Novaia Zhizn',* MATM, Collection of Press Reviews.

106. *SS,* I, p. 340.

107. Ibid., I, p. 341. This accords well with the rehearsal notes published in Vinogradskaia, *Zhizn'i tvorchestvo,* II, pp. 308-9.

108. Senelick, *Gordon Craig's Moscow "Hamlet,"* p. 167.

109. Russkie Vedomosti, Moscow, Jan. 6, 1912 (O.S.). MATM, Collection of Press Reviews.

110. Koonen, "Stranitsy iz zhizni," p. 81.

111. Summary of the scores of reviews appearing in Russian newspapers and journals in 1912. Complete collection in MATM, Collection of Press Reviews.

112. Ibid.

113. V. Briusov, "Gamlet v Moskovskom khudozhestvennom teatre," MATM, Collection of Press Reviews.

114.. *SS*, I, p. 346.

115. Ibid., VII, p. 489.

116. As printed in a Russian translation by M. Lykiardopoulo in *Russkoe Slovo*, December 24, 1911 (O.S.). MATM, Collection of Press Reviews.

117. Gordon Craig, *A production, being thirty-one collotype plates of designs projected or realized for "The Pretenders" of Henrik Ibsen, and produced at the Royal Theatre, Copenhagen, 1926* (London, 1930), p. 5.

118. Stroeva, *Rezhissërskie iskaniia*, I, p. 264.

Chapter 4

1. Birman, *Put' aktrisy*, p. 134.

2. As described by Vadim Vasil'evich Shverubovich in an interview on April 15, 1966.

3. Vinogradskaia, *Zhizn' i tvorchestvo*, III, p. 88.

4. Birman, *Put' aktrisy*, p. 134.

5. *Tvorchestvo aktëra i teoriia Stanislavskogo* by Fëdor Fëdorovich Komissarzhevskii was published in Petrograd in 1916.

6.. Stroeva, *Rezhissërskie iskaniia*, II, p. 15..

7. The first of these was set in Orsino's palace—a drapery of Renaissance tapestries, carelessly tossed over a throne, up right. A blue curtain, left, swung fanlike to the right on a movable pivot, up center, to reveal the second scene: a bit of seashore, with a glow from a beach fire illuminating the faces of Sebastian and Antonio. Scene 3 was a cave, and 4 was the Duke's palace once more. The fifth episode took place at Olivia's house, worked in delicately carved lattices and mullioned windows. The delicacy of the latticework was carried over into the costumes, which were an attempt at Elizabethan dress. Episode 6 took place at the Duke's palace, and was followed by an intermission.

   Scene 7 was an outside entrance to Olivia's house, and the set consisted of a single heavy door whose upper half was crossbarred, plus a bench and a lamppost. Olivia's cellar, the next scene, was suggested by stairs, right, and assorted baggage and the barrel into which Malvolio was wedged at one point. A short street scene was followed by an episode in Olivia's garden, for which almost the entire stage was used. A low wall, up left, with robes thrown over it to break its severe line, ended at right in an arched passageway into the house. Columns of the same carved latticework seen previously stood in front of the house.

   After another intermission, the curtain rose on a corner of the same garden, in which a little of the wall was visible. Covering the entire left part of the stage, however, was a raised platform behind which was a covered passageway in which Malvolio disported himself. Several street scenes comprised the twelfth episode: the set was dominated by the dark blue curtains, in front of which the street began up right, past the house and out into the foyer, left. A single window frame, center, indicated a corner of Olivia's house. The stage was richly decorated for the reunion scene of the thirteenth episode, but still set in suggestive bits rather than as a realistic environment.

8. David Magarshack, *Stanislavsky: a Life* (New York, 1951), p. 350.

9. *O Stanislavskom,* p. 170.

10. "Soviet's War on Art," December 18, 1928.

11. Vinogradskaia, *Zhizn' i tvorchestvo,* IV, p. 178.

12. Ibid., IV, p. 205.

13. *SS,* VIII, p. 191.

14. One analogy of Leonidov's (the train and the rails) was praised by Stanislavski at the time, and was eventually used in *Creating a Role* (*SS,* IV, pp. 335-36).

15. *SS,* VIII, pp. 205-6.

16. Leonidov, *Vospominaniia, stat'i,* p. 325.

17. Stan, *Rezhissërskii plan "Otello"* (Moscow-Leningrad, 1945), p. 6.

18.. See Boris Isaakovich Zingerman, "Analiz rezhissërskogo plana 'Otello' K. Stanislavskogo" in *Shekspirovskii sbornik,* ed. A.A. Anikst and A.L. Shtein (Moscow, 1958), pp. 364-96, for a thorough presentation of this point.

19. *SS,* VIII, p. 242.

20. Leonidov, *Vospominaniia, stat'i,* p. 332.

21. Ibid., p. 338.

22. Ibid., p. 342.

23. See V.G. Sakhnovskii's letter to Leonidov, Ibid., pp. 339-40.

24. Vinogradskaia, *Zhizn' i tvorchestvo,* IV, p. 200.

25. Ibid., IV, p. 201.

Chapter 5

1. *SS,* I, p. 270.

2. Ibid.

Bibliography

Books and Articles

Abalkin, Nikolai Aleksandrovich, ed. *Nasledie Stanislavskogo i praktika sovetskogo teatra.* Moscow, 1953.

———. *Sistema Stanislavskogo i sovetskii teatr.* Moscow, 1954.

Aikhenval'd Iurii et al. *V sporakh o teatre: Sbornik statei.* Moscow, 1910.

Akademiia nauk SSSR, Institut istorii iskusstv. *K.S. Stanislavskii: Materialy, pis'ma, issledovaniia.* Moscow, 1955.

Alekseev, M.P., ed. *Shekspir i russkaia kultura.* Moscow-Leningrad, 1965.

Alpers, Boris Vladimirovich. *Aktërskoe iskusstvo v Rossii.* Moscow, 1945.

———. *Mikhail Semënovich Shchepkin (1788-1863).* Moscow-Leningrad, 1943.

Altaev, A. *Ot tsepei k slave: Kartiny iz zhizni artista M.S. Shchepkina.* Petersburg, 1920.

Amfiteatrov, Aleksandr Valentinovich. "Aleksandr Pavlovich Lenskii." In *Gallereia stsenicheskikh deiatelei,* Vol. I, Moscow, (1915).

———. *Znakomyia muzy.* Paris, 1928.

Arapov, Pimen. *Letopis' russkago teatra.* St. Petersburg, 1861.

Aseev, B.N. *Russkii dramaticheskii teatr XVII–XVIII vekov.* Moscow, 1958.

Ashukin, Nikolai Sergeevich. *Khrestomatiia po istorii russkogo teatra XVIII i XIX vekov.* Moscow-Leningrad, 1940.

Bablet, Denis. *Edward Gordon Craig.* Trans. Daphne Woodward. New York, 1966.

Bakshy, Aleksandr. *The Path of the Modern Russian Stage.* London, 1916.

Belinskii, Vissarion Grigor'evich. *Polnoe sobranie sochinenii,* Vol. II. Moscow, 1953.

Beskin, Emmanuil Martynovich. *Istoriia russkogo teatra.* Moscow-Leningrad, 1928.

Birman, Serafima Germanovna. *Put' aktrisy.* Moscow, 1959.

———. *Trud aktëra.* Moscow, 1939.

——— and Giatsintova, Sof'ia Vladimirovna. *Tvorcheskie besedy masterov teatra,* Vol. VIII-IX. Moscow-Leningrad, 1939.

Bibikov, I. *Iulii Tsezar' v istorii i na stsene v postanovke M X T-a.* Moscow, 1904.

Blok, Vl. *Sistema Stanislavskogo i problemy dramaturgii.* Moscow, 1963.

Brodskii, Aleksandr, ed. *M.N. Ermolova.* Leningrad, 1925.

———. *Moskovkii Malyi Teatr, 1824–1924.* Moscow, 1924.

Bulgakov, A.S. "Rannee znakomstvo s Shekspirom v Rossii." In Gosudarstvennyi akademicheskii teatr dramy. *Teatral'noe nasledstvo,* I. Leningrad, 1934.

Chambers, E.K. *Shakespeare: A Survey.* 1925; rpt. New York, 1958.

Chekhov, Anton Pavlovich. *Polnoe sobranie sochinenii i pisem,* Vols. XI and XX. Moscow, 1948 and 1951.

Cheney, Sheldon. *Stage decoration.* New York, 1928.

Chushkin, Nikolai Nikolaevich. *Gamlet-Kachalov: Iz stsenicheskoi istorii "Gamleta" Shekspira.* Moscow, 1966.

_____, ed. *Moskovskii khudozhestvennyi teatr,* Vol. I: 1898-1917. Moscow, 1955.

_____ and B. Rostotskii. *"Iulii Tsezar'* na stsene Moskovskogo Khudozhestvennogo Teatra," in Nemirovich-Danchenko, Vladimir Ivanovich. *Rezhissërskii plan postanovki tragedii Shekspira "Iulii Tsezar'."* Moscow, 1964, pp. 5-200.

Craig, Edward. *Gordon Craig. The Story of His Life.* New York, 1968.

Craig, Edward Gordon. *Books and Theatres.* London-Toronto, 1925.

_____. *Catalogue of an Exhibition of Drawings and Models for "Hamlet" and Other Plays.* London, 1912.

_____. *Index to the Story of My Days; Some Memoirs.* New York, 1957.

_____. "Kto Gamlet: uchenik ili neudachnik?" Trans. M. L-o. *Studiia,* 1911, No. 9, p. 3.

_____. *A Living Theatre.* Florence, 1913.

_____. *On Eight Pages from the Story of the Theatre by Glenn Hughes.* Seattle, 1931.

_____. *A production, being thirty-two collotype plates of designs projected or realized for "The Pretenders" of Henrik Ibsen, and produced at the Royal Theatre, Copenhagen 1926.* London, 1930.

_____. *Scene.* London, 1923.

_____. *Stsenicheskoe iskusstvo.* No trans. given. St. Petersburg, 1906.

_____. *On the Art of the Theatre.* Chicago, 1912.

_____. *The Art of the Theatre.* London, 1905.

_____. *The Theatre—Advancing.* Boston, 1919.

_____. *Towards a New Theatre.* London-Toronto, 1913.

Danilov, Sergei Sergeevich. *Mikhail Semënovich Shchepkin (1788-1938): K 150-letiiu so dnia rozhdeniia.* Moscow-Leningrad, 1938.

_____. *Ocherki po istorii russkogo dramaticheskogo teatra.* Moscow, 1948.

_____. *Russkii dramaticheskii teatr XIX veka.* Leningrad, 1957.

Derman, A. *Moskovskogo Malogo teatra aktër Shchepkin.* Moscow, 1951.

Desnitskii, V.A., ed. *Klassiki russkoi dramy.* Leningrad, 1940.

Dmitriev, Iu. *Mochalov, aktër-romantik.* Moscow, 1961.

_____ and Klinchin, A., comp. *Pavel Stepanovich Mochalov.* Moscow, 1953.

Doroshevich, V.M. *Staraia teatral'naia Moskva.* Petrograd, 1923.

Dramaticheskoi slovar'. Moscow, 1787.

Drizen, Nikolai Vasil'evich. *Dramaticheskaia tsenzura dvukh epokh, 1825-1881.* Petrograd, 1917.

_____. *Materialy k istorii russkago teatra.* Moscow, 1905.

_____. *Stopiatidesiatiletie Imperatorskikh Sanktpeterburgskikh Teatrov.* St. Petersburg, 1906.

_____. *Sorok let teatra: Vospominaniia 1875-1915.* St. Petersburg, (1916?).

Durylin, S.N. *Mariia Nikolaevna Ermolova, 1853-1928.* Moscow, 1953.

_____. *Mastera M.Kh.A.T.-a.* Moscow-Leningrad, 1939.

Efros, Nikolai. *K.S. Stanislavskii: Opyt kharakteristiki.* Petersburg, 1918.

_____. *M.S. Shchepkin: Opyt kharakteristiki.* Petersburg, 1920.

_____. *Moskovskii khudozhestvennyi teatr, 1898-1923.* Moscow-Petersburg, 1924.

_____. *V.I. Kachalov, fragment.* Petersburg, 1919.

Ezhegodnik Moskovskogo khudozhestvennogo teatra, 1944. Moscow, 1946.

Ezhegodnik Moskovskogo khudozhestvennogo teatra, 1948. Moscow, 1951.

Fedotova, Glikeriia Nikolaevna. *G.N. Fedotova: 25 let na stsene Malogo teatra.* Moscow, 1887.

Filippov, Vl. *Malyi teatr.* Moscow, 1928.

Fovitzky, A.L. *The Moscow Art Theatre and its Distinguishing Characteristics.* New York, 1922.

Freidkina, L.M. *Dni i gody Vl. I. Nemirovicha-Danchenko.* Moscow, 1962.

_____. *Vladimir Ivanovich Nemirovich-Danchenko (1858-1943).* Moscow-Leningrad, 1945.

Gassner, John. *Directions in Modern Theater and Drama.* New York, 1956.

Giliarovskaia, Nadezhda Vladimirovna. *Teatral'no-dekoratsionnoe iskusstvo za 5 let*. Kazan', 1924.

Gnedich, Petr Petrovich. *Kniga zhizni*. Leningrad, 1929.

Gorchakov, Nikolai Mikhailovich. *Rezhissërskie uroki K.S. Stanislavskogo*. Moscow, 1950.

_____. *Stanislavski Directs*. Trans. Miriam Goldina. New York, 1954.

Gorelik, Mordecai. *New Theatres for Old*. New York, 1962.

Gourfinkel, Nina. *Constantin Stanislavski*. Paris, 1955.

Gregor, Joseph. "Edward Gordon Craigs Hamlet." In *Phaidros*. Vienna, 1947, Folge 2, pp. 153-75.

_____ and Fülöp-Miller, René. *Das russische theater*. Zurich-Leipzig-Vienna, 1928.

Gremislavskii, Ivan Iakovlevich. *Kompositsiia stsenicheskogo prostranstva v tvorcchestve V.A. Simova*. Moscow, 1953.

_____. *Sbornik statei i materialov*. Ed. A.G. Guliev. Moscow, 1967.

Grindval'd, Ia. *Tri veka Moskovskoi stseny*. Moscow, 1949.

Gurevich, Liubov' Iakovlevna. *Istoriia russkogo teatral'nogo opyta*. Moscow-Leningrad, 1939.

_____. *Comp. and ed. O Stanislavskom: Sbornik vospominanii*. Moscow, 1948.

Gzovskaia, Ol'ga Vladimirovna. *Puti i pereput'ia. Portrety, Stat'i i vospominaniia ob O.V. Gzovskoi*. Moscow, 1976.

Iartsev, A.A. *M.S. Shchepkin, ego zhizni i stsenicheskaia deiatel'nost' v sviazi s" istoriei sovremennago emu teatra*. St. Petersburg, 1893.

Ignatov, I.N. *Pavel Stepanovich Mochalov*. Petersburg, 1922.

Iur'ev, Iurii Mikhailovich. *Tvorcheskaia beseda s molodymi aktërami*. Leningrad, 1939.

_____. *Zapiski 1872-1893*. 2 vols. Moscow-Leningrad, 1939 and 1945.

Iuzhin-Sumbatov, Aleksandr Ivanovich. *Zapisi, stat'i, pis'ma*. Ed. V. Filippova. Moscow, 1951.

Kachalov, Vasilii Ivanovich. *Sbornik statei, vospominanii, pisem*. Comp. and ed. V. Ia. Vilenkin. Moscow, 1954.

Kalashnikov, Iurii Sergeevich. *Esteticheskii ideal K.S. Stanislavskogo*. Moscow, 1965.

_____. *Teatr budushchego; sistema K.S. Stanislavskogo, metod realisticheskogo tvorchestva*. Moscow, 1962.

Kizevetter, Aleksandr Aleksandrovich. *M.S. Shchepkin: Episod iz istorii russkogo stsenicheskogo iskusstva*. Prague, 1925.

_____. *Teatr*. Moscow, 1922.

Knebel', Mariia Osipovna. *Slovo v tvorchestve aktëra*. Moscow, 1964.

Komissarzhevskii, F. *Tvorchestvo aktëra i teoriia Stanislavskogo*. Petrograd, 1916.

Koonen, Alisa Georgievna. "Stranitsy iz zhizni," VI. In *Teatr*. Moscow, 1967, No. 10, pp. 77-91.

Kozintsev, Grigorii Mikhailovich. *Shakespeare: Time and Conscience*. Trans. J. Vining. New York, 1966.

Kristi, G. *K.S. Stanislavskii*. (Moscow), 1962.

Kugel', Aleksandr Rafailovich. (Homo Novus). *Teatral'nye portrety*. Petrograd, 1923.

_____. *Utverzhdenie teatra*. (Moscow, 1923).

_____. *V. Kachalov: Zhizn' i tvorchestvo*. Moscow, 1927.

_____ and Filippov, V., eds. *Sto let Malomu teatru*. Moscow, n. d.

Lavrent'eva, S.I. *Perezhitoe*. St. Petersburg, 1914.

Leeper, Janet. *Edward Gordon Craig, Designs for the Theatre*. Harmondworth, Middlesex, 1948.

Lenskii, Aleksandr Pavlovich. *Stat'i, pis'ma, zapiski*. Moscow, 1950.

Leonidov, Leonid Mironovich. *Proshloe i nastoiashchee: iz vospominanii*. Moscow, 1948.

_____. *Vospominaniia, stat'i, besedy, perepiska, zapisnye knizhki*. Comp. and ed. V. Ia. Vilenkin. Moscow, 1960.

Leont'evskii, Nikolai, comp. *Mariia Petrovna Lilina*. Moscow, 1960.

Lirondelle, André. *Shakespeare en Russie 1748-1840*. Paris, 1912.

Lunacharskii, Anatolii Vasil'evich et al. *Teatr, kniga o novom teatre: Sbornik statei*. St. Petersburg, 1908.

Macdougall, Allen Ross. *Isadora: A Revolutionary in Art and Love.* New York, 1960.

Magarshack, David. *Stanislavsky: a Life.* New York, 1951.

Mardzhanishvili, K.A. *Tvorcheskoe nasledie: vospominaniia, stat'i i doklady.* Tbilisi, 1958.

Markov, Pavel Aleksandrovich. *Noveishie teatral'nye techeniia, 1898-1923.* Moscow, 1924.

──────. *Pravda teatra.* Moscow, 1965.

──────and Chushkin, N. *Moskovskii khudozhestvennyi teatr 1898-1948.* Moscow-Leningrad, 1950.

Markov, V.D. *Kratkaia istoriia teatra.* Moscow, 1929.

Marotti, Ferruccio. *Edward Gordon Craig.* (Bologna, 1961).

Meyerhold, V.E. "Naturalistic Theater and Theater of Mood." In *Chekhov. A Collection of Critical Essays.* Ed. Robert L. Jackson. Englewood Cliffs, N.J., 1967, pp. 62-68.

Meierkhol'd, Vsevolod Emil'evich. *O teatre.* St. Petersburg, 1913.

Melik-Zakharov, Sergei Vaganovich, and Bogatyrev, Sh. Sh., comps. *Stanislavskii: Pisateli, artisty, rezhissëry o velikom deiatele russkogo teatra.* Moscow, 1963.

Morozov, Mikhail Mikhailovich, ed. *Mastera teatra v obrazakh Shekspira: Sbornik.* Moscow-Leningrad, 1939.

Morozov, Petr Osipovich. *Istoriia russkago teatra.* St. Petersburg, 1889.

Moskovskii khudozhestvennyi teatr. Moscow, 1955.

Moskovskii khudozhestvennyi teatr: istoricheskii ocherk ego zhizni i deiatel'nosti. 2 vols. Moscow, 1913 and 1914.

Moskovskii khudozhestvennyi teatr v illiustratsiiakh i dokumentakh 1898-1938. 2 vols. Moscow, 1938 and 1945.

Moskovskii Malyi teatr, 1824-1924. (Moscow, 192 ?)

Nemirovich-Danchenko, Vladimir Ivanovich. *Iz proshlogo.* (Moscow), 1936.

──────. *Izbrannye pis'ma v dvukh tomakh (1879-1943),* Moscow, 1979.

──────. *My Life in the Russian Theatre.* Trans. John Cournos. London, 1937.

──────. *Rezhissërskii plan postanovki tragedii Shakspira Iulii Tsezar', M Kh t, 1903 god.* Comp. and ed. N.N. Chushkin and B. Rostotskii. Moscow, 1964.

──────. *Teatral'noe nasledie.* 2 vols. Moscow, 1952 and 1954.

Novitskii, Pavel Ivanovich. *Sovremennye teatral'nye sistemy.* (Moscow), 1933.

Ostrovskii, Aleksandr Nikolaevich. *Polnoe sobranie sochinenii,* Vol. XII. Moscow, 1952.

Poliakova, Elena Ivanovna. *Stanislavskii.* Moscow, 1977.

──────. *Stanislavskii—aktër.* Moscow, 1972.

Prokof'ev, Vladimir Nikolaevich. *V sporakh o Stanislavskom.* Moscow, 1962.

Prygunov, M.D. *Russkaia stsena na poslednie sorok let, 1880-1920 gg.* Kazan', 1921.

Pushkin, Aleksandr Sergeevich. "Table talk." In *Polnoe sobranie sochinenii,* Vol. V. Moscow-Leningrad, 1938, pp. 458-60.

Rodina, Tat'iana Mikhailovna. *Russkoe teatral'noe iskusstvo v nachale XIX veka.* Moscow, 1961.

Rose, Enid. *Gordon Craig and the Theatre.* New York, 1931.

Saylor, Oliver. *Inside the Moscow Art Theatre.* New York, 1925.

Senelick, Laurence. *Gordon Craig's Moscow "Hamlet."* Westport, Connecticut, 1982.

Shchepkin, Mikhail Semënovich. *Zapiski aktëra Shchepkina.* Ed. A.B. Derman. Moscow, 1938.

──────. *Zapiski i pis'ma.* Moscow, 1864.

──────. *Zapiski, pis'ma; sovremenniki o M.S. Shchepkine.* Moscow, 1952.

Sheringham, George. *Designs in the Theatre.* London, 1927.

Simonov, P.V. *Metod K.S. Stanislavskogo i fiziologiia emotsii.* Moscow, 1962.

Simonson, Lee. *The Stage Is Set.* New York, 1932.

Slonim, Marc. *Russian Theater.* Cleveland, 1961.

Sobolev, Iurii Vasil'evich. *Moskovskii khudozhestvennyi teatr: Ocherki.* Moscow-Leningrad, 1938.

Sobolev, Iurii Vasil'evich. *Pavel Mochalov.* Moscow, 1937.

_____. *Vl. I. Nemirovich-Danchenko.* Petersburg, 1918.

Stanislavskii, Konstantin Sergeevich. *An Actor Prepares.* Trans. Elizabeth Reynolds Hapgood, introd. John Gielgud. New York, 1948.

_____. "Beseda K.S. Stanislavskogo s Gordonom Kregom, zapisannaia L.A. Sulerzhitskim, o 'Gamlete'. Beseda 10 apr. 1909 g." In *Teatr i dramaturgiia.* Moscow, 1934, No. 3, p. 131.

_____. *Besedy K.S. Stanislavskogo.* Ed. L. Ia. Gurevich. Moscow-Leningrad, 1939.

_____. *Building a Character.* Trans. Elizabeth Reynolds Hapgood, introd. Joshua Logan. New York, 1949.

_____. *Creating a Role.* Trans. Elizabeth Reynolds Hapgood, ed. Hermine I. Popper, introd. Robert Lewis. New York, 1961.

_____. *Khudozhestvennye zapisi, 1877-1892.* Ed. L. Ia. Gurevich. Moscow, 1939.

_____. *My Life in Art.* Trans. J.J. Robbins. Boston, 1924.

_____. *My Life in Art.* Trans. G. Ivanov-Mumjiev. Moscow, n.d.

_____. *Rezhissërskii plan "Otello."* Ed. N. Zograf. Moscow-Leningrad, 1945.

_____. *Stanislavsky Produces Othello.* Trans. Helen Nowak. London, 1948.

_____. *Sobranie sochinenii v vos'mi tomakh.* Ed. M.N. Kedrov. 8 vols. Moscow, 1954-1961.

_____. *Stat'i, rechi, besedy, pis'ma.* Comp. G. Kristi and N. Chushkin, introd. Vl. Prokof'ev. Moscow, 1953.

"Stanislavski on Hamlet." *The Daily Worker,* New York, Oct. 4, 1938.

Stroeva, Marina Nikolaevna. *Rezhissërskie iskaniia Stanislavskogo.* 2 vols. Moscow, 1973 and 1977.

Sulerzhitskii, Leopol'd Antonovich, *Povesti i rasskazy, stat'i i zametki o teatre, perepiska, vospominaniia o L.A. Sulerzhitskom.* Moscow, 1970.

Syrkina, Flora Iakovlevna. *Russkoe teatral'no-dekoratsionnoe iskusstvo vtoroi poloviny XIX veka.* Moscow, 1956.

Talanov, Aleksandr Viktorovich. *Kachalov.* Moscow, 1962.

Tal'nikov, D. *Sistema Shchepkina.* Moscow-Leningrad, 1939.

Tanieev, S.V. *Iz proshlogo imperatorskikh teatrov.* 5 Vols. St. Petersburg, 1885-1890.

Teliakovskii, V.A. *Vospominaniia (1898-1917).* Petersburg, 1924.

Toporkov, Vasilii Osipovich. *Chetyre ocherka o K.S. Stanislavskom.* Moscow, 1963.

_____. *K.S. Stanislavskii na repetitsii: Vospominaniia.* Moscow, 1950.

Tsimbal, Sergei L'vovich. *Teatral'naia novizna i teatral'naia sovremennost'.* (Leningrad), 1964.

Tsinkovich, V.A. "Narodnyi teatr i dramaticheskaia tsenzura," in *Teatral'noe nasledstvo: Soobshcheniia; Publikatsii.* Moscow, 1956, pp. 375-401.

Turovskaia, M. *Ol'ga Leonardovna Knipper-Chekhova, 1868-1959.* Moscow, 1959.

Vakhtangov, Evgenii Bagratsionovich. *Zapiski, pis'ma, stat'i.* Moscow-Leningrad, 1939.

Varneke, Boris Vasil'evich. *Istoriia russkogo teatra XVII–XIX vekov.* 3rd ed. Moscow, 1939.

Vilenkin, Vitalii Iakovlevich. *I.M. Moskvin na stsene Moskovskogo khudozhestvennogo teatra.* Moscow, 1946.

_____. *Kachalov.* Moscow, 1962.

_____. *V.I. Nemirovich-Danchenko: Ocherk tvorchestva.* Moscow 1941.

Vinogradskaia, Irina Nikolaevna. *Zhizn' i tvorchestvo K.S. Stanislavskogo: Letopis.* 4 vols. Moscow, 1971-1976.

Vlasov, V.N., comp. *Voprosy rezhissury, sbornik statei rezhissërov sovetskogo teatra.* Moscow, 1954.

Vol'kenshtein, Vladimir Mikhailovich. *Stanislavskii.* 2nd ed. Leningrad, 1927.

Volkov, Nikolai. *Meierkhol'd.* Vol. I: 1874-1908. Moscow-Leningrad, 1929.

Vsevolodskii-Gerngross, Vsevolod Nikolaevich. *Istoriia russkogo teatra.* Moscow-Leningrad, 1929.

_____. *Istoriia teatral'nogo obrazovaniia v Rossii.* Vol. I XVII–XVIII vv. St. Petersburg, 1913.

_____. *Khrestomatiia po istorii russkogo teatra.* Moscow, 1936.

Zingerman, Boris Isaakovich. "Analiz rezhissërskogo plana 'Otello' K. Stanislavskogo." In *Shekspirovskii sbornik.* Ed. A.A. Anikst and A.L. Shtein. Moscow, 1958, pp. 364-96.
———. *Shekspir na sovetskoi stsene.* Moscow, 1956.
Znosko-Borovskii, E. *Russkii teatr nachala XX veka.* Prague, (192-?).
Zograf, Nikolai Georgievich. *Aleksandr Pavlovich Lenskii.* Moscow, 1955.
———. *Malyi teatr vtoroi poloviny XIX veka.* Moscow, 1960.

Periodicals

The Mask, Florence, 1908-1929.
The Page, London, 1898-1901.
The Marionnette, Florence, 1918-1919.

Archives

Biblioteka Vserossiiskogo Teatral'nogo obshchestva. Moscow, USSR.
  Bulgakov, A.S. "Shekspir na russkoi stsene."
  Chushkin, Nikolai Nikolaevich. "Kachalov v roli Gamleta," report.
  ———and Rostotskii, B.I. "'Iulii Tsezar' ' v M Kh T," report.
  Freidkina, L.M. "Rabota V.I. Nemirovicha-Danchenko nad 'Iuliem Tsezarem,'" report.
  Ivanova, E. and Kuznetsova, I. "'Gamlet' v M Kh A T 1940-1945 g."
  Samarin-Volzhskii, A.M. "Russkie Gamlety na rubezhe dvukh vekov," report.
  Subbotina, E.M. "Stsenicheskaia istoriia komedii 'Mnogo shuma iz nichego' v Rossii," monograph.
  Troitskii, Z.L. "Iz stsenicheskoi istorii komedii 'Dvenadtsataia noch' '," report.
  Zagorskii, M.B. "Russkaia kritika o Shekspire," monograph.
  ———. "Shekspir v russkoi kritike."
  ———. "Sovetskaia teatral'naia kritika o Shekspire," report.
Dana Collection, Houghton Rare Book Library, Harvard University, Cambridge, Massachusetts.
Gordon Craig Collection, Bibliothèque de l'Arsenal, Paris, France.
  Transcripts of the *Hamlet* conversations.
Leningradskii gosudarstvennyi teatral'nyi muzei, Fond zvukozapisei. Leningrad, USSR.
  Kachalov, Vasilii Ivanovich. *Hamlet,* II, 2, 542-601, reading, n.d.
  Sats, Il'ia Aleksandrovich. Three marches from the music for *Hamlet* at the Moscow Art Theater, 1911.
Muzei pri Moskovskom khudozhestvennom teatre. Moscow, USSR.
  Arkhiv Vl. I. Nemirovicha-Danchenko
  Arkhiv K.S. Stanislavskogo.
  Collection of Press Reviews.
  Sulerzhitskii, Leopol'd Antonovich. Dekoratsii k 'Gamletu'. Nos. 1287-90.
Tsentral'nyi teatral'nyi muzei imeni A.A. Bakhrushina. Moscow, USSR.
  Collection of Production Photographs.

Index

Abbey Theater (Dublin), 88
Acting, 21-25, 27, 82; and Gordon Craig's new
  abstract scenery, 86, 89, 96, 124; education
  of actors, 8-10, 129, 133; problems in *Julius
  Caesar,* 62-63, 72; in Russian theatrical
  tradition, 6-12. *See also* "Method" (acting);
  "System" (Stanislavski's)
"Actor and the *Über-Marionette,* The"(Craig),
  86
Actor Prepares, An. See *Actor's Work on
  Himself, An*
*Actor's Creative Work and Stanislavski's
  Theory,* 128
*Actor's Work on Himself, An (An Actor
  Prepares,* Stanislavski), xiii, 130, 131, 133,
  137
Aleksandrinski Theater, 3, 29-30
Alekseev, Konstantin Sergeevich. *See*
  Stanislavski
Alexander II, 2
"All-Russian Conference of Theater Workers,"
  12
Andreev, Leonid Nikolaevich, 84; *Life of Man,*
  87, 88
Antony and Cleopatra: 1887 Maly Theater
  production, 5
Appia, Adolphe: and symbolism, xxiii
"Art": Gordon Craig's mystical view of, 85
Art and Literature, Society of, xiv, xx, 8, 11-12
Art of the Theater, The (Craig), 85-86
Art Theater. *See* Moscow Art Theater
Audience, involvement of: in Stanislavskian
  theater, 32, 67-69, 81, 128

Ballet: as source of acting trainees, 8, 9
Belinski, Vissarion Grigorievich, 13, 14; on
  historical naturalism in Shakespeare, 50-51
Bely, Andrei, 76
Benefit system, in Imperial theaters, 3,
  139-40 n. 5
Besnard, Lucien, 19, 20, 25

Birman, Serafima Germanovna, 128
Blue Bird, The (Maeterlinck), 87, 98
Boborykin, Pyotr Dmitrievich, 9
Boris Godunov (Pushkin), 42, 53, 70
Brenko, Anna, 2; and the Pushkin Theater, 6
Bruisov, Valery Iakovlevich, 124
Brutus, 50, 51, 52, 53, 62, 63, 70. *See also Julius
  Caesar:* 1903 Moscow Art Theater
  productions; Stanislavski: as Brutus
Building a Character. See *Actor's Work on
  Himself, An*
Burdzhalov, Georgi Sergeevich (né
  Burdzhalyan), 38, 39, 40

Caesar, Julius (in Shakespeare), 41, 45, 50, 51;
  as political and mythic superman, 52-53,
  70, 74. See also *Julius Caesar:* 1903
  Moscow Art Theater production;
  Kachalov: as Caesar
Censor, Imperial, 1-2, 33, 50; and Shakespeare,
  139 n. 2, 140 n. 18
Chekhov, Anton Pavlovich, 29-30, 34-35, 43,
  75, 142 n. 59; interest in 1903 *Julius Caesar,*
  49, 50; plays in Moscow Art Theater
  productions, 29, 31, 32, 35, 36, 42, 43, 44,
  90, 136; on Stanislavski's naturalism, 30,
  45, 83, 136. Works: *The Cherry Orchard,*
  45, 136; *Ivanov,* 14-15; *The Seagull,* xxii,
  29-32, 43, 131, 136; *Three Sisters,* 37, 129-
  30; *Uncle Vanya,* 43, 44, 136
Chushkin, Nikolai Nikolaevich, 35-36,
  148 n. 48
Classicism, European: in eighteenth-century
  Russian acting and literature, 7
Comédie Française: acting style of, 9
Coriolanus: Lenski's 1902 production, 16
Costumes, 5-6; in 1912 *Hamlet,* 96, 97, 101-102;
  in 1903 *Julius Caesar,* 37, 46, 47
Cox, Ursula, 89
Craig, Edward Gordon: "Actor and the *Über-
  Marionette,* The," 86; *Art of the Theater,*

85-86; visual approach to 1912 *Hamlet,* 88,
98, 100, 104, 107, 137; reactions to 1912
Hamlet, 101-3, 124-25; *The Mask* (journal),
86; introduced to Stanislavski by Isadora
Duncan, xxiii, 85, 86-87; begs funds of
Stanislavski to found a theater school, 94-
95, 98; influence on Stanislavski and
Russian theater, 125-26; symbolical and
stylized approach to acting, xxiii, 81, 86,
96, 124. *See also Hamlet:* 1912 Moscow Art
Theater production; Stanislavski: working
relationship with Craig
Creating a Role. See *Actor's Work on Himself,
An*
"Creative motor," 84
  Crowd scenes: in 1912 *Hamlet,* 107; in 1903
  Julius Caesar, 42, 43, 46, 47, 48, 65-70, 72,
  73-74, 78; in 1896 *Othello,* 19-21; in 1930
  Othello, 132, 133
Cronegk, Ludwig, 17, 18, 39

Daily Telegraph, 130
Dalmatov, Vasili Panteleimonovich: as
  Hamlet, 15
Death of Tintagiles (Maeterlinck), 81
Diaghilev, Sergei: criticisms of 1903 *Julius
  Caesar,* 76-77
Director, function of: in Craig's "Art of the
  Theater," 85-86; in work of Lenski, 10-11;
  in Russian theater, 3; in Stanislavski's
  "theater of experience," 31-32, 82
Drama of Life (Hamsun), 88
Duncan, Isadora, xxiii, 84, 85, 86-87, 92

Efros, Nikolai Efimovich: criticisms of 1903
  Julius Caesar, 50-54, 75, 76
Elizabethan production styles, 38, 129
English theater: historical costuming in, 5-6
Ensemble (acting), 2, 8, 10-11, 18; in 1897
  Twelfth Night, 27; in "theater of
  experience," 32
Ermolova, Maria Nikolaevna, 12, 75, 135
"Experimental Guide to Dramatic Art, An"
  (Stanislavski), 83
Externalism, 27, 29, 31, 33-34, 69; in 1903 *Julius
  Caesar,* 79; in Stanislavski's early work,
  135-36, 137; and inner truth, 83-84, 99-100

Faust, 5
Fedotov, Aleksandr Filippovich: theater of, 2
Fedotov, A.G., 11
Fedotova, Glikeria Nikolaevna (née
  Pozdniakova), 12, 135; teaches Shchepkin's
  system, 8, 9
First Studio of the Moscow Art Theater, 127-29
French theater: historical costuming in, 5-6
Fruits of Enlightenment (Lev Tolstoy), 12

Garrick, David, 6
Giatsintova, Sofia Vladimirovna: as Maria in
  1917/1918 *Twelfth Night,* 128
Gogol', Nikolai Vasilievich: *Inspector General,*
  99
Golovin, Aleksandr Iakovlevich, 131, 133, 134
Gorky, Maksim (né Aleksei Maksimovich
  Peshkov), 31, 102; plays in Moscow Art
  Theater productions, 29, 31, 32, 35, 36, 136;
  on Stanislavski's naturalism, 83
Griboyedov, Aleksandr Sergeevich: *Woe from
  Wit,* 6
Gurevich, Liubov' Iakovlevna, 89, 93-94, 128,
  129; review of 1903 *Julius Caesar,* 72, 77
Gzovskaia, Olga Vladimirovna: as Ophelia in
  1912 *Hamlet,* 98, 101, 109

Hamlet, xiv-xv, xxiii-xxiv, 13, 14, 73, 87-126,
  127, 132
—V.G. Belinski's interpretation of title
  character, 14
—1912 Moscow Art Theater production, xxiii-
  xxiv, 87-126, 127, 132; audience reactions
  to, 110-23, 127; costumes, 96, 97, 101-2;
  Craig's visual approach, 88, 98, 100, 104,
  107, 137; critical reception of, 104, 106-7,
  108, 109, 110-11; crowd scenes in, 107;
  presentation of Elsinore in, 92; character of
  Hamlet in, 90, 91-92, 93, 104-6, 107-8;
  lighting, 88, 93, 95, 96, 101, 104; music in,
  90, 92-93, 96, 103, 104, 105, 108, 109-10;
  sets, 88, 89, 93, 95, 96, 103, 104, 106; sound
  effects, 92, 104; treatment of text, 89, 90,
  110; interpretive discussions of Stanislavski
  and Craig, 89-93, 96, 99, 100
—Nemirovich-Danchenko's interpretation of
  title character, 73; plans for staging in the
  1940s, 111-24
—In Polevoi's translation, 13
—Turgenev's interpretation of title character,
  14
Hamsun, Knut, 84; *Drama of Life,* 88
Hauptmann, Gerhardt: *Schluck and Jau,* 81
Historicism. *See* Naturalism, historical
Hour Glass, The (Yeats): at the Abbey Theater
  in Dublin, 88
Huguenots, Les, 5
Hunter's Club, 20, 26

Ibsen, Henrik: *Pillars of Society,* 35
"If," magic: in Stanislavski's system, 83
Imperial Theater system, 2, 3, 4; benefit system
  in, 3, 139-40 n. 5; reforms in actor
  education, 9
Inspector General (Gogol'), 99

Internalism, 99-100, 136-37. *See also* Acting; "Creative motor"; Externalism; Realism, psychological; "System" (Stanislavski's)
Irving, Sir Henry, 85; as romantic actor, 6, 7
Iur'ev, Iurii Mikhailovich, 9, 14
Ivanov (Chekhov), 14-15

Jonson, Ben, 25
Julius Caesar, xiv-xv, xxii, 13, 31-79, 81, 83, 136
—1885 Meininger troupe production, 38, 45, 47, 64, 67, 75-76; externalism in, 31, 33-34, 69
—1903 Moscow Art Theater production, xxii, 32-79; acting problems in, 62-63, 72; involvement of audience in, 81, character of Brutus in, 41, 45-46, 67, 73-75; character of Caesar in, 41, 45, 70-71; Chekhovian tones of, 42, 43, 44-45, 54-75, 79; costumes, 37, 46, 47; critical reception of, 75-79; crowd scenes in, 42, 43, 46, 47, 48, 65-70, 72, 73-74, 78; first dress rehearsal, 49-50; reviewed by N.E. Efros, 50-54; lighting, 39, 43-44, 49; naturalism in, 34, 37-44, 50-54, 62-65, 69, 71, 76-79, 83, 136; organization of preparatory work for, 36-37; presentation of Rome in, 38-42, 46, 50, 57, 67, 70, 72, 75, 79; Roman society as principal character in, 38, 41, 42, 52, 53-54, 65-70, 77; sets, 35, 38, 44, 46-47, 49, 51, 53-54, 63; sound effects, 39, 43-45, 67; treatment of text and monologues, 54-62, 65
—as interpreted by Nemirovich-Danchenko, 51-54, 70-79
—political themes in, 52-54, 69-70
—in Russian theatrical tradition, 32-33

Kachalov, Vasili Ivanovich (né Shverubovich): as Caesar, 41, 49, 50, 70-76, 77, 79; as Hamlet, xxiii, 93, 97-111, 124, 137
Karatygin, Vasili Andreevich, 7
Kean, Edmund, 6
Kemble, John Philip, 6
King Lear, 13
Komissarzhevskaia Theater, 128
Komissarzhevski, Fyodor Petrovich, 11
Knipper-Chekhova, Olga Leonardovna, 30, 40, 43, 49; as Gertrude, 111; on pre-dress reading of *Julius Caesar*, 49-50
Konstantin Sergeevich. *See* Stanislavski
Koonen, Alisa, 95, 101-103, 110
Koreshchenko, Arseni Nikolaevich, 27
Korsh Theater, 2

Leonidov, Leonid Mironovich (né Volfenzon): as Cassius, 49, 54; as Othello in 1930 production, 129, 130, 131, 133, 134

Lenski, Aleksandr Pavlovich, 6, 15-16, 135; articles on theater practice and theory, 10-11; criticisms of 1885 Meininger production of *Julius Caesar*, 34
Lentovski, Mikhail Valentinovich, 20
Life of Man (Andreev), 87, 88
Lighting: in 1912 *Hamlet*, 88, 93, 95, 96, 101, 104; in 1903 *Julius Caesar*, 39, 43-44, 49; and the Meininger troupe, 17-18; Stanislavski's postnaturalist experimentation with, 84
Lozinski, Mikhail Leonidovich: prose translations of Shakespeare, 13
Luzhski, Vasili Vasilievich (né Kaluzhski), 40
Lykiardopoulo, Mikhail Fyodorovich, 89, 98

Maeterlinck, 84; *The Blue Bird*, 87, 98; *Death of Tintagiles*, 81, 84, 87
Maid of Orleans (Schiller), 4
Maly Theater, 3-4, 5, 6; and Lenski's Novy Theater, 10, 11
Mardzhanov, Konstantin Aleksandrovich (né Kote Mardzhanishvili), 95, 96, 97; views on Craig, 100-101
Mask, The (Craig's journal), 86
Meiningen (Saxe-Meiningen), Duke of: naturalistic methods of, xxi, 17-29, 135. *See also* Meininger troupe
Meininger troupe, 5, 25, 42; 1885 production of *Julius Caesar*, 31, 33-34, 35, 38, 69; innovations in historical realism, 5, 6, 17-29, 64; influence on Stanislavski, 12, 26, 135, 137
Merchant of Venice, The, xxii, 28; *Jew of Venice*, 13
Merezhkovsky, Dmitri Sergeevich, 90
Meshcherski, Prince Prokopii Vasilievich, 7
"Method" (acting), xix, xxii. *See also* "System" (Stanislavski's)
Meyerhold, Vsevolod Emilievich, 29, 30, 31, 86; and "theater of mood," 29; criticisms of 1903 *Julius Caesar*, 79; joins Stanislavski to form experimental studio, 81
Midsummer Night's Dream, A: at Lenski's Novy Theater, 15-16
Mise-en-scène. *See* Sets
Mochalov, Pavel Stepanovich, 7; as Hamlet, 14
Molière, 5
Month in the Country, A (Turgenev), 99
Moscow Art Theater: administration and repertory, 29, 36, 47, 87, 94, 98, 100-101; artistic paralysis of, 81; backstage esprit, 36-37; and classic theater, 127; and Chekhov's plays, 29, 31, 32, 35, 36, 42, 43, 44, 90, 136; foundation of, xxi-xxii, 10-11, 16; and Gorky's plays, 29, 31, 32, 35, 36, 136; production of 1912 *Hamlet*, xxiii-xxiv,

87-126, 127, 132; production of 1903 *Julius Caesar,* xxii, 32-79, 81, 83, 136; influenced by Meininger troupe, 18; production of 1898 *Merchant of Venice,* 28; production of 1930 *Othello,* 129-34; relation to Soviet government, 129, 130, 133-34; production of 1898 *Tsar Fyodor,* xxii, 29, 43, 72, 79, 83; production of 1897 and 1899 *Twelfth Night,* xxi, 27-28; First Studio production of 1917/1918 *Twelfth Night,* 127-29

Moscow Philharmonic Society, 9

Moscow Polytechnic Exhibit, 2

Moscow Theater School, 9, 10

Moskvin, Ivan Mikhailovich, 101-2

Much Ado About Nothing: 1897 production, xxi, 26-27, 28

Muratova, Elena Pavlovna, 98

Music, use of: in 1912 *Hamlet,* 90, 92-93, 96, 104, 105, 108, 109-10; in Lenski's Shakespearean productions, 15-16; in nineteenth-century Russian theater, 6; in 1897 *Twelfth Night,* 27

My Life in Art (Stanislavski), 25, 26, 36-37, 42, 50, 108

Mysticism: in Craig's view of *Hamlet* and the theater, 90, 92, 104, 106, 111

Naturalism, historical: in 1903 *Julius Caesar,* 34, 37-44, 50-54, 62-65, 69, 71, 76-79, 83, 136; and the Meininger troupe, 5, 6, 17-29, 64; in 1898 *Merchant of Venice,* 28; in 1897 *Much Ado About Nothing,* 26-27; in 1896 *Othello,* 25; in 1930 *Othello,* 131-32, 134; in Shakespeare, 50-52, 53; in 1898 *Tsar Fyodor,* 29

Naturalism (realism): rejected by Craig's symbolism, 86, 91, 109; passé, 81; in 1898 *Seagull,* 30, 31; in Stanislavski's early work, 135

Navrozov, F.N., 28

Nemirovich-Danchenko, Vladimir Ivanovich, 9, 127, 130, 135, 136; response to Efros's criticisms of *Julius Caesar,* 51-54; plans for a 1940s production of *Hamlet,* 111-124; directs *Julius Caesar,* 32-79; criticisms of the Meininger production of *Julius Caesar,* 33-34; *Out of the Past,* 36; and Russian theatrical tradition, 29; working relationship with Stanislavski, 34, 35-36, 45, 46, 47, 48

"Neskuchnoe," 40

Novosti Dnia (News of the Day), 50-51

Novy Theater, 10, 11, 15-16

Ostrovski, Aleksandr Nikolaevich, 3, 4-5, 9; criticisms of Meininger troupe, 18, 34

Othello, xv, xxi, xxiv, 13, 19-27, 29-35, 79, 129-34, 135; Stanislavski's production of 1896, xxi, 19-26, 79, 131-32, 135; of 1930, xxiv, 129-34; title role as played by Salvini, 19; Pushkin's interpretation of title character, 20

Out of the Past (Nemirovich-Danchenko), 36

Pasternak, Boris: verse translations of Shakespeare, 13

Pchelnikov, Pavel Mikhailovich, 50

Pillars of Society (Ibsen), 35

Piot, 88

Polevoi, Nikolai Alekseevich, 13

Poliakova, Elena Ivanovna, xii-xiv, xv

Pompeii: Moscow Art Theater research expedition for 1903 *Julius Caesar,* 40

Power of Darkness (Lev Tolstoy), 52

Promptbooks: defined, xv; Nemirovich-Danchenko's, for 1903 *Julius Caesar,* 38, 39, 40-41, 45, 54, 66, 69, 70, 78; for 1912 *Hamlet,* 103; for 1897 *Much Ado About Nothing,* 267; for 1896 *Othello,* 19-20; for 1930 *Othello,* xxiv, 127, 130-33; Stanislavski's, evidence of dictatorial style of direction in, 82; Stanislavski's, record of experimentation with "system," 99, 126

Pushkin, Aleksandr Sergeevich, 5; *Boris Godunov,* 42, 53, 70; interpretation of Othello, 20

Pushkin Theater, 2, 6

Rationalism, in nineteenth-century Russian acting, 7

Realism, 86, 91, 109; versus romanticism, xix-xx; in nineteenth-century Russian acting, 8. *See also* Naturalism

Realism, historical: in Russian theater, 5-6. *See also* Naturalism, historical

Realism, psychological, 12, 32; and Chekhov's plays, 31, 32, 79, 90; in 1930 *Othello,* 131-33; in Stanislavskian acting, 89, 94, 96, 111, 124, 126, 137

Romanticism, 5-6, 42; in nineteenth-century Shakespearean criticism, 50-51, 52, 53; in Russian Shakespearean productions, xix-xx, 15; in Russian theater, 7, 8, 9, 111, 124

Romeo and Juliet, 13

Rossi, Ernesto, 20, 26, 135

Rostotski, Boleslav Norbert Iosifovich, 35

Russian theater: debts to Gordon Craig, 125-26; nineteenth-century, xix-xx, 1-16; administration and repertory, 1-6; acting and production styles, 5-12; and Shakespeare, xix-xx, 1, 13-16

Russkie Vedomosti (Russian News), 50

Russkoe Slova (Russian World), 50, 104

Salvini, Tommaso, 135; as Othello, xxi, 19, 129
Sats, Ilya Aleksandrovich: music for *The Blue Bird*, 87; music for *Hamlet*, 90, 92-93, 96, 103, 104, 105, 108, 109-10
Saxe-Meiningen (Meiningen), Duke of: naturalistic methods of, xxi, 17-29, 135. *See also* Meininger troupe
Schiller, Friedrich von, 42; *Maid of Orleans*, 4
Schluck and Jau (Hauptmann), 81
Seagull, The (Chekhov): 1898 Moscow Art Theater production, xxii, 29-32, 43, 131, 136
Senelick, Laurence, xv, 108
Sets: in 1912 *Hamlet*, 88, 89, 93, 95, 96, 103, 104, 106; in 1903 *Julius Caesar*, 35, 38, 44, 46-47, 49, 51, 53-54, 673; in 1897 *Much Ado About Nothing*, 26-27, 28; in 1896 *Othello*, 21-25, 267; in 1930 *Othello*, 131, 133, 134; Stanislavski's postnaturalist experimentation with, 84, 89; in 1898 *Tsar Fyodor*, 29; in 1897 and 1899 productions of *Twelfth Night*, 27-28; in 1917/1918 *Twelfth Night*, 127-28, 149 n. 7
Shakespeare, William: treatment of history, 50-52, 53, 54, 71; humanity of characters, 42, 79; problem of performing famous monologues, 62; Moscow Art Theater's reputed inadequacy with plays, 127; taste in production styles, 25; and the psychological realism of Chekhov and Gorky, 32, 87; in Russian theater, xiv-xv, xix-xx, 1, 13-16. Works: *Antony and Cleopatra*, 5; *Coriolanus*, 16; *Hamlet*, xiv-xv, xxiii-xxiv, 13, 14, 73, 87-126, 127, 132; *Julius Caesar*, xiv-xv, xxii, 13, 31-79, 81, 83, 136; *King Lear*, 13; *Macbeth*, 13, 33; *Merchant of Venice*, xxii, 13, 28; *A Midsummer Night's Dream*, 15-16; *Much Ado About Nothing*, xxi, 26-27, 28; *Othello*, xv, xxi, xxiv, 13, 19-27, 29-35, 79, 129-34, 135; *Romeo and Juliet*, 13
Shchepkin, Mikhail Semyonovich, 7-8, 9, 10
Shchubert, A.I., 8
Shumski, Sergei Vasilievich, 8
Simov, Viktor Andreevich, 28; sets for 1903 *Julius Caesar*, 35, 38, 39, 40, 41, 44, 46, 49, 88
Sollogub, Fyodor (né F.K. Teternikov), 6, 11
Solodovnikov Theater, 20
Sound effects: in 1912 *Hamlet*, 92, 104; in 1903 *Julius Caesar*, 39, 43-45, 67; and the Meininger troupe, 17-18; in 1896 *Othello*, 19-20
Soviet government: relation to Moscow Art Theater, 129, 130, 133-34
Sovnarkom: correspondence from Stanislavski, 130

Stanislavski, Igor Konstantinovich (son), 130
Stanislavski, Kira Konstantinovna (daughter), 98
Stanislavski, Konstantin Sergeevich, xiii-xiv, xix; and Anton Chekhov, xxii, 30, 43, 45, 49, 50, 75, 83, 1367; directorial style of, 27, 82; and Isadora Duncan, xxiii, 84, 85, 86-87, 92; production styles of, xxiv; and Russian theatrical tradition, 25, 29; on Shakespearean scholarship, 25, 26. Career: work with the Society of Art and Literature, xx, 8-11, 17-29; founds Moscow Art Theater with Nemirovich-Danchenko, 11-12, 16; introduced to the Meininger troupe, 17-29; as Trigorin in *The Seagull*, 30; decision to produce the 1903 *Julius Caesar*, 33-35; studies of Rome, 38-41; contributions to 1903 *Julius Caesar*, 42-43, 46, 48; as Brutus, 46, 49, 50, 73, 75, 77, 78, 79, 143 n. 87; working relationship with Nemirovich-Danchenko, 34, 35-36, 45, 46, 47, 48; artistic crisis of 1904-6, 81-84; decision to assist Meyerhold in theatrical experimentation, 81; retires to Finland to work out theories, xxii, xxiv, 82-83; meets Gordon Craig, turns to symbolism for 1912 *Hamlet*, xxiii, 85, 86-87; working relationship with Craig, 87-88, 90-95, 98, 99, 101-3, 124-25, 126; suffers typhus, 98, 99; directs 1917/1918 *Twelfth Night*, 127-29; onset of poor health during work on *Othello* in 1928, 129-30; culmination of theoretical work in *An Actor's Work on Himself*, 137. Works: *Actor's Work on Himself, An (An Actor Prepares)*, xiii, 130, 131, 133, 137; "Experimental Guide to Dramatic Art, An," 83; *My Life in Art*, 25, 26, 36-37, 42, 50, 108
Stanislavski, Lilina (wife), 19, 26, 48, 84, 98
Star system: and the Meininger troupe, 18; in Russian theater, 3
Storozhenko, Nikolai Ilich, 15
Stroeva, Marina Nikolaevna, xii-xiv, xv, 126, 148 n. 96
Sudakov, Ilya Iakovlevich, 129, 130, 133
Sulerzhitski, Leopold Antonovich: assistant director of 1912 *Hamlet*, 88, 89, 93, 96, 97, 98, 100, 110; disputes with Craig, 101-2
Sushkevich, Boris Mikhailovich, 127
Suvorin, Aleksei Sergeevich, 33
Symbolism: in Craig's new acting style, xxiii, 81, 86, 96, 124; in 1912 *Hamlet*, 87-126; in Stanislavski's postnaturalist work, xxiii, 137
"System" (Stanislavski's): foundation of, xxii, xxiv, 83; Stanislavski's difficulty in interpreting for his actors, 96-97;

experimentation in 1912 *Hamlet*, 98-101, 102, 124, 126; distorted in *The Actor's Creative Work and Stanislavski's Theory*, 128; taught by Stanislavski to student actors of the Moscow Art Theater, 129; in *An Actor's Work on Himself*, 130-31, 133, 134, 136-37

Teatr i Zhizn' (Theater and Life), 33
Terry, Ellen, 85
"Theater of experience" (Stanislavski's), xxiii, 85, 110, 137; developed in Moscow Art Theater productions of Chekhov and Gorky plays, 29, 31-32, 136
"Theater of the future" (Craig's), 85, 124
"Theater of mood" (Meyerhold's), 29
Three Sisters (Chekhov), 37, 129-30
Tikhomirov, I.A., 49
Tolstoy, Aleksei Konstantinovich: *Tsar Fyodor*, xxii, 29, 43, 77, 79, 83
Tolstoy, Lev Nikolaevich: *Fruits of Enlightenment*, 12; *Power of Darkness*, 52; *War and Peace*, 42
Tree, Beerbohm, 6
Truth, sense of: in Stanislavski's system, 83, 99-100, 124
Tsar Fyodor (Aleksei Tolstoy): 1898 Moscow Art Theater production, xxii, 29, 43; naturalism in, 77, 79, 83

Turgenev, Ivan Sergeevich: interpretations of Hamlet and Lear, 14; *A Month in the Country*, 99
Turin: as inspiration for 1897 *Much Ado About Nothing*, 26
Twelfth Night: 1897 and 1899 productions, xxi, 27-28; 1917/1918 First Studio productions, xv, xxiv, 127-29, 131, 149 n. 7

Über-Marionette, in Craig's theory, 86, 87-88, 97
Uncle Vanya (Chekhov), 43, 44, 136

Vakhtangov, Evgeny Bagratsionovich, 99
Varneke, Boris Vasilievich, 76
Venice: as inspiration for Stanislavski's 1897 *Othello*, 19-20
Verigina, V.P., 48
Vinogradskaia, Irina Nikolaevna, 134
Vishnevski, Aleksandr Leonidovich (né Vishnevetski), 39; as Antony in 1903 *Julius Caesar*, 50, 72, 99
Voronov, Evgeny Ivanovich, 9

War and Peace (Lev Tolstoy), 42
Woe from Wit (Griboyedov), 6

Yeats, William Butler: *The Hour Glass*, 88